Technology Management

Developing and Implementing Effective Licensing Programs

Intellectual Property–General, Law, Accounting & Finance, Management, Licensing, Special Topics Series

Early-Stage Technologies: Valuation and Pricing by Richard Razgaitis

Edison in the Boardroom: How Leading Companies Realize Value from Their Intellectual Assets by Julie L. Davis, Suzanne S. Harrison

From Ideas to Assets: Investing Wisely in Intellectual Property by Bruce Berman

Intellectual Property Assets in Mergers and Acquisitions by Lanning Bryer and Melvin Simensky

Intellectual Property in the Global Marketplace, Volume 1: Valuation, Protection, Exploitation, and Electronic Commerce, 2e by Melvin Simensky, Lanning Bryer, Neil J. Wilkof

Intellectual Property in the Global Marketplace, Volume 2: Country–by–Country Profiles, 2e by Melvin Simensky, Lanning Bryer, Neil J. Wilkof

Intellectual Property Infringement Damages: A Litigation Support Handbook, Second Edition by Russell L. Parr

Intellectual Property: Licensing and Joint Venture Profit Strategies, 2e by Gordon V. Smith, Russell L. Parr

Licensing Intellectual Property: Legal, Business, and Market Dynamics by John W. Schlicher

Patent Strategy: The Manager's Guide to Profiting from Patent Portfolios by Anthony L. Miele

Profiting from Intellectual Capital: Extracting Value from Innovation by Patrick H. Sullivan

Technology Licensing: Corporate Strategies for Maximizing Value by Russell L. Parr, Patrick H. Sullivan

Technology Management: Developing and Implementing Effective Licensing Programs by Robert C. Megantz

Trademark Valuation by Gordon V. Smith

Valuation of Intellectual Property and Intangible Assets, Third Edition by Gordon V. Smith, Russell L. Parr

Value–Driven Intellectual Capital: How to Convert Intangible Corporate Assets into Market Value by Patrick H. Sullivan

Technology Management

Developing and Implementing Effective Licensing Programs

Robert C. Megantz

John Wiley & Sons, Inc.

This publication is designed to provide accurate and authoritative information in regard
to the subject matter covered. It is sold with the understanding that the publisher is not
engaged in rendering legal, accounting, or other professional services. If legal advice or
other expert assistance is required, the services of a competent professional person
should be sought.

ISBN: 0-471-20018-2

Printed in the United States of America

10 9 8 7 6 5 4 3 2 1

For my wife Naomi,
our sons Thomas and Andrew,
and my parents Sam and Ruth

About the Author

R obert C. Megantz has more than 20 years experience in technology development and licensing, primarily in the electronics, telecommunications, and computing industries, working with established and start-up companies. His responsibilities have ranged from product development to intellectual property management to marketing and executive management.

Starting in 1978, he worked at Dolby Laboratories Licensing Corporation, San Francisco, CA, in various engineering and management positions, including General Manager. While at Dolby, he directed a large, successful international licensing operation with more than 125 licensees in the consumer and professional audio markets. In the technical area, he directed or assisted in the development of several key audio technologies, including the Dolby Surround, HX Pro, and C- and S-type noise reduction systems, and developed and implemented quality control procedures to ensure compliance with trademark licensing requirements.

In 1991, he left Dolby Labs to help other technology-driven companies more effectively utilize their intellectual property. As a principal at TacTec, a licensing and business development consultancy, his activities have included assisting the Stanford University Office of Technology Licensing (Stanford, CA) in developing and implementing a licensing program for their Sondius™ physical modeling synthesis technology, working with iM Networks, Inc. (Mountain View, CA) in developing and implementing a licensing-based business model for its Internet radio technologies, and providing Kestrel Institute (Palo Alto, CA) with technical and licensing services related to their software technologies. From 1997 to 1999, he served as acting CEO of Neural Systems Corporation, Los Altos, CA. In addition to his consulting work, he is an Adjunct Lecturer at the Leavey School of Business at Santa Clara University, where he teaches the course "How to License Technology."

He is active in the Licensing Executives Society and the Audio Engineering Society. He holds a B.S.E.E. degree from Cornell University, Ithaca, NY, and has published several articles and the book *"How to License Technology."*

Contents

Preface

WHAT IS TECHNOLOGY?

Trying to define technology reminds me of the parable of the blind men and the elephant—the elephant seemed to be a tree, a snake, a rope, a fan, or something else depending on from what perspective it was viewed.

To a scientist, technology is the end product of research—inventions and know-how that may be developable into a commercial product. The embodiment of scientific research is often research papers, patent disclosures, and demonstration units that were used to prove the inventive concepts.

To an engineer, technology is a tool or process that can be employed to build better products. Better products could be products whose performance is superior, that cost less, or that allow the manufacturer to sell in previously inaccessible markets. Engineers turn research results into marketable products. In the course of product development and manufacturing, engineers often develop new technologies that have a significant effect on the company's revenues and profitability.

Marketing personnel must look at technology as a challenge. On the one hand, it offers them an opportunity to gain an advantage over competitors by differentiating products or quickly entering new markets. On the other hand, they need to fully understand the marketing implications of the technology and determine whether the advantage associated with using the technology will outweigh the cost of doing so. Marketers must determine the market value of the technology and how it can be profitably used in their company's products.

To an attorney, technology is intellectual property to be protected and guarded. Patents, trademarks, copyrighted works, mask works, and know-how are all legal embodiments of technology that are widely used to control its dissemination and use. Intellectual property permeates our lives, from the entertainment we enjoy to the clothes and food we buy to the medicines we take when sick. The legal system is responsible for making sure that intellectual property is used properly and fairly; a substantial amount of time and effort is expended to that end.

To the business executive, technology may be the most important, yet least understood, company asset. Most executives understand that the future of their company depends to a great extent on its use of technology, yet many companies have not developed or implemented a technology strategy or a meaningful method for measuring and valuing technology assets. Other executives understand very well the technological issues in their business and markets, but fail to understand the opportunities and methods for leveraging technology assets in other markets. The successful professional with vision and commitment understands the importance of technology and devotes the resources and attention necessary to ensure that technology is nurtured, utilized, protected, and leveraged for maximum advantage.

Finally, to those who use and enjoy it, technology is a wonderful, amazing, always-changing bag of tricks that help us to live healthier, happier, safer, and more fulfilling lives. All the individual perspectives that make up the world of technology, like the blind men's observations, describe a wisdom far greater than the sum of its parts.

The effective use of technology is perhaps the most important issue faced by technology-based companies today, and will undoubtedly become even more critical in years to come. Intellectual capital can be a company's most valuable asset, yet it is far more difficult to quantify and exploit than buildings, machinery, capital, and other assets that can be readily defined and listed on a balance sheet. Those of you who are not yet convinced of the value of intellectual property should check the market value of companies with significant intellectual property assets. Just to offer one example, the Coca-Cola brand name has been valued at almost $40 billion!

Licensing is one of several intellectual property strategies that are increasingly being used to utilize technology assets in new, creative ways. Used in such industries as electronics, computing, telecommunications, bio-technology, pharmaceuticals, chemicals, and many others, licensing has allowed firms to enter and develop markets previously restricted to those with significant proprietary technology assets or to develop markets not even in existence because of the need for standardization.

Over the years, many colleagues, clients, and other friends and acquaintances have expressed to me the need for a resource that clearly and succinctly explains how to develop and implement a technology licensing program. Although a number of excellent resources are available that present in-depth discussion of various legal and financial aspects of technology licensing, a step-by-step, how-to treatment seemed lacking.

Technology Management: Developing and Implementing Effective Licensing Programs is intended to fill this gap by offering an accessible yet complete description of all aspects of a technology licensing program, starting with issues that must be addressed in the early stages of licensing and ending with long-term concerns. Chapter 1 discusses alternatives to licensing and how to determine whether licensing is in fact the appropriate strategy to pursue. Chapter 2 introduces the various intellectual property components of a licensing strategy, such as patents and trademarks, and how they can and should be managed. Chapter 3 discusses conducting market research to learn more about markets, competitive technologies, and prospective licensees, and how to use the information gathered. Chapter 4 outlines methods commonly used to determine the value of intellectual property, information critical to developing a licensing strategy, which is discussed in Chapter 5. Chapter 6 offers some ideas on how to market technology, and Chapter 7 discusses negotiating and drafting license agreements. Organizational requirements for administering long-term license agreements are the subject of Chapter 8.

In addition to the main eight chapters, four appendices provide more specific information. Appendix A contains case studies on a number of well-known licensing programs, including Stanford University's and Dolby Laboratories'. Appendix B lists sources of information that can be used in the market research phase, including organizations, publications, and online resources. Appendix C contains two annotated sample license agreements, one adapted from an agreement used in a well-known and successful consumer electronics licensing program, and the other used to license computer software. They offer insight into many of the issues that must be addressed in license agreements. Appendix D is a glossary of terms commonly used in licensing.

I wrote this book with three target audiences in mind. The first consists of individuals at companies who own or use intellectual property but have not yet had the time or need to develop and implement an overall intellectual property strategy. Using this book, I would hope that such readers would be able to obtain a good basic understanding of all aspects of a licensing program. I would also like to think that these readers could use *Technology Management* to decide whether licensing is an appropriate strategy and, if so, to go a long way toward designing and implementing an effective program. The second target audience consists of professionals with experience in one aspect of licensing who would like to learn more about other aspects. For example, the information on valuing technology might be of interest to an intellectual property attorney who, although well-versed in the legal aspects of licensing, might want to learn more about valuation. The information in the Appendices should also be of interest to professionals. The third target audience is individual inventors, who can use the book to cost-effectively learn what they need to do to protect and market their inventions. Often on tight budgets, inventors can use *Technology Management* to become better educated on the licensing process and improve their capability to market their inventions and negotiate with prospective licensees.

In my 20-plus years in technology licensing I have worked as part of a major licensing organization, as an independent consultant, for two start-up companies, and have lectured in a business school. Throughout my career I have been asked to recommend a source of basic information on how to license technology, but have never found a book that included all the necessary information presented in a clear, concise manner. So, I now offer you my (and many of my friends' and colleagues') views on the basics of technology licensing.

Technology Management is for all who are, or want to become, involved in this fascinating and rewarding occupation. I hope you find the book enlightening and enjoyable, and wish you great success in your technology ventures.

Bob Megantz
San Jose, CA

Acknowledgments

Many friends and colleagues have generously assisted me in writing this book and its predecessor, *How to License Technology*. My sincere thanks go out to all, and especially to:

Douglas Aguilera of Andersen (San Jose, CA), for writing the patent audit section of Chapter 8 and for the use of Exhibit 8.1.

Michael Amiri of DSI Technology Escrow (Norcross, GA), for writing the escrow section of Chapter 7.

Stephen E. Baldwin (San Carlos, CA), for updating Chapter 2.

Robert S. Bramson of Bramson and Pressman (Conshohocken, PA), for reviewing Chapter 2, the auction and conducting a patent auction sections of Chapter 4, the ideas and much of the text for the section on selling infringed patents in Chapter 7, for writing the Wang case study in Appendix A, and for Appendix D.

Robert A. Christopher, partner, Coudert Brothers (San Jose, CA), for updating and editing the section on anti-trust/restraint of trade in Chapter 5.

Greg Franklin of Intellect Partners (Palo Alto, CA), for his help with Chapter 1 and the use of Exhibits 1.1 and 1.2 and for his help in explaining the net present value calculation described in Chapter 4.

Tony Grimani of Performance Media Industries (San Anselmo, CA), for updating the Home THX case study in Appendix A.

Martin Lindsay of Dolby Laboratories (San Francisco, CA), for updating the Dolby case study.

Laura Majerus of Fenwick & West LLP (Palo Alto, CA), for the use of Exhibit 2.6.

William F. Morrison of the College of Business at San Jose State University (San Jose, CA), for writing the negotiation section of Chapter 7 and for the use of Exhibit 7.1.

Niels Reimers, founder of the Stanford University Office of Technology Licensing, who helped in many ways, including writing the university licensing section of Chapter 5 and providing many of the ideas used in Chapter 1.

Jon Sandelin, of the Stanford Office of Technology Licensing (Stanford, CA), for updating the Stanford case study in Appendix A and for his help with the university licensing section of Chapter 5.

Ed Schummer of Dolby Laboratories (San Francisco, CA), who provided the ideas and the initial drafts for the hybrid versus separate licensing section of

Chapter 7 and the corporate licensing section of Chapter 5, and who helped with the Dolby case study in Appendix A.

Robert A. Spanner, of Trial & Technology Law Group (Menlo Park, CA), for the use of Exhibits 2.3 and 2.4.

And, finally, to Susan McDermott, my editor at John Wiley & Sons, for her help and enthusiasm in general, and in particular for her contributions to Appendix B.

Technology Management

Developing and Implementing Effective Licensing Programs

1

To License or
Not to License . . .

Licensing is just one of several strategies for exploiting and commercializing intellectual property. Before discussing how to license, the question of whether to license should be addressed. This chapter discusses alternative approaches to commercializing and managing IP, because only by carefully considering all options can you be assured that the decision to license is correct.

ALTERNATIVE APPROACHES

A company or individual can profitably exploit intellectual property in several ways:

- Initiating a new venture to develop, manufacture, and sell products
- Buying an existing company with the required assets
- Establishing a joint venture
- Licensing
- Forming a strategic alliance
- Selling the intellectual property rights to a third party

Each approach involves a degree of risk and the potential for reward. The relationship between risk and reward for each alternative is shown in Exhibit 1.1.

New Venture

Both risk and potential return are highest with a new venture. Both the products and the supporting business infrastructure must be developed, at considerable up-front cost in both time and money, before any products can be sold and rev-

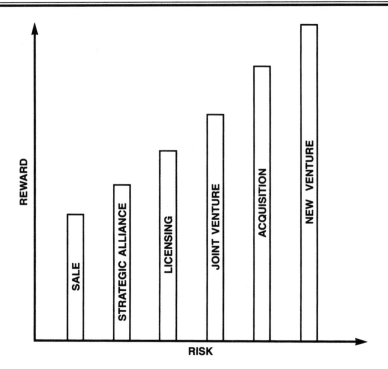

Exhibit 1.1   Risk versus Reward for Various Approaches

enues generated. If successful, however, profits and other benefits will be maximized in a new venture, and total control will be maintained.

Acquisition

Buying an existing company or product line is slightly less risky because much of the required development has been completed and the business infrastructure may be largely in place. Thus, time-to-market can be much shorter than with a new venture, while still maintaining total control. However, a substantial investment is required, decreasing the potential reward. In addition, the marriage of two different corporate cultures required for a successful acquisition can be rocky, especially when a large, established company buys a smaller, more entrepreneurial organization. The buyer also may be required to acquire undesired assets and liabilities as part of the purchase.

Joint Venture

In a joint venture two or more companies work together in a new company, sharing risks, rewards, and control of the operation. Although the risk is still relatively high, it is lowered for each of the participants and the potential for success is enhanced if the skills and resources of the participants are complementary. However, joint ventures can be difficult to manage because of the differing goals and degrees of control of the participants and, just as with risk, reward is lower than the previous alternatives because it will be divided among the owners.

Licensing

Licensing lowers risk still more, because less investment and fewer resources are needed to implement a licensing program than to manufacture. Much of the risk is transferred to the licensee, who is responsible for developing, manufacturing, and marketing the licensed products. Naturally, a proportional measure of the potential reward is also transferred, limiting the licensor's reward. Different licensing strategies engender different levels of risk for both the licensor and licensee. For example, large initial license payments coupled with low or no running royalties shift more of the risk to the licensee, while a low initial payment together with higher running royalties is riskier for the licensor. Choosing the correct balance of risk and reward in licensing arrangements is explored further in Chapters 5 and 7.

Strategic Alliance

Two or more companies can also form a strategic alliance, in which they cooperate in a limited way in return for a share of the profits associated with the alliance. Alliances can be horizontal or vertical. For example, in a vertical alliance company A might agree to market and sell products developed by company B in return for a share of the profits. In a horizontal alliance two firms might take advantage of each others' specialized manufacturing skills to more efficiently and competitively exploit a market. The risks in a strategic alliance are limited to the areas of mutual cooperation, as are the potential rewards.

Sale

Finally, unneeded technology can be sold outright, which is the least risky approach. Because of the high risk assumed by the purchaser, this approach offers relatively less reward as well.

TECHNOLOGY MANAGEMENT STRATEGIES

All alternatives to exploiting intellectual property should be carefully considered before deciding to license. One analysis technique involves mapping the technology position against "complementary assets," assets that are needed to successfully exploit the technology, such as capital, marketing and sales resources, and manufacturing capabilities. Exhibit 1.2 illustrates the relationships between technology position, complementary assets, and technology strategy.

If both the technology position and complementary assets are strong, manu-

COMPLEMENTARY ASSETS

		WEAK	STRONG
TECHNOLOGY POSITION	**STRONG**	**ACQUIRE COMPLEMENTARY ASSETS** • Develop • Strategic Alliance • Joint Venture OR **LICENSE-OUT**	**MANUFACTURE AND SELL**
	WEAK	**SELL OR ABANDON TECHNOLOGY ASSET**	**ACQUIRE TECHNOLOGY** • Develop • Strategic Alliance • Joint Venture OR **LICENSE-IN**

Exhibit 1.2   Technology Management Strategy Options

facturing and selling is the best strategy. If both are weak, technology assets should be sold or abandoned.

If the technology position is strong but complementary assets are weak, there are two choices: complementary assets can be acquired (via development, strategic alliance, or joint venture) and products can be made and sold, or the technology assets can be licensed to another company with suitable complementary assets.

If a company has strong complementary assets but a weak technology position, technology can be acquired by licensing or by forming a strategic alliance or joint venture with a firm capable of supplying the necessary technology.

TYPES OF LICENSING

This book deals with two types of licensing: licensing-out, in which an individual or company licenses its intellectual property to another in return for royalties and/or other considerations; and licensing-in, in which an individual or company actively seeks out an intellectual property owner to supply key products or technologies under license. Much of the material presented is applicable to both situations, but we have noted comments that apply to one or the other.

Licensing-Out

As mentioned above, before deciding to license-out it is best first for you to clearly determine whether licensing is the preferred approach. Although seemingly obvious, the importance of this first step should not be underestimated, and you should apply diligence in researching all available alternatives. The research should begin with the assumption that it is generally most profitable for a company to manufacture and sell products incorporating its intellectual property. Only when manufacturing and selling have been rejected should you investigate the other alternatives already listed, including licensing-out.

Before you decide to pursue licensing-out, it must be understood that licensing is not the simple, inexpensive yet highly profitable business model that many people believe it to be. The licensor must allocate resources, both financial and personnel, to perform the many tasks associated with a successful licensing effort, which include supplying information and assistance to licensees both before and after agreements are signed, protecting intellectual property, negotiating the licenses themselves, and providing for additional expenditures required during the life of the agreement and, unfortunately, sometimes after the agreement terminates.

The licensor must also consider the potential useful life of the technology. In the current climate of explosive technology development, a more useful or cost-effective technology could be offered by a competitor much sooner than expected. If the licensed technology can be easily replaced and does not need a whole industry and a large infrastructure to support it, its life expectancy will be relatively short. If, on the other hand, an infrastructure is necessary and several industries must participate in order to fully exploit the technology, both the introductory phase and the overall life expectancy will be longer.

Perhaps most importantly of all, licensing-out must be considered a long-term commitment which, although it offers the potential for a stable long-term revenue stream, requires substantial ongoing effort and expense.

Reasons for licensing-out include the following:

1. *To generate income from intellectual property resources.* If a company is not making or selling products incorporating its intellectual property for whatever reason, including the lack of sufficient resources, no income will be generated unless the intellectual property is licensed.
2. *To provide a second source of supply.* If production capacity is limited, it is uneconomical or impractical to manufacture the product, or the market is reluctant to accept a device that is single-sourced, a company may elect to license its design and underlying intellectual property to a competitor.
3. *To exploit other markets.* If an invention can be used in several areas, it may be difficult for one company to make and sell products for all markets. Granting a license to a company that is expert in the markets not covered is attractive in this case.

4. *To gain side benefits.* Licensing can result in significant side benefits to the licensor, including increased visibility of a licensed trademark because of advertising by the licensee, the use of improvements developed by the licensee, and so forth.

5. *To minimize legal expenses.* Infringers can be licensed, thereby avoiding legal expenses associated with infringement actions. This strategy can be useful when trademarks are being infringed, in which case the infringement must be stopped or the protection can be lost. Even a royalty-free license can be preferable to losing the trademark. Although this can reduce legal expenses, if the licensee is a competitor, the effect on the licensor's business should be factored into the overall cost of licensing. If the infringer is active in other markets, an agreement can be negotiated that restricts activities in the licensor's market. Other strategies for dealing with infringement are discussed in Chapter 7.

6. *To generate revenue in foreign markets.* Licensing can be used in foreign markets to generate revenue when there is insufficient justification for any other activity, to protect foreign patents by "working" (the requirement in some countries that a patent be used in that country to remain in effect), to take advantage of the (foreign) licensee's knowledge of the local market, and to avoid problems with local currencies, exchange controls, taxes, labor considerations, and restrictions on ownership.

Licensing-In

Licensing-in is a way to acquire products or technologies without expending the time and resources necessary to develop them independently. In some cases licensing-in is required in order to gain access to technologies that are proprietary but standardized in products in the market of interest. In return, the licensee is required to channel some of its profits from the sale of licensed products back to the licensor in the form of royalties.

Many of the observations already offered with regard to licensing-out apply equally to licensing-in. In addition, the prospective licensee must answer several important questions:

- Can the technology or product be developed in-house and, if so, how much time will it take and what will it cost?
- Does the product or technology to be licensed fulfill all of the requirements, both technologically and from a marketing perspective? Are the license terms reasonable, and can competitive licensed products be manufactured and marketed?
- Will the licensor be willing and able to fulfill all its obligations under the license? If support is required, does the licensor have the resources in place to provide the support, and are those resources compatible with the licensee's personnel and operations?

Reasons for licensing-in include the following:

1. *To be able to manufacture standardized products.* Many current standards specify proprietary technologies. In order to compete in the market, all vendors must obtain licenses for all such technologies incorporated in their products. Usually (but not always) technologies that are incorporated in standards are licensed under standard terms to all qualified licensees.
2. *To reduce time-to-market.* By licensing a product or technology, the time required to bring a product to the market can often be reduced substantially.
3. *To legalize infringement.* Frequently a manufacturer will unknowingly (or, sometimes, knowingly) introduce a product that infringes on others' intellectual property. Licensing can be a cost-effective way to legalize such infringement without severe disruption of the business and without incurring excessive legal costs.

WHAT TO DO AFTER DECIDING TO LICENSE

Once licensing has been chosen, several important decisions must be made:

- *What to license.* When choosing a product or technology for licensing, consider product lines and markets in which the licensor is currently active, the potential for competition with licensees, and the importance of a technology or product to the licensor's overall business strategy.
- *Counsel.* Legal counsel will be needed to advise on business and intellectual property issues, and assistance will be required to determine the tax consequences of various licensing strategies. Counsel should assist in assessing the strengths and weaknesses of the intellectual property that will be licensed and (when licensing-out) in preparing and implementing an intellectual property protection strategy.
- *Licensing strategy.* The overall goals of the licensing program should be developed. For example, the prospective licensor should consider whether its goal is to become a licensing conduit for its own and perhaps others' technologies over the long term (10 to 20 years) or to exploit a single idea or invention to its maximum and then move on to something else. Are short-term revenues required, or can a longer-term strategy be considered? Strategies for any given approach can be devised to maximize the chances of success. Such strategies are discussed in Chapter 5.
- *Market analysis.* In what markets can the technologies be licensed, and what companies are active in those markets? Identify and analyze competitive technologies, and estimate the size of the market opportunity. There should be a clear understanding of the advantages the technology offers to the user, and the value of these advantages. More information on market analysis techniques can be found in Chapter 3.
- *Revenue potential estimation.* Based on the strength of the intellectual property and the competitive analysis, what is the size of the potential market opportunity and what royalty rates can you justify?

- *Resource requirements.* To license-out, what additional staffing do you need, both to administer the licensing program and to fulfill the obligations of the license? Do the anticipated returns justify the expense and effort necessary to implement the licensing program? When licensing-in, who will be responsible for finding the product or technology to license, for effectively transferring the technology, and for fulfilling the payment and reporting (and any other) obligations of the license?

FINANCIAL CONSIDERATIONS

The major costs associated with licensing include:

- *Personnel.* This can include management, administration of agreements, intellectual property, and technical information related to the licensed products or technologies; and engineering and marketing personnel resources diverted to support the licensing effort.
- *Travel, entertainment, and communications.* You may incur high expenses when you contact and meet prospective licensees and licensors, negotiate agreements, and provide services (such as technology transfer and trademark-related quality control) after the agreement has been signed. In addition, those involved in licensing should join and participate in the activities of the various trade organizations related to technology licensing (such as the Licensing Executives Society (LES) and the Association of University Technology Managers (AUTM)).
- *Professional fees.* This includes legal counsel, tax counsel, and any consultants whom you might retain to assist in the licensing program.

Exhibit 1.3 illustrates a typical relationship between time and licensor's net cash flow in long-term licensing-out arrangements. Initially cash flow will be negative, as licensing revenues will not offset technology development, marketing, and legal expenses. As revenues increase, net cash flow will become positive and will grow for several years as markets are more effectively addressed by increasing numbers of licensed products and/or licensees. In later years new technologies may replace the licensed technology or patents may expire, resulting in flat (or decreasing) revenues.

When licensing-in, your expenses associated with developing and marketing licensed products and royalty payments to the licensor will be offset by revenues that are generated from licensed product sales. Product sales typically will grow relatively slowly at first, enter a period of more rapid growth, and then level off and decrease as the technology reaches the end of its life cycle. Cash flow for the licensee could be similar to Exhibit 1.3 as well: negative at first, followed by increasing positive cash flow as sales revenues increase, and finally leveling off and dropping.

Quantifying the risks and rewards of a business strategy that utilizes licensing

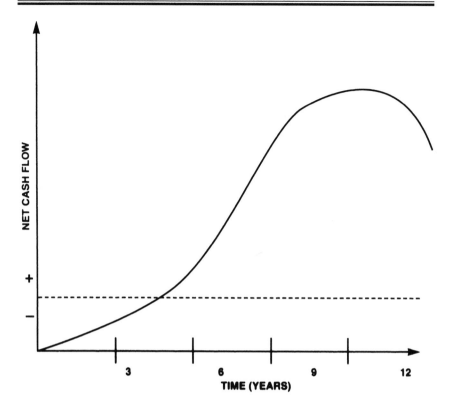

Exhibit 1.3   Typical Relationship between Time and Licensor's Net Cash Flow in a Long-Term Licensing Arrangement

is key to achieving success. In order to do this, the prospective licensor must understand the legal issues associated with protecting and licensing intellectual property and how to find and analyze relevant market information, value the technologies of interest, and develop a suitable licensing strategy. A chapter of this book is devoted to each of these subjects, followed by further information on how to implement a licensing program.

So, now that you've decided to license, let's see exactly what's involved.

2

Intellectual Property

The development, protection, and proper utilization of intellectual property (IP) are of fundamental importance to companies active in technology licensing. In fact, intellectual property provides both the basis for technology licensing and its components. Before any licensing effort is contemplated, a thorough review of existing intellectual property should be performed and an IP strategy developed.

The first half of this chapter introduces and briefly explains the legal concepts behind trademarks, patents, copyrights, know-how, and mask works. Then, issues relating to IP maintenance are explored, including the goals of an IP management program, IP auditing, the development of an IP strategy, and IP administration. Finally, typical guidelines for protecting, evaluating, and handling intellectual property are listed.

More information on patents and trademarks can be found at the U.S. Patent and Trademark Office Web site (www.uspto.gov), and more information on copyrights can be found at the U.S. Copyright Office Web site (www.loc.gov/copyright/). IP assessment is discussed further in Chapter 3, a discussion of valuation appears in Chapter 4, and details of licensing strategies are in Chapter 5.

PATENTS

Background

Patents are intended to encourage innovation by protecting the property rights of inventors while allowing the benefits of the invention to be utilized by the public (via disclosure of its details and the sale of products incorporating the invention). A patent gives its holder the right to exclude others from making, using, or selling the invention for a fixed period of time.

A typical patent has several sections:

• Cover page that lists the patent number, the name of the inventor, the filing date and the date the patent was issued, previous inventions and publications that relate to the invention (prior art), an abstract of the invention, and other related information.
• Drawings that describe and illustrate the invention.
• Background information, including a discussion of the general field of knowledge to which the invention is addressed and related inventions.
• Summary description of the invention.
• List of the drawings.
• Detailed description of the invention and its implementations described in the patent.
• "Claims" that list the part of the subject matter described in the specification believed by the inventor to be the invention.

Exhibit 2.1 is a concise U.S. patent showing the various sections described (with the exception of the drawings).

The inventor (and his or her patent counsel) generally try to make the claims as broad as possible to extend the scope of the patent, while avoiding claims that are the subject of prior art. The patent examiner, on the other hand, attempts to restrict the claims to what is truly new, useful, non-obvious, and supported by a complete written description of the invention. These four requirements will be discussed in more detail later in this chapter.

United States Patent [19]

Brown et al.

[11] **Patent Number:**   **4,692,262**

[45] **Date of Patent:**   **Sep. 8, 1987**

[54] **SKIN CLEANSER CAPABLE OF SOFTENING AND REMOVING SMEGMA**

[76] Inventors: Robert L. Brown, 3917 Evergreen, Irving, Tex. 75061; Elizabeth C. Stewart, No. 6 Pinecreek La., Houston, Tex. 77055

[21] Appl. No.: 908,697

[22] Filed: Sep. 18, 1986

[51] Int. Cl.⁴ C11D 3/48
[52] U.S. Cl. 252/106; 252/173;
         252/550; 252/559; 252/DIG. 5; 424/149;
                                                          514/358
[58] Field of Search 252/106, 107, 173, 174.21,
         252/542, 550, 559, DIG. 5, DIG. 14; 424/149;
                                                          514/358

[56]   **References Cited**

             U.S. PATENT DOCUMENTS

3,147,124 9/1964 Wentworth 424/149
3,787,566 1/1974 Oeuvraes 514/358

FOREIGN PATENT DOCUMENTS

188316 9/1985 Japan .

Primary Examiner—Paul Lieberman
Assistant Examiner—Hoa Van Le
Attorney, Agent, or Firm—Pravel, Gambrell, Hewitt, Kimball & Krieger

[57]   **ABSTRACT**

A cleansing composition capable of removing smegma comprises in an aqueous solution a cleansing agent comprising a mixture of surface active agents in the indicated amounts as follows:
(i) from a trace to 0.2% by weight, based on the total weight of said composition, as an active material of cetylpyridinium chloride,
(ii) from a trace to not more than 20 ppm chlorine dioxide,
(iii) from a trace to 1% by weight, based on the total weight of said composition as an active material, of polyoxyethylene (20) sorbitan monosterate, and
(iv) sodium lauryl sulfate from a trace to 2%.

4 Claims, No Drawings

Exhibit 2.1   United States Patent—Brown et al.

1

SKIN CLEANSER CAPABLE OF SOFTENING AND REMOVING SMEGMA

BACKGROUND OF THE INVENTION

1. Field of the Invention

The present invention relates to a cleansing composition suitable for use as a topical cleanser for removing smegma from human skin.

2. Description of the Prior Art

There have been proposed several cleaning agents for cleaning and/or removing oily secretions from human skin, particularly the facial area, such as U.S. Pat. No. 3,988,255 and U.S. Pat. No. 4,495,079 as well as U.S. Pat. No. 4,287,101 which discloses a detergent composition for removing sebum or smegma from soil spots in fabrics. None of these, however, are considered suitable for topical application to human skin and particularly where traces of such material may be ingested.

SUMMARY OF THE INVENTION

The present invention relates to a new and improved cleaning composition for removing accumulations of smegma from the surface of human skin and particularly from the skin in the genital area. Because of the waxy or cheese-like nature of smegma, which is secreted from sebaceous glands, ordinary bath soap is not always effective in the complete removal of this material. Also, because of the fatty constituents formed in smegma, it is a host for the growth of a mycobacteria. This invention will also act as a deodorizer.

The present invention is effective as a topical cleanser suitable for removal of smegma from human skin and, because of the particular constituents is hypoallergenic and non-irritating to the skin as well as cavities in the human body.

An object of the present invention is to provide a skin cleanser which combines cleansing agents which are hypoallergenic and non-irritating to the human skin, particularly in sensitive areas such as about the genitals and which is suitable for human ingestion and is germicidal, tuberculocidal, fungicidal and virocidal. Yet another object is to provide a skin cleanser capable of removing smegma from the genital area without irritating the skin which in that area is particularly sensitive.

The present invention provides a skin cleanser for topical application which is capable of softening and removing smegma from human skin without causing irritation to the treated area or to body cavities. The preferred cleanser is a mixture of water with the following amounts of cleansing agents:

(i) from a trace to 0.2% by weight, based on the total weight of said composition, as an active material of cetylpyridinium chloride,

(ii) from a trace to not more than 50 ppm chlorine dioxide,

(iii) from a trace to 1% by weight, based on the total weight of said composition as an active material, of polyoxyethylene sorbitan monostearate (tween-60).

2

Also, artificial coloring or flavors or natural, non-sugar sweetener may be added if desired, and

(iv) sodium lauryl sulfate from a trace to 2%.

DESCRIPTION OF THE PREFERRED EMBODIMENT

The genital skin cleanser formulation of this invention may be in the form of a lotion, spray, cream, gel, or foam, as desired. The cleansing function of the composition is provided principally by the active ingredients of cetylpyridinium chloride sodium lauryl sulfide, chlorine dioxide, and polysorbate 60 (tween 60) which is a polyoxyethylene sorbitan monosterate.

It is also possible to include small amounts of other additives such as fragrances, flavors, sweeteners, coloring agents or foaming agents or the like.

This cleanser is to be applied topically to the genital area to clean such areas including the removal of accumulated smegma and the microbiological organisms which may be accumulated therewith. Smegma provides a culture medium or host material for such microbiological organisms. It will be appreciated that the cleanser composition of the present invention is hypoallergenic and non-irritating both to the human skin and to the tissue forming body cavities (mucosal lining tissue).

What is claimed is:

1. A skin cleanser capable of softening and removing smegma and microbiological organisms which may be associated therewith from the human skin which comprises a mixture containing:

  from a trace to 0.2% by weight, based on the total weight of said composition, as an active material of cetylpyridinium chloride,

  from a ttace to not more than 20 ppm chlorine dioxide,

  from a trace to 2% by weight, based on the total weight of said composition as an active material, of polyoxyethylene (20) sorbitan monostearate; and

  from a trace to not more than 2% sodium lauryl sulfate.

2. The invention of claim 1 wherein the mixture is suitable for oral ingestion.

3. The invention of claim 1 wherein the mixture is non-irritating to the skin in the genital area or the body cavities.

4. A topical skin deodorizer reducing or eliminating the odor from human skin caused by accumulation of smegma and microbiological organisms which may be associated therewith which deodorizer comprises a mixture containing:

  from a trace to 0.2% by weight, based on the total weight of said composition, as an active material of cetylpyridinium chloride,

  from a trace to not more than 20 ppm chlorine dioxide,

  from a trace to 2% by weight, based on the total weight of said composition as an active material, of polyoxyethylene (20) sorbitan monostearate; and

  from a trace to not more than 2% sodium lauryl sulfate.

* * * * *

Exhibit 2.1 *(Continued)*

In any litigation involving a patent, the claims are used to define the invention and determine whether another product or technology is covered by the patent. In such litigation, the patentee tries to show that the claims of its patent cover the accused product, whereas the defendant tries to show that they do not or that they are invalid for some reason (e.g., they cover prior art).

Even after being granted a patent, its owner does not necessarily have the right to make, use, or sell the patented invention, as the patented invention may be only an improvement on an existing patent, whose claims would cover any product made incorporating the patented improvement. The ultimate determination that a product or technology is covered by the claims of a patent (that it infringes a claim) is determined by litigation, which is not only expensive but can be dangerous for the patent holder, as there is a risk of having the claims declared invalid for any of a number of reasons. Therefore, negotiation should be considered first in a patent dispute, and litigation should be instigated only when negotiations fail. The reader is referred to the Compton's NewMedia case study in Appendix A3.1 for further discussion on patent validity.

There are three different types of U.S. patents, the most common being the utility patent, which covers functional inventions and new compositions, including drugs and genetically engineered plants and animals. Recently, computer software programs, which were generally protected by copyright, have been found in many cases to be patentable as well. The term of a utility patent was, until recently, 17 years from the date of issue (except for certain drugs requiring FDA approval), and now begins from the date of issue and expires 20 years from the date of application for applications filed after June 8, 1995. Design patents protect the ornamental, non-functional aspects of manufactured products, and are valid for 14 years. Certain aspects of product design may also be additionally protected as trademarks. Plant patents can be obtained for new varieties of asexually reproduced plants, and are valid for 17 years.

You must file a U.S. patent application in the U.S. Patent and Trademark Office (PTO) within one year of the first public use, sale, or offer for sale of the invention. However, most foreign countries require that an application be filed before any public use, sale, or publication occurs.

WARNING: If you want foreign patent protection, you must not disclose the invention prior to filing the U.S. application.

In the past, the U.S. patent application was kept secret until the patent was granted. In an important change in U.S. patent law made in November, 2000, U.S. patent applications are now published 18 months after the U.S. filing date unless the applicant files a document, at the time of filing the U.S. patent application, that states that the application will not be subject to foreign filings. If such a document is filed with the patent application at the time of filing, the PTO will not publish the U.S. patent application until the patent is allowed.

This change in U.S. patent law makes the U.S. more consistent with most foreign countries, where patent applications are generally published 18 months after the U.S. or earliest foreign filing date. After expiration, anyone can use the invention.

There is another type of patent application, called a provisional patent application, that allows an inventor to file a complete written description of the invention with the PTO. It is not required that claims be filed with a provisional patent application. The provisional application provides the inventor with patent pending status for one year, and must be converted into a utility application within one year after filing if the applicant wants to obtain utility patent protection and still claim priority based on the filing date of the provisional application.

Provisional applications are useful for several reasons. First, the costs to file a provisional application are usually lower than to file a utility application. Second, when time is of the essence (e.g., when an invention is about to be disclosed publicly), a provisional application can be used to quickly obtain patent pending status. Also, a provisional application, when converted into a utility application within one year, can provide the inventor with up to 21 years of patent protection.

Patents are applied for by the inventor and, in the absence of any agreement to the contrary, become the property of the inventor. However, an invention developed by an employee as part of the employee's work is usually assigned to the employer under the terms of the employment contract. Inventions developed by an employee outside the scope of his or her work can in some cases be retained as personal property, especially if the development occurred outside the workplace and the subject of the patent is not related to the employee's work duties. If the invention is developed using the employer's resources, a so-called shop right may be acquired by the employer, allowing royalty-free use of the patent. If outside consultants participate in product development, ownership of any IP rights should be clearly defined in the consulting agreement.

When more than one person develops a patented invention, each inventor's interest is undivided, that is, each has the right to sell or license rights to the patent independently. As this can cause problems when licensing, multiple inventors can assign their patent rights (e.g., as tenants in common) to a common organization that can take responsibility for all patent-related activities.

Patents that are the result of research performed at educational institutions can be owned either by the inventors or the institution. If the institution retains ownership, a portion of any revenues generated by the patent is often given to the inventors and/or their departments. If the research was funded by the government, a non-exclusive, royalty-free license for government use is retained.

Patents must be applied for and obtained separately in each country in which protection is desired. There are several international treaties and conventions relating to patents. The Paris Convention gives an applicant one year from the date of the first application filed in a convention country to file all subsequent applications in convention countries. The Patent Cooperation Treaty (PCT) provides a means for filing international patent applications. Nearly all countries of commercial significance (with the exception of Taiwan) are signatories of the Paris Convention and the PCT.

Once an application has been filed in one PCT country, a single additional application can be filed that lists all additional PCT countries in which protection is desired. Individual applications with their fees, translations, and other requirements can be delayed, saving substantial time and money in the short term. The application will be published 18 months after its initial (not PCT) filing date. It is possible to delay the 18-month publication date by renouncing the initial priority date, but this tactic should only be considered if you are relatively certain that no outside developments that may be construed as prior art have occurred in the interim. If foreign applications are not filed within the one-year grace period, the applicant cannot claim priority of the original application.

The term of a foreign patent varies from 15 to 20 years. Taxes and maintenance fees must be paid for foreign (and U.S.) patents, and in some countries the patent must be "worked" (i.e., shown to have been utilized in that country) to remain valid.

Requirements for Patenting

To obtain a U.S. patent, an invention must meet all four of the following requirements (foreign requirements may be slightly different):

1. *Novelty.* The claimed invention must be original and not previously known to anyone. It must not have been disclosed in prior art. Publication anywhere in the world of a description of the invention, sale (or even an offer to sell), or use of the invention in the United States more than one year before the application is filed nullifies the novelty of the invention. In addition, if anyone can show that the invention was described in any publication or made public in any other way by someone other than the inventor prior to the invention date, the patent can be denied or, if already issued, invalidated.

   It is practically impossible for the patent examiner to find all prior art when reviewing a patent application, and, therefore, it is not uncommon for undiscovered prior art to surface after the patent has been issued. In fact, this is one of the more common defenses offered by infringers. Furthermore, if the invention was discovered previously by someone else but kept secret (rather than patented), the later inventor may still be able to receive patent protection and prevent the original inventor from using the patented invention. To avoid such problems, it is important to obtain patent protection.

2. *Non-obviousness.* If a reference can be found that is close to the invention and that, with minor modifications, results in the invention, the invention is obvious. Or, if the elements of the invention are collectively shown in two or more references and someone with ordinary skill can combine these multiple references to create the invention, it is obvious. The invention cannot be obvious to someone with ordinary skill in the art, but it can be obvious to someone with extraordinary skill.

   Determining the difference between an invention that is obvious to someone with extraordinary skill and one obvious to someone with mere ordinary skill can be difficult. The test of obviousness is whether the prior art suggests or teaches the claimed invention to someone of ordinary skill in the art. Because it is a judgment test, court decisions for determining the obviousness or non-obviousness of a claimed invention are frequently difficult to reconcile. Again, the prior art is checked, and if someone with normal skill, referring to all pertinent prior art, could have developed the invention, it is considered obvious.

The patent can overcome a claim of obviousness in several ways, such as by determining whether the invention solves a problem that has long been known but previously has been unsolved, by measuring commercial success (an obvious invention would tend to be less successful), or by determining the existence of a successful licensing program for the invention (a successful licensing program would imply that others agree that the invention is not obvious).

3. *Utility.* The invention must be capable of being operated or used to achieve some minimally useful purpose. This purpose cannot be illegal or against public policy. For most licensable inventions this requirement is easily met. However, some statutory subject matter (such as algorithms and paper with printing) and inventions with no known purpose (such as new drugs with no known application), cannot be patented. In an important case law development in 1998, it was found that methods of doing business may be patentable, as long as the other requirements of patentability are met. As a result, there have been thousands of patent applications filed for business methods, many in the dot-com area. It remains to be seen how many of these method patents will ultimately stand up in litigation.

4. *Enabling disclosure.* The fourth requirement is that an enabling disclosure of the invention must be provided in the patent application originally filed with the PTO, so that someone with ordinary skill in the art would be able to make or use the claimed invention without undue experimentation. This means that the content of the application must be sufficiently detailed in the written specification and drawings that only ordinary design skill would be needed to make or use the invention in a straightforward fashion. The explanation must include the best method of implementing the patented technology known to the inventor at the time of application.

An applicant for a patent cannot add new descriptions (called new matter) later to an application and still claim priority on the original filing date. Because of this prohibition on new matter, it is important that the patent application be as complete as possible as of the filing date in order to satisfy the enabling disclosure requirement. If the enabling disclosure requirement is not met, any resulting patent issued may be invalidated later.

Factors in Determining Whether to Patent

Filing patent applications is an expensive process. The first step is usually a search for prior art and related patents to determine whether the invention is patentable. Then, the application must be prepared and filing fees paid. For a simple application, the total cost to this point will be a minimum of $3000 to

$4000, with complex filings costing many times this figure. Responses to questions from the patent office, foreign filing and translation fees, and issuance and maintenance fees will all add many times to the cost of obtaining a patent.

In addition to cost, many other commercial factors should be considered when deciding whether to file a patent application for a particular invention:

- Is there demand? Does the invention represent a technical breakthrough in its field? Does using the invention result in a significant decease in cost, a dramatic increase in performance, or a very wide extension of the field of application? If so, the economic prospects for a patent covering the invention are bright, and wide-range protection should be considered.
- Is the invention fully developed from both a design and production standpoint? If not, its implementation cost may be unclear and some patentable aspects of the invention may not yet be fully developed. On the other hand, waiting too long to file a patent application may result in the loss of the opportunity due to a similar invention by someone else, a publication, or some other disclosure. If development is complete and patenting is not justified, it may be advantageous to purposely disclose the invention to protect against later-filed patent claims by others covering the invention.
- Are there alternatives available? If so, what advantages does the invention offer? The advantages must be compelling enough to justify the costs of developing and protecting the invention. In addition, alternatives under development should be examined to determine their effect on the invention's prospects and novelty.
- Is the demand limited? Is the invention based on obsolescent art (an improvement to the LP record, for example)? If demand is limited, is there a market "niche" sufficiently lucrative to justify development and patent protection costs? If not, it might be preferable to maintain the invention as a trade secret (if possible) rather than pursuing patenting.
- Is the invention's commercial value proven? A patent covering technology for which there is a large proven market is more valuable than one for which there is a smaller proven market. If not proven, what will the consumer reaction be? Marketing considerations should exert great influence over IP protection decisions. How to conduct market research to determine a technology's prospects is addressed in Chapter 3.
- Can the invention be maintained as proprietary? Is there prior art? If so, can the claims of the patent application be made narrow enough to avoid prior art and still provide adequate protection? If it is not clear that protection can be obtained, two factors must be considered: First, should resources be devoted to developing and patenting technology of questionable originality; and second, does someone else own proprietary technology that is needed to commercialize the invention being developed?
- Can the invention be manufactured without using any special components? If so, it may be difficult to control its use by others, even if patented. A special component could be an integrated circuit necessary to implement a technology or a raw material available from only limited sources. By con-

trolling the ability to produce products covered by the patent, the owner enhances control over the technology and anyone licensed to use the technology. If special components are not required, remedies for unauthorized use of the patents must be pursued in court.

A thorough analysis of commercial factors will assist in determining the importance of the invention to the overall business strategy. Generally, patent protection can be sought for these reasons:

- To protect innovations that are important to the company's business.
- For future use, or as a candidate for licensing.
- To use as a bargaining tool when negotiating with other companies.

Unfortunately, it is often unclear at the time a patentable invention is developed what its prospects will be. The inventor may perceive some value and may envision some notion of breadth, but an accurate determination of the invention's value must often be delayed until after the patent is granted or later. Inventions that seem of primary importance when patent applications are filed may be less important when the patent is granted, because of changing market conditions. Conversely, applications filed for future use may end up being much more important than originally envisioned. Of course, when examining an existing patent portfolio (e.g., for licensing or valuation) the importance of a patent can be more easily judged.

In spite of uncertain prospects, some guidelines are necessary to allow a reasonable and intelligent patent policy to be developed and instituted. Early classification is desirable. In this spirit, the following observations are offered.

Patents that are important to a company's business usually represent real advances and include claims that cover a wide range of applications and markets. Owners of these patents can use their exclusionary power to establish and maintain a superior and more profitable market position or to form the basis of a successful licensing program. Because of their value, these patents are challenged more frequently (and ardently) than less significant patents.

Patents that may be useful in the future or that may be candidates for licensing often cover improvements to existing patents or inventions which are narrower in scope in terms of their application or market. In many cases these patents are sought to protect future product developments by preventing others from obtaining exclusionary rights. In addition, when licensing technology it is desirable to develop a "portfolio" of patents, most likely including one or more significant patents, which can be licensed together and which will provide a more comprehensive and defensible set of intellectual property rights. These patents can be useful in augmenting a portfolio. More information on the strategic aspects of licensing intellectual property can be found in Chapter 5.

Patents intended to be used as bargaining tools, also known as defensive patents, are generally narrow in scope and of limited usefulness by themselves. However, they can be relatively easy to obtain and, in industries where cross-licensing is prevalent, can be traded with other patent holders to avoid financial obligations. Defensive patents covering a small aspect of a standard technology—for example, the Motion Picture Experts Group (MPEG) video and audio compression technology standards—can be leveraged to ensure access to all other intellectual property required to implement the technology.

Patent Marking

Products incorporating a patented technology can be marked with the patent numbers or, if an application is pending, with the words "patent applied for." Marking is not required to protect the patent, but does provide certain advantages in infringement proceedings, such as defining the period for which damages may be collected ("constructive notice").

TRADEMARKS

Background

A trademark is a word or symbol that identifies the source or quality of goods or services. (Technically, *service marks* identify services, but *trademark* is often colloquially used for both goods and services.) Its function is to distinguish the product or service bearing the trademark and sold by the owner and/or its licensees from articles of the same general nature sold by others. A trademark serves the commercial interests of the owner or licensee by protecting their good will, and also allows the public to select goods of a known quality and prevents deception of the public by similar marks.

Trademarks should be distinguished from *trade dress* and *trade names*. *Trade dress* generally refers to a product's packaging (shape, color, and so forth), and can also be protected (through use). McDonald's Golden Arches is an example of trade dress. A *trade name* is the name of a business or organization, and can either be the same as the trademark used to identify its products or services (in which case the trade name is protected via the trademark registration) or different (in which case the trade name cannot be registered at the PTO but can be protected by state law).

In the United States, common-law rights to a trademark can be established and maintained by commercial use of the mark. Common-law rights accrue from the date of first use, which should be carefully documented. In addition, if the mark is used in interstate commerce, it can be registered and protected under federal trademark law. Registration in one or more classes determines the type of goods on which use of the mark will be protected. The registration is valid for 10 years and can be renewed for additional 10-year periods indefinitely as long as the trademark is still in use.

A trademark's property rights are maintained by its continued use on the goods. An affidavit must be filed in the fifth year following registration, showing that the trademark is being used on the goods in interstate commerce; otherwise the registration will be automatically canceled. Until 1988 trademarks could only be registered in the United States based on their use. Since then applications have been accepted based on the "bona fide intent to use (ITU)," with registration granted after use. When an ITU application is allowed by the PTO, the owner must file a statement of use, and pay required fees, within three years of the date of allowance or the ITU application will go abandoned.

ITU applications can be useful business tools. When the ITU application matures to a federal registration, based upon actual use of the mark at a later date, a presumption of enforceability attaches with the registered mark. This presumption of enforceability is based on the filing date of the ITU application, and not on the federal registration date, which may occur several years after the ITU filing date. Thus the protection offered by an ITU filing is superior to that offered by common-law trademark protection, which begins on the date of first use of the mark.

U.S. trademark registration only protects the use of the trademark in the United States; registrations must be obtained in each country in which protection is desired. In foreign countries, protection is usually granted to the first to file for registration, rather than the first to use the mark, as in the United States. For this reason it is important to register in all countries in which protection is desired before the mark becomes well-known (and valuable) because waiting may result in registration of the mark by someone else and then in an expensive procedure to be able to register your own mark.

Many countries require that the trademark be used in that country to maintain protection, and that the trademark holder submit data showing use from time to time. In addition, the product marking and other trademark usage requirements vary, so requirements must be researched and suitable trademark usage guidelines developed for each country in which the marks will be used.

In the United States, unregistered trademarks can be acknowledged using the "TM" symbol (™), and the "circle-R" (®) can, and should, be used with registered trademarks. Trademarks can also be acknowledged using a statement such as "[Trademark] is a trademark of [Company]." As already noted, requirements in other countries vary.

Because a trademark is so closely tied to the reputation of the owner, licensing of trademarks was traditionally forbidden as an attempt to deceive customers. More recently, however, licensing has been permitted as long as the licensor exercises quality control over the licensee's trademarked goods. Quality control includes both ensuring that the products bearing the marks meet minimum performance requirements and that the marks are used and acknowledged correctly. If the trademark owner fails to exercise the required control, the mark is considered abandoned and protection is lost. In addition, to maintain its trademark the owner must either license or extinguish any infringing uses. More information on trademark quality control can be found in Chapter 8.

Using Trademarks in Technology Licensing

Intellectual property associated with technology licensing is often thought to be limited to patents, copyrighted works, and know-how. However, licensing trademarks together with other IP can offer the following significant advantages:

- Trademarks are additional intellectual properties that can be licensed, adding value to the license and justifying higher payment by the licensees.
- Trademarks can be renewed indefinitely and thus never expire (unlike patents). Trademark licenses can also last indefinitely.
- The use of a trademark by the licensee increases its value. All advertising by the licensee serves to increase the public awareness of the trademark, which benefits the trademark owner.
- Over the life of an agreement, the value of the trademarks can increase because of their enhanced public image, and the value of the patents may decrease because of subsequent inventions or approaching expiration. The increased trademark value can justify maintaining the royalty rates and extending the license (often at an adjusted royalty rate) beyond the expiration of the patents.
- Use of the same trademarks on licensed products and manufactured products can have a symbiotic effect; that is, recognition of the marks on licensed products can enhance sales of manufactured products and vice versa. For example, the "Dolby Digital" trademark used on films and theater surround processors complements its use on licensed consumer audio equipment.

On the other hand, a sizeable investment is required to develop, register, and maintain trademarks internationally. Further discussion of the strategic aspects of trademark licensing can be found in Chapter 5.

Trademark Development

Once the decision is made to include a trademark with other licensed intellectual property, the next step is to choose an appropriate mark. Existing trademarks might be licensable. If so, development and registration costs will be minimized and existing public recognition of the trademarks can be leveraged to the advantage of both licensor (the trademark will be more valuable and more desirable to prospective licensees) and licensees (licensed products bearing the trademarks will be perceived by purchasers as being of higher quality). Many firms use and license their trade name as a trademark (Coca-Cola, for example).

The art of designing effective trademarks is a subject beyond the scope of this book. Firms specializing in both trademark naming and their design can be consulted. However, some suggestions and observations that may be of help are offered as an introduction to the subject.

To obtain the maximum commercial benefit from a trademark, it is advantageous to develop either a single stylized name or a set consisting of a symbol and a name that can be used individually or together as a logo. The name chosen may or may not be that of the company. Different technologies can be identified using either generic descriptors (common terms such as *type I* or *system* that impart little information by themselves) or by another trademark in conjunction with the logo. The advantage of this approach is that the trademark system developed can be used on a variety of products, resulting in maximum exposure of the mark with minimum cost for development and protection. In addition, arbitrary or fanciful names or symbols make good trademarks, as they are often easier to register than marks that are more descriptive.

A well-designed logo should have the following characteristics:

- It must be distinctive, that is, easily distinguished from other trademarks.
- It must project an accurate impression of the company and business, but it should be general enough to be useable with a variety of technologies.
- It must be reproducible in a variety of sizes, and in color (if desired) as well as black and white.
- It must be able to be displayed and transmitted convincingly using a variety of media, including television and facsimile.
- It must be original and registrable in all countries of interest.

The costs associated with developing a trademark can vary substantially. The trademark and logo development can be done in-house or by hiring an outside firm. Both methods have advantages and disadvantages, and, in fact, the best approach may be a combination of the two. The cost to develop a trademark name in conjunction with a naming consultant is typically a minimum of $10,000, with at least an additional $10,000 required to develop a logo based on the name.

Once developed and protected, the logo can be used on products and collateral materials, and licensed to others for use on their products. In addition, the individual elements of the logo can be used alone if desired. As already mentioned, generic terms can be used together with the logo to discriminate between products or technologies. In some cases trademarked descriptors may be used as well, as long as the owner understands that additional development and protection costs will be associated with the use of additional trademarks.

Trademark Protection

The trademarks used in the logo should be registered in all countries where products bearing the logo will be made or sold, and in all classes necessary. Assuming two trademarks are registered in a single class in 24 countries (the United States, the European Economic Community countries, the European Free-Trade Agreement countries, and several Asian countries), the cost for the filings plus local legal work is typically around $35,000. Legal advice regarding problems in filings, registration fees in some countries, and the cost of obtaining and providing registered user evidence are not included in this estimate. Furthermore, trademarks must be maintained by renewing registrations when necessary, with associated fees and proof-of-use requirements, and by dealing with infringement. Finally, do not overlook costs associated with internal administration of the trademarks and legal representation.

In addition to the legal protection mentioned above, a trademark quality control program must be instituted. The quality control program should ensure first, that the trademarks are used properly, and second, that the products bearing the trademarks perform adequately to protect the quality image of the trademarks.

To ensure proper usage, trademark artwork and guidelines should be developed for use by product designers, marketing personnel, and licensees. All usage of the trademarks on products, marketing materials, and in other areas should be checked for conformance to the guidelines, and an aggressive program should be initiated to identify and rectify trademark misusage and infringement.

Finally, a technical quality control program for licensed products must be instituted. This will require either support from the inventor or from product-development engineers (to evaluate licensed products, prepare reports for the licensees, and take care of technical follow-up) or the establishment of a dedicated engineering support organization. The latter is the better long-term solution, assuming the trademark licensing activities will become substantial. Technical licensing personnel perform the following tasks:

- Prepare technical descriptions and applications information for licensed technologies.
- Develop performance specifications and test procedures.
- Conduct sample product evaluations and prepare associated documentation.
- Ensure that all problems noted are rectified.
- Analyze new product designs.
- Visit licensees to discuss evaluations, new product plans, new technologies, and to check production lines.

More information on the organization and function of a licensing trademark quality-control program can be found in Chapter 8.

COPYRIGHTS

Copyright is used to protect a wide variety of works including books, musical compositions, performances, and movies. Copyright protection is also very important in the realm of technology, where it is used for computer software, firmware (microcode used in computer processors), and written materials such as manuals and marketing brochures. This section will concentrate on the uses of copyright in technology licensing.

Background

Copyright in the United States is founded on a provision of the United States Constitution that authorizes Congress to enact laws to give authors exclusive rights to their writings for limited times. The Copyright Act has counterparts in most other countries and is tied to its foreign counterparts by international treaties, creating a network of world copyright laws.

To qualify for protection a work must be original to the author and fixed in a tangible medium of expression. *Original* means that the author created the work; there are no requirements for novelty or ingenuity. Only expressive elements of a work are protected by copyright, not the ideas or concepts contained in the work. If protection of the idea or concept is desired, it can be realized by patenting (if a patent can be obtained) or by maintaining the ideas and concepts as trade secrets. Protection begins at the moment the work is fixed (printed on paper, recorded, and so on).

There is a bundle of rights associated with a copyright that can be subdivided into separate parts that are individually protected. These include the right to reproduce the work, the right to prepare derivative works, and the right to distribute copies to the public. *Publication* refers to the distribution of a work to the public, and is not required to obtain copyright protection.

Copyright is a property right; the author not only has the exclusive right to reproduce, distribute, and prepare derivatives of the work but also has the exclusive right to commercially exploit those rights. As with patents, ownership of copyrighted works often depends on the employment status of the author. Works prepared by an employee within the scope of his or her employment are called *works made for hire* and are generally the property of the employer, subject to certain exceptions. Works created outside the scope of employment (e.g., a musical composition written by a chemist) would usually belong to the author. Ownership becomes more difficult to ascertain if copyrighted works are created by an outside consultant under contract with an employer, and it is recommended that in this situation legal counsel be retained to assist in drafting the copyright assignment clause of a suitable consulting arrangement.

Copyrights for works created after 1978 are valid for the life of the author plus 50 years. The term of the copyright of a work made for hire is 75 years from the date of first publication or 100 years from the date of creation, whichever comes first. After the term of the copyright, the work enters the public domain.

Protecting Copyright

As already mentioned, copyright protection begins at the moment a work is fixed. However, copyright is best protected by placing a notice on every piece of copyrightable material generated, including all written copies of programs, schematics, and other technical documentation; media such as disks, tapes, and ROMs; programs themselves (e.g., the notice appears on the screen when booted up); and manuals.

The following are typical copyright notices:

- Simple notice (e.g., for a published paper or product manual):
  © [year] [Company]. All Rights Reserved.
- More comprehensive notice (e.g., for a computer disk containing code used to program a digital signal processor (DSP)):
  This product contains one or more programs protected under international and U.S. copyright laws as unpublished works. They are confidential

and proprietary to [Company]. Their reproduction or disclosure, in whole or in part, or the production of derivative works therefrom without the express permission of [Company] is prohibited. Copyright [year] by [Company]. All rights reserved.

It is not necessary to register a copyright with the Copyright Office to obtain protection. However, there are important benefits made available through registration. An infringement claim cannot be filed until the copyright has been filed, and registration authorizes the court to presume that the registrant is the owner of the work. In addition, if an infringement claim is pursued, higher (statutory) damages and attorneys' fees can be collected on a successful verdict.

To register the work, you must fill out a simple application form (form TX for computer software) and send it together with one copy of the unpublished work (two copies if the work is published) and the registration fee to the Registrar of Copyrights, United States Copyright Office, Library of Congress, Washington, DC 20559. A sample registration form is shown in Exhibit 2.2.

At a minimum, copyrighted works associated with each major commercial release of a product should be registered if any changes to the works have been made. Application can be made as soon as the design has been completed and released for manufacture.

KNOW-HOW

Background

The term *know-how* is used broadly to designate all industrial information and data, including trade secrets. Protectable know-how (trade secrets) includes formulas, unpatented inventions and techniques, business and marketing plans intended for internal use, and all other intellectual property, not protected in other ways, that is particular and essential to the operation of the business.

Unprotectable know-how (also sometimes referred to as *show-how*) includes everything else such as consulting and other assistance given to licensees during the transfer of technology, employees' skills that are of general use in the practice of a profession, and advertising and marketing materials and capability.

The use of protectable know-how can be restricted, while the use of unprotectable know-how generally cannot be. Both can be provided under a license agreement, however.

Exhibit 2.3 lists many of the types of information and data that could be considered know-how.

Protecting Know-How

Unlike patents, trademarks, and copyrighted works, there are no formal application or registration procedures for protecting know-how. Instead, know-how is protected by keeping it secret. Secrecy is maintained by instituting policies about

Filling Out Application Form TX

Detach and read these instructions before completing this form.
Make sure all applicable spaces have been filled in before you return this form.

BASIC INFORMATION

When to Use This Form: Use Form TX for registration of published or unpublished nondramatic literary works, excluding periodicals or serial issues. This class includes a wide variety of works: fiction, nonfiction, poetry, textbooks, reference works, directories, catalogs, advertising copy, compilations of information, and computer programs. For periodicals and serials, use Form SE.

Deposit to Accompany Application: An application for copyright registration must be accompanied by a deposit consisting of copies or phonorecords representing the entire work for which registration is to be made. The following are the general deposit requirements as set forth in the statute:

Unpublished Work: Deposit one complete copy (or phonorecord).

Published Work: Deposit two complete copies (or one phonorecord) of the best edition.

Work First Published Outside the United States: Deposit one complete copy (or phonorecord) of the first foreign edition.

Contribution to a Collective Work: Deposit one complete copy (or phonorecord) of the best edition of the collective work.

The Copyright Notice: For works first published on or after March 1, 1989, the law provides that a copyright notice in a specified form "may be placed on all publicly distributed copies from which the work can be visually perceived." Use of the copyright notice is the responsibility of the copyright owner and does not require advance permission from the Copyright Office. The required form of the notice for copies generally consists of three elements: (1) the symbol "©," or the word "Copyright," or the abbreviation "Copr."; (2) the year of first publication; and (3) the name of the owner of copyright. For example: "©1995 Jane Cole." The notice is to be affixed to the copies "in such manner and location as to give reasonable notice of the claim of copyright." Works first published prior to March 1, 1989, **must** carry the notice or risk loss of copyright protection.

For information about notice requirements for works published before March 1, 1989, or other copyright information, write: Information Section, LM-401, Copyright Office, Library of Congress, Washington, D.C. 20559-6000.

PRIVACY ACT ADVISORY STATEMENT
Required by the Privacy Act of 1974 (Public Law 93-579)

AUTHORITY FOR REQUESTING THIS INFORMATION:
• Title 17, U.S.C., Secs. 409 and 410

FURNISHING THE REQUESTED INFORMATION IS:
• Voluntary

BUT IF THE INFORMATION IS NOT FURNISHED:
• It may be necessary to delay or refuse registration
• You may not be entitled to certain relief, remedies, and benefits provided in chapters 4 and 5 of title 17, U.S.C.

PRINCIPAL USES OF REQUESTED INFORMATION:
• Establishment and maintenance of a public record
• Examination of the application for compliance with legal requirements

OTHER ROUTINE USES:
• Public inspection and copying
• Preparation of public indexes
• Preparation of public catalogs of copyright registrations
• Preparation of search reports upon request

NOTE:
• No other advisory statement will be given you in connection with this application
• Please keep this statement and refer to it if we communicate with you regarding this application

---

Exhibit 2.2   Filling Out Application Form TX

LINE-BY-LINE INSTRUCTIONS

Please type or print using black ink.

1 SPACE 1: Title

Title of This Work: Every work submitted for copyright registration must be given a title to identify that particular work. If the copies or phonorecords of the work bear a title or an identifying phrase that could serve as a title, transcribe that wording *completely* and *exactly* on the application. Indexing of the registration and future identification of the work will depend on the information you give here.

Previous or Alternative Titles: Complete this space if there are any additional titles for the work under which someone searching for the registration might be likely to look or under which a document pertaining to the work might be recorded.

Publication as a Contribution: If the work being registered is a contribution to a periodical, serial, or collection, give the title of the contribution in the "Title of this Work" space. Then, in the line headed "Publication as a Contribution," give information about the collective work in which the contribution appeared.

2 SPACE 2: Author(s)

General Instructions: After reading these instructions, decide who are the "authors" of this work for copyright purposes. Then, unless the work is a "collective work," give the requested information about every "author" who contributed any appreciable amount of copyrightable matter to this version of the work. If you need further space, request Continuation sheets. In the case of a collective work such as an anthology, collection of essays, or encyclopedia, give information about the author of the collective work as a whole.

Name of Author: The fullest form of the author's name should be given. Unless the work was "made for hire," the individual who actually created the work is its "author." In the case of a work made for hire, the statute provides that "the employer or other person for whom the work was prepared is considered the author."

What is a "Work Made for Hire"? A "work made for hire" is defined as (1) "a work prepared by an employee within the scope of his or her employment"; or (2) "a work specially ordered or commissioned for use as a contribution to a collective work, as a part of a motion picture or other audiovisual work, as a translation, as a supplementary work, as a compilation, as an instructional text, as a test, as answer material for a test, or as an atlas, if the parties expressly agree in a written instrument signed by them that the works shall be considered a work made for hire." If you have checked "Yes" to indicate that the work was "made for hire," you must give the full legal name of the employer (or other person for whom the work was prepared). You may also include the name of the employee along with the name of the employer (for example: "Elster Publishing Co., employer for hire of John Ferguson").

"Anonymous" or "Pseudonymous" Work: An author's contribution to a work is "anonymous" if that author is not identified on the copies or phonorecords of the work. An author's contribution to a work is "pseudonymous" if that author is identified on the copies or phonorecords under a fictitious name. If the work is "anonymous" you may: (1) leave the line blank; or (2) state "anonymous" on the line; or (3) reveal the author's identity. If the work is "pseudonymous" you may: (1) leave the line blank; or (2) give the pseudonym and identify it as such (for example: "Huntley Haverstock, pseudonym"); or (3) reveal the author's name, making clear which is the real name and which is the pseudonym (for example, "Judith Barton, whose pseudonym is Madeline Elster"). However, the citizenship or domicile of the author must be given in all cases.

Dates of Birth and Death: If the author is dead, the statute requires that the year of death be included in the application unless the work is anonymous or pseudonymous. The author's birth date is optional but is useful as a form of identification. Leave this space blank if the author's contribution was a "work made for hire."

Exhibit 2.2 *(Continued)*

Author's Nationality or Domicile: Give the country of which the author is a citizen or the country in which the author is domiciled. Nationality or domicile must be given in all cases.

Nature of Authorship: After the words "Nature of Authorship," give a brief general statement of the nature of this particular author's contribution to the work. Examples: "Entire text"; "Coauthor of entire text"; "Computer program"; "Editorial revisions"; "Compilation and English translation"; "New text."

3 SPACE 3: Creation and Publication

General Instructions: Do not confuse "creation" with "publication." Every application for copyright registration must state "the year in which creation of the work was completed." Give the date and nation of first publication only if the work has been published.

Creation: Under the statute, a work is "created" when it is fixed in a copy or phonorecord for the first time. Where a work has been prepared over a period of time, the part of the work existing in fixed form on a particular date constitutes the created work on that date. The date you give here should be the year in which the author completed the particular version for which registration is now being sought, even if other versions exist or if further changes or additions are planned.

Publication: The statute defines "publication" as "the distribution of copies or phonorecords of a work to the public by sale or other transfer of ownership, or by rental, lease, or lending"; a work is also "published" if there has been an "offering to distribute copies or phonorecords to a group of persons for purposes of further distribution, public performance, or public display." Give the full date (month, day, year) when, and the country where, publication first occurred. If first publication took place simultaneously in the United States and other countries, it is sufficient to state "U.S.A."

4 SPACE 4: Claimant(s)

Name(s) and Address(es) of Copyright Claimant(s): Give the name(s) and address(es) of the copyright claimant(s) in this work even if the claimant

6 SPACE 6: Derivative Work or Compilation

General Instructions: Complete space 6 if this work is a "changed version," "compilation," or "derivative work" and if it incorporates one or more earlier works that have already been published or registered for copyright or that have fallen into the public domain. A "compilation" is defined as "a work formed by the collection and assembling of preexisting materials or of data that are selected, coordinated, or arranged in such a way that the resulting work as a whole constitutes an original work of authorship." A "derivative work" is "a work based on one or more preexisting works." Examples of derivative works include translations, fictionalizations, abridgments, condensations, or "any other form in which a work may be recast, transformed, or adapted." Derivative works also include works "consisting of editorial revisions, annotations, or other modifications" if these changes, as a whole, represent an original work of authorship.

Preexisting Material (space 6a): For derivative works, complete this space and space 6b. In space 6a identify the preexisting work that has been recast, transformed, or adapted. An example of preexisting material might be: "Russian version of Goncharov's 'Oblomov'." Do not complete space 6a for compilations.

Material Added to This Work (space 6b): Give a brief, general statement of the new material covered by the copyright claim for which registration is sought. Derivative work examples include: "Foreword, editing, critical annotations"; "Translation"; "Chapters 11-17." If the work is a compilation, describe both the compilation itself and the material that has been compiled. Example: "Compilation of certain 1917 Speeches by Woodrow Wilson." A work may be both a derivative work and compilation, in which case a sample statement might be: "Compilation and additional new material."

7 SPACE 7: Manufacturing Provisions

Due to the expiration of the Manufacturing Clause of the copyright law on June 30, 1986, this space has been deleted.

Exhibit 2.2   *(Continued)*

is the same as the author. Copyright in a work belongs initially to the author of the work (including, in the case of a work made for hire, the employer or other person for whom the work was prepared). The copyright claimant is either the author of the work or a person or organization to whom the copyright initially belonging to the author has been transferred.

Transfer. The statute provides that, if the copyright claimant is not the author, the application for registration must contain "a brief statement of how the claimant obtained ownership of the copyright." If any copyright claimant named in space 4 is not an author named in space 2, give a brief statement explaining how the claimant(s) obtained ownership of the copyright. Examples: "By written contract"; "Transfer of all rights by author"; "Assignment"; "By will." Do not attach transfer documents or other attachments or riders.

5 SPACE 5: Previous Registration

General Instructions: The questions in space 5 are intended to show whether an earlier registration has been made for this work and, if so, whether there is any basis for a new registration. As a general rule, only one basic copyright registration can be made for the same version of a particular work.

Same Version: If this version is substantially the same as the work covered by a previous registration, a second registration is not generally possible unless: (1) the work has been registered in unpublished form and a second registration is now being sought to cover this first published edition; or (2) someone other than the author is identified as copyright claimant in his or her earlier registration, and the author is now seeking registration in his or her own name. If either of these two exceptions apply, check the appropriate box and give the earlier registration number and date. Otherwise, do not submit Form TX; instead, write the Copyright Office for information about supplementary registration or recordation of transfers of copyright ownership.

Changed Version: If the work has been changed and you are now seeking registration to cover the additions or revisions, check the last box in space 5, give the earlier registration number and date, and complete both parts of space 6 in accordance with the instructions below.

Previous Registration Number and Date: If more than one previous registration has been made for the work, give the number and date of the latest registration.

8 SPACE 8: Reproduction for Use of Blind or Physically Handicapped Individuals

General Instructions: One of the major programs of the Library of Congress is to provide Braille editions and special recordings of works for the exclusive use of the blind and physically handicapped. In an effort to simplify and speed up the copyright licensing procedures that are a necessary part of this program, section 710 of the copyright statute provides for the establishment of a voluntary licensing system to be tied in with copyright registration. Copyright Office regulations provide that you may grant a license for such reproduction and distribution solely for the use of persons who are certified by competent authority as unable to read normal printed material as a result of physical limitations. The license is entirely voluntary, nonexclusive, and may be terminated upon 90 days notice.

How to Grant the License: If you wish to grant it, check one of the three boxes in space 8. Your check in one of these boxes together with your signature in space 10 will mean that the Library of Congress can proceed to reproduce and distribute under the license without further paperwork. For further information, write for Circular 63.

9,10,11 SPACE 9,10,11: Fee, Correspondence, Certification, Return Address

Deposit Account: If you maintain a Deposit Account in the Copyright Office, identify it in space 9. Otherwise leave the space blank and send the fee of $20 with your application and deposit.

Correspondence (space 9) This space should contain the name, address, area code, and telephone number of the person to be consulted if correspondence about this application becomes necessary.

Certification (space 10): The application can not be accepted unless it bears the date and the **handwritten signature** of the author or other copyright claimant, or of the owner of exclusive right(s), or of the duly authorized agent of author, claimant, or owner of exclusive right(s).

Address for Return of Certificate (space 11): The address box must be completed legibly since the certificate will be returned in a window envelope.

Exhibit 2.2 *(Continued)*

FORM TX
For a Literary Work
UNITED STATES COPYRIGHT OFFICE

REGISTRATION NUMBER

TX   TXU

EFFECTIVE DATE OF REGISTRATION

_____
Month   Day   Year

DO NOT WRITE ABOVE THIS LINE. IF YOU NEED MORE SPACE, USE A SEPARATE CONTINUATION SHEET.

1   TITLE OF THIS WORK ▼

PREVIOUS OR ALTERNATIVE TITLES ▼

PUBLICATION AS A CONTRIBUTION If this work was published as a contribution to a periodical, serial, or collection, give information about the collective work in which the contribution appeared.   **Title of Collective Work** ▼

If published in a periodical or serial give: Volume ▼   Number ▼   Issue Date ▼   On Pages ▼

2 **a**   NAME OF AUTHOR ▼

DATES OF BIRTH AND DEATH
Year Born ▼   Year Died ▼

Was this contribution to the work a "work made for hire"?
☐ Yes
☐ No

AUTHOR'S NATIONALITY OR DOMICILE
Name of Country
OR { Citizen of ▶ _____
Domiciled in ▶ _____

WAS THIS AUTHOR'S CONTRIBUTION TO THE WORK
Anonymous? ☐ Yes ☐ No
Pseudonymous? ☐ Yes ☐ No
If the answer to either of these questions is "Yes," see detailed instructions.

NATURE OF AUTHORSHIP Briefly describe nature of material created by this author in which copyright is claimed. ▼

NOTE

Exhibit 2.2   *(Continued)*

Under the law, the "author" of a "work made for hire" is generally the employer, not the employee (see instructions). For any part of this work that was "made for hire" check "Yes" in the space provided, give the employer (or other person for whom the work was prepared) as "Author" of that part, and leave the space for dates of birth and death blank.

b

NAME OF AUTHOR ▼

DATES OF BIRTH AND DEATH
Year Born ▼   Year Died ▼

Was this contribution to the work a "work made for hire"?
☐ Yes
☐ No

AUTHOR'S NATIONALITY OR DOMICILE
Name of Country
OR { Citizen of ▶ _____
      Domiciled in▶ _____

WAS THIS AUTHOR'S CONTRIBUTION TO THE WORK
Anonymous? ☐ Yes ☐ No
Pseudonymous? ☐ Yes ☐ No
If the answer to either of these questions is "Yes," see detailed instructions.

NATURE OF AUTHORSHIP   Briefly describe nature of material created by this author in which copyright is claimed. ▶

c

NAME OF AUTHOR ▼

DATES OF BIRTH AND DEATH
Year Born ▼   Year Died ▼

Was this contribution to the work a "work made for hire"?
☐ Yes
☐ No

AUTHOR'S NATIONALITY OR DOMICILE
Name of Country
OR { Citizen of ▶ _____
      Domiciled in▶ _____

WAS THIS AUTHOR'S CONTRIBUTION TO THE WORK
Anonymous? ☐ Yes ☐ No
Pseudonymous? ☐ Yes ☐ No
If the answer to either of these questions is "Yes," see detailed instructions.

NATURE OF AUTHORSHIP   Briefly describe nature of material created by this author in which copyright is claimed. ▶

3

a YEAR IN WHICH CREATION OF THIS WORK WAS COMPLETED
This information must be given ▼ Year in all cases.

b DATE AND NATION OF FIRST PUBLICATION OF THIS PARTICULAR WORK
Complete this information ONLY if this work has been published.
Month ▶ _____ Day ▶ _____ Year ▶ _____ ◀ Nation

4

See instructions before completing this space.

COPYRIGHT CLAIMANT(S) Name and address must be given even if the claimant is the same as the author given in space 2. ▼

TRANSFER If the claimant(s) named here in space 4 is (are) different from the author(s) named in space 2, give a brief statement of how the claimant(s) obtained ownership of the copyright. ▶

DO NOT WRITE HERE
OFFICE USE ONLY

APPLICATION RECEIVED

ONE DEPOSIT RECEIVED

TWO DEPOSITS RECEIVED

FUNDS RECEIVED

MORE ON BACK ▶   • Complete all applicable spaces (numbers 5-11) on the reverse side of this page.
      • See detailed instructions.   • Sign the form at line 10.

DO NOT WRITE HERE
Page 1 of _____ pages

Exhibit 2.2   *(Continued)*

EXAMINED BY   **FORM TX**

CHECKED BY

☐ **CORRESPONDENCE**
☐ Yes

FOR
COPYRIGHT
OFFICE
USE
ONLY

5

DO NOT WRITE ABOVE THIS LINE. IF YOU NEED MORE SPACE, USE A SEPARATE CONTINUATION SHEET.

PREVIOUS REGISTRATION Has registration for this work, or for an earlier version of this work, already been made in the Copyright Office?

☐ **Yes** ☐ **No** If your answer is "Yes," why is another registration being sought? (Check appropriate box) ▶

a. ☐ This is the first published edition of a work previously registered in unpublished form.

b. ☐ This is the first application submitted by this author as copyright claimant.

c. ☐ This is a changed version of the work, as shown by space 6 on this application.

If your answer is "Yes," give: **Previous Registration Number** ▶   **Year of Registration** ▶

6

DERIVATIVE WORK OR COMPILATION Complete both space 6a and 6b for a derivative work; complete only 6b for a compilation.
a. **Preexisting Material** Identify any preexisting work or works that this work is based on or incorporates. ▶

b. **Material Added to This Work** Give a brief, general statement of the material that has been added to this work and in which copyright is claimed. ▶

—space deleted—

7

See instructions
before completing
this space.

8

REPRODUCTION FOR USE OF BLIND OR PHYSICALLY HANDICAPPED INDIVIDUALS A signature on this form at space 10 and a check in one of the boxes here in space 8 constitutes a non-exclusive grant of permission to the Library of Congress to reproduce and distribute solely for the blind and physically handicapped and under the conditions and limitations prescribed by the regulations of the Copyright Office: (1) copies of the work identified in space 1 of this application in Braille (or similar tactile symbols); or (2) phonorecords embodying a fixation of a reading of that work; or (3) both.

Exhibit 2.2   *(Continued)*

9   See instructions.

a ☐ Copies and Phonorecords   b ☐ Copies Only   c ☐ Phonorecords Only

DEPOSIT ACCOUNT If the registration fee is to be charged to a Deposit Account established in the Copyright Office, give name and number of Account.
Name ▼   **Account Number ▼**

CORRESPONDENCE Give name and address to which correspondence about this application should be sent.   Name/Address/Apt/City/State/ZIP ▼

Be sure to give your daytime phone number ▼

Area Code and Telephone Number ▲

10

CERTIFICATION* I, the undersigned, hereby certify that I am the

Check only one ▶
☐ author
☐ other copyright claimant
☐ owner of exclusive right(s)
☐ authorized agent of _____
   Name of author or other copyright claimant, or owner of exclusive right(s) ▲

of the work identified in this application and that the statements made
by me in this application are correct to the best of my knowledge.

Typed or printed name and date ▼ If this application gives a date of publication in space 3, do not sign and submit it before that date.

_____ Date ▶ _____

Handwritten signature (X) ▼

11

MAIL CERTIFI-CATE TO

Name ▼

Number/Street/Apt ▼

City/State/ZIP ▼

Certificate will be mailed in window envelope

YOU MUST
• Complete all necessary spaces
• Sign your application in space 10

SEND ALL 3 ELEMENTS IN THE SAME PACKAGE:
1. Application form
2. Nonrefundable $20 filing fee in check or money order payable to Register of Copyrights
3. Deposit material

MAIL TO
Register of Copyrights
Library of Congress
Washington, D.C. 20559-6000

May 1995—300,000   ♻ PRINTED ON RECYCLED PAPER   ☆U.S. GOVERNMENT PRINTING OFFICE: 1995-387-237/47

Exhibit 2.2 *(Continued)*

Exhibit 2.3   Potential Sources of Proprietary Information

1. Financial Information

Material costs.
Supplier discounts.
Supplier identities.
Overhead costs.
Profit margins.
Financing plans.
Banking arrangements.
Present and future pricing policies.
Distributor and dealer discounts.
Identities of equity or debt holders.
Share holdings.
Capital contributions.
Management information systems.

2. Organizational Information

Opening and closing of facilities.
Number and type of employees per shift.
Equipment types and utilization rates.
Mergers.
Acquisitions.
Expansion plans.
Key employee acquisitions.
Key employee terminations.
Personnel information.
Transfers of key employees or functional
    groups.
Methods of operation.

3. Marketing Information

New product developments.
Delivery schedules.
Product shortages or oversupply.
Customer lists.
Confidential customer information.
Identities of licensees.
Terms of licenses.
Market research and forecasts.
Contracts and contract negotiations.
New geographic or niche market penetration.
Marketing and advertising plans.
Marketing and advertising budgets.

4. Technical Information

Plant organization and design.
Processes and methods of manufacture.
Machinery design and specifications.
Tolerance data.
The ingredients of materials.
The source of components.
Performance characteristics.
Service and repair records.
Scientific theorems.
Experimental constants.
Chemical formulas.
Software.
Research and development reports.
Research and development plans and
    objectives.
Research and development budgets.

disclosure and use of know-how that maintain confidentiality and minimize the chance of inadvertent disclosure. Typical techniques employed internally include keeping know-how under lock and key, restricting access to those with a need to know, and requiring sign-out of sensitive documents. Risks associated with outside disclosure of know-how are mitigated through the use of non-disclosure agreements and confidentiality provisions in license agreements. Exhibit 2.4 lists representative security measures that can be used to protect know-how, and a typical corporate policy regarding the protection and use of know-how can be found in Exhibit 2.6.

Using these techniques, know-how can be broadly protected and its protection can last indefinitely. However, if the know-how is independently discovered by someone else, he or she cannot be prohibited from using it, licensing it to others, publicizing it, and even (possibly) obtaining patent protection and preventing others from using it. Therefore, the decision to protect intellectual property as know-how rather than seeking patent protection should not be taken lightly. Trade secrets can be fickle friends.

Exhibit 2.4   Representative Security Measures

1. *Physical Security Measures*
   (a) Fences, barriers, and other physical restraints against unauthorized entry onto the premises.
   (b) Guards, particularly to restrict access to sensitive areas and to record in logs the identity of persons entering the premises.
   (c) Physical barriers around secret devices or processes or other physical segregations of such trade secrets to prevent access by the public and other employees.

2. *Strategic Security Measures*
   (a) Maintenance of documents containing proprietary data in locked files or restricting access to files by placing the files in supervised areas.
   (b) Requiring that files be used in a protected area.
   (c) Requiring that files be signed out before removal.
   (d) Restricting access to copiers, particularly at night.
   (e) Using electronic copier keys so that the identity of the user can be traced.
   (f) Requiring users to identify what has been copied.
   (g) The utilization of confidentiality stamps.
   (h) Escorting visitors on company premises.
   (i) Recording what a visitor observed in the way of equipment and processes, what documents he reviewed, and which persons he talked to.
   (j) Having visitors sign confidentiality agreements.
   (k) Control of the manner in which sensitive documents are discarded.
   (l) Locking up notebooks, data, and manuals when not in use.
   (m) Limiting the distribution and number of copies of written materials.
   (n) Restricting access to research materials and instruments.
   (o) Not committing information to writing.
   (p) Procuring confidentiality agreements from third parties, such as manufacturers of equipment, customers in possession of proprietary material, and sales prospects.
   (q) Physical dispersion of the steps in a proprietary process so that few employees are aware of the entire process.
   (r) Obliteration of identifying characteristics, part numbers, or manufacturer's identification of component parts before delivery to the customer.
   (s) Licensing, rather than sale, of documentation relating to company trade secrets, such as operating or training manuals, under a confidentiality agreement.

3. *Computer Security*
   (a) Restricting physical access to computer terminals and other peripheral devices.
   (b) Placing computers, terminals, and other peripheral devices in secure locations under constant supervision.
   (c) Using passwords, software "keys," and data encryption.
   (d) Putting "fuses" into software to detect unauthorized access.
   (e) Using unusual formats for recording data.
   (f) Using hidden serial numbers to trace the source of the software or hardware used.

4. *Employee Procedures*
   (a) Informing employees what is considered confidential prior to commencement of employment, keeping employees informed as categories of confidential information are added or deleted, enumerating what is considered confidential at employment termination, and extracting the employee's agreement to keep it confidential.
   (b) Restricting employee access to areas where secret manufacturing processes or sensitive R & D is being conducted.
   (c) Requiring employees to document R & D development so that a record of the information they had access to and the discoveries they participated in developing is readily available.
   (d) Adopting procedures to monitor communications between the technical staff and sales personnel.
   (e) Directing employees to report all attempts by any unauthorized person to obtain proprietary company business information.
   (f) Excluding disaffected or terminated employees from access to proprietary or confidential information.
   (g) Conducting an audit for each departing employee to insure that he has returned all materials that might contain proprietary or confidential information and extracting from the employee a pledge that all such materials have in fact been returned.
   (h) Requiring all consultants to sign nondisclosure agreements.
   (i) Limiting the information consultants shall have access to.

MASK WORKS

Background

Mask works are the topological drawings used to manufacture integrated circuits and their embodiments in the integrated circuits. The Semiconductor Chip Protection Act of 1984 provides protection for mask works. Mask work protection is in many ways similar to copyright protection. The protection begins on the date of first commercial exploitation or the date of registration, whichever comes first, and ends 10 years later. The owner has the exclusive rights to reproduce the mask work, to import or distribute a chip in which the mask work is embodied, and to allow others to reproduce the mask work or distribute a chip.

Protecting Mask Works

Mask works can be protected through registration. The procedure used to register a mask work is very similar to that used with copyrighted works. Registration is not required, but if the mask work is not registered, protection ends two years from the date of first commercial exploitation.

In addition, a *mask work notice* should be affixed to the mask:

M (or the letter M in a circle) _____ (company name or abbreviation).

INTELLECTUAL PROPERTY MANAGEMENT

Intellectual property is the cornerstone on which a licensing program is built. As such, effective management of intellectual property is critical to the success of any licensing strategy.

Goals

The overall goal of an IP management program is to utilize intellectual assets to maximum benefit. Specifically, this would include the following:

- *Identification.* Identifying proprietary IP assets, both those that are important to implementing the business strategy and those that are superfluous.
- *Protection.* Determining the appropriate type and level of protection for each IP asset based on its characteristics and importance, and modifying and/or maintaining protection as needed.
- *Development.* Assisting in identifying additional key intellectual assets needed to implement the business plan and deciding whether to develop them in-house or to obtain them by licensing-in. If the latter option is chosen, locating and obtaining the assets needed.
- *Utilization.* Maximizing revenue generation through the most efficient use of intellectual property. Actively promoting the development, use, and protection of intellectual assets throughout the organization.

IP management is comprised of several components. First, the role of intellectual property in the business must be assessed; the focus of an IP management program will depend on the company's situation. The importance of and benefits derived from investing in IP assets must be compared to the benefits from investing in other assets (e.g., a new factory). The following general areas should be considered:

- Where are investments currently being made? To what extent is the company focused on developing products, establishing markets for its products, and defining and projecting a company image to its customers? The balance of investment dedicated to intellectual property and to other pursuits will depend on the relative importance of intellectual property to the overall business strategy.
- What competitive advantage will be exploited? If the strategy is to compete based on cost, then IP may be less important than investment in manufacturing and marketing resources (although proprietary process improvements could be important). If product differentiation by technical excellence or market image will be key, intellectual property could be of great importance. Are the markets targeted IP-intensive or served by low-cost, mass-produced products?
- Will success be achieved by focussing on producing excellent products or the superior execution of the business strategy? In the first case, competitors with superior execution skills must be prevented from competing by protecting the IP assets of the products being made. In the second case, intellectual property may be of less importance, so fewer resources should be devoted to its development and protection.

Second, competitors' IP assets and the importance of intellectual property in their business strategies should be examined to help confirm that the strategy being considered is correct.

Information on determining the role of intellectual property in a business can be found in Chapter 1, while Chapter 3 describes how to research competitors' strategies. The rest of this section will discuss how to conduct an IP audit and how to develop an IP strategy. Typical guidelines for the handling and protection of intellectual property appear in Exhibit 2.6.

Auditing Intellectual Property

An audit determines the importance and value of IP assets. The auditor should have technical, legal, and marketing skills to be able to understand the underlying technology, recognize the proprietary aspects of the technology and the proper means of protection, and assess its commercial prospects and effect on the overall business strategy. The output of an audit consists of a report, listing all current assets and their status, and recommendations for developing and implementing an IP strategy that will assist in achieving the objectives of the overall business plan. The audit process should be continually repeated to refine both the strategy and implementation based on changes in the market and the development of new IP assets.

The results of the audit can be used for both defensive and offensive planning. Defensive issues would include identifying key IP issues that need to be addressed in order to implement the overall business plan. This may include finding outside patents that must be licensed or designed around in planned or current products, or avoiding copyright infringement by noting the need for a so-called clean room development effort (duplicating others' ideas using a different mode of expression). Offensive issues include ways in which intellectual property can be used to generate a market advantage, to produce licensing revenues, to add value in an asset sale, and the like.

An IP audit can illuminate several different areas in need of attention. Patents, trademarks, copyrights, and other protected intellectual assets may be found that are not being maintained properly. Important assets may be found that are not protected at all. License agreements may have been executed whose terms either are not being complied with or may affect current and future plans in unanticipated ways. Existing in-house methods for documenting and protecting IP assets may be inadequate or poorly implemented. Products may be found that infringe on others' intellectual property. The effort devoted to an intellectual property audit is usually more than repaid by more efficient use and protection of IP assets and the avoidance of future IP-related problems.

To begin, all existing intellectual property and procedures related to intellectual property such as the following should be examined and listed:

- *Issued patents and patent applications, both domestic and foreign.* Expiration dates, maintenance fee schedules, and litigation history should be included.
- *Trademarks.* All countries in which trademarks are registered should be listed, along with usage requirements and details of usage in those countries. The litigation history should be included. The date of first use and supporting documentation should be provided for unregistered trademarks. Any known infringement of registered or unregistered trademarks should be noted.
- *Copyrighted works, both registered and unregistered.* These include computer software and firmware and written materials such as product manuals, technical papers, marketing materials, and so forth. If registered, proof and date of registration should be included. Litigation history and any known infringement should be noted.
- *Semiconductor mask works, both registered and unregistered.* If registered, proof and date of registration should be included. Litigation history and any known infringement should be noted.
- *Proprietary know-how (trade secrets).* It can be difficult to identify all proprietary know-how. However, an attempt should be made, starting with know-how that is currently used in products or has been licensed previously.
- *Non-proprietary know-how ("show-how").* Employee skills, marketing materials and distribution networks, quality control procedures and equipment, and so on.

In addition to the intellectual property itself, the following are three other areas of interest to an auditor:

1. Where is the intellectual property currently being used in the organization and to what advantage. If not used, why not?
2. Existing and pending license agreements. The terms and histories of all licenses granted or taken should be listed.
3. Corporate policies for the protection of intellectual property, including:
   - Terms of the contract signed by new employees regarding disposition of intellectual property, and any existing employee contracts that do not conform to the current guidelines.
   - Procedures for disclosing intellectual property to outside parties.
   - Lab notebook management procedures.
   - Invention disclosure and review procedures.
   - IP protection policies, including means for protecting trade secrets, trademark protection procedures, use/protection of software, and so on.

Developing an IP Strategy

Once existing IP assets and policies have been identified and cataloged, a strategy should be developed that provides the protection necessary to implement the desired business and licensing strategies. Elements of IP strategies related to patents, trademarks, copyrighted works, mask works, and proprietary know-how are discussed in the following sections:

Patents
Policies should be developed for the proper handling, disclosure, and review of patentable inventions and guidelines instituted for determining which inventions should be patented and when and how international protection will be sought. The existing patent portfolio should be reexamined based on the new guidelines, and for each patent or application a decision should be made whether to maintain existing protection, seek further protection (if possible), or pursue an exit strategy (sale, license, or abandonment). Exhibit 2.5 shows a typical form used to disclose potentially patentable inventions for review.

Trademarks
First, a decision should be made whether to pursue a trademark strategy. Once the decision to proceed has been made, existing trademarks should be examined to see if they should be used for licensing. If not, names may have to be developed, logos designed, and an international trademark protection strategy implemented (as outlined earlier in this chapter). Trademark quality control and maintenance programs should be implemented, as discussed in Chapter 8. If trademarks are currently being used, their protection and use should conform to the new guidelines.

Exhibit 2.5   Typical Patent Disclosure Form

This form should be filled out any time you think you may have made an invention. The earlier you fill out this form, the better. An invention need only be conceived to warrant disclosure. **Implementation is not a prerequisite.** Because you may be overly conservative in determining what constitutes an invention, you should fill out this disclosure form even if you aren't sure that your work is sufficiently novel, significant, or valuable to be an invention.

In filing patent applications, time is of the essence. This form should preferably be completed before the following:

- Any public use, advertisement, or non-confidential distribution of your software.
- Any beta-test, marketing test, or similar evaluations.
- Any sale, license, or other commercialization of the software, regardless of whether under confidentiality or not.

Even if any of these events have occurred, you should still complete this form.
If you have any questions or concerns while completing this form, please contact _____.

INVENTION IDENTIFICATION FORM

1. **Title of the Invention:**

2. **Applicable Product or Project:**

3. **Summary of Invention:** Describe in clear and simple terms what the invention does, and how does the invention do it. State the advantages of the present invention over any previously existing methods or apparatus.

4. **Commercial Advantage:** What competitive edge does the invention give the company?

5. **Longevity:** Will the invention provide that competitive advantage three to seven years from now?

6. **Disclosure:** When was the invention first non-confidentially disclosed or used, including using the invention in-house to produce a product that was publicly used?

7. **Commercialization:** When was the invention first used, demonstrated, or promoted for a commercial purpose? This includes presenting to a potential customer a new product or service that employs the invention even before the invention was implemented.

8. **Inventors:** Who are the people who conceived, or substantially assisted in implementing the invention?

Inventor's Name	Title

Please forward this completed form to _____.

An Effective Patent Protection Strategy
for Companies and Individuals on a Budget

Companies and inventors who want to maximize protection of their inventions while minimizing short-term expenses associated with patent filings should consider the following strategy:

- Begin by filing a provisional patent application with the U.S. PTO. This will establish an early priority date while delaying part of the expense associated with preparing a utility application for up to one year. Caveat: you must ensure that the provisional patent application includes the required enabling disclosure of the invention as of the date of filing. New matter cannot be added later to a pending patent application and still claim priority on the original filing date for that new matter.
- Just before the end of the one-year grace period, convert the provisional application to a utility application.
- At the same time, consider filing a PCT application to preserve foreign filing rights.
- If foreign rights are desired, pursue foreign filings in countries of interest as required by the PCT.

More information on domestic and foreign patent application procedures can be found in the "Patents" section of this chapter.

The advantage of this approach is that a substantial portion of the expenses associated with comprehensive international patent protection is delayed (up to 30 months after the original U.S. filing date) without jeopardizing the protection. While the provisional application (and, later, the PCT application) matures, the applicant has more time to better judge the importance and value of the invention, and can therefore make a more well-informed decision as to the appropriate scope of patent protection required. Unnecessary expense to protect less important inventions is avoided, while the ability to protect important inventions is preserved.

Copyrighted Works

Policies should be developed and implemented regarding which copyrighted works will be registered and which works will be protected as unpublished. All personnel involved in preparing, copying, and distributing copyrighted works should be instructed as to how to mark the works properly. Existing copyrighted works should be protected and used according to the new policy.

Exhibit 2.6   Intellectual Property Policy Guidelines

A. Patent Policy

   1. [Company] will aggressively build an international patent portfolio to protect its inventions and to provide technology for licensing. The emphasis will be on protecting innovations that are important to [Company]'s current and future business or that will be candidates for licensing.

   2. Every engineer will be responsible for the proper handling of proprietary information, following the guidelines below:

      a. All engineers involved in research will keep all notes and data in a bound lab notebook with numbered pages. Notebooks will be sent periodically to corporate headquarters to be read, signed, and dated by a qualified engineer or manager to establish the earliest possible date of invention.

      b. Engineers involved in handling outside confidential information as a result of joint development activities will do so in such a way as to not compromise any related development activities in other groups. Outside confidential information will only be accepted after a disclosure or license agreement has been signed, and will be distributed internally on a need-to-know basis. Confidential information will be kept in a secure location, copying will be limited, and records will be kept of its location.

      c. All unsolicited outside disclosures will be immediately resealed upon opening without detailed reading of the contents and given to [assistant to Vice President, R&D]. The material will then be returned to the sender without being read and with a standard cover letter outlining [Company]'s policies regarding such disclosures and a Non-Disclosure Agreement, which must be signed and returned before any further communications regarding the disclosure.

   3. [Vice President, Engineering] will regularly check recent in-house research to determine whether any developments may qualify for patenting. Any patentable ideas will be submitted to the Patent Committee, consisting of [Vice President, Engineering], [Vice President, Marketing], [Vice President, Finance], [Vice President, Licensing], and [Vice President, Manufacturing] for determination of whether patent protection will be pursued.

   4. Once the decision has been made to patent an invention, liaison with the inventor and outside counsel will be the responsibility of [Vice President, Licensing]. If a development is an extension of a previous invention, it will be handled by the person who took care of the original patent.

   5. Applications will be filed first in the country in which the research was performed, and in additional countries as needed. Consideration will be given to countries in which similar products to those incorporating the technology are manufactured and sold. Applications will be structured in such a way as to minimize the cost of filing (by filing provisional applications when appropriate, combining related inventions where possible, and maximizing the number of claims per filing).

   6. Incentives will be provided to inventors and supervisors to recognize the achievement of inventions and to encourage participation in the process.

   7. Granted patents and details of applications will be kept in a safe location in the office handling the patent.

   8. Patent notices (e.g., "U.S. Pat. no. . . . .") will be placed on all products (when possible), data sheets, advance information, and evaluation boards when a patent has been granted or an application has been filed (in which case "Pat. Pend." is used). Samples of all the above materials will be submitted to [Vice President, Licensing] for confirmation, and [Vice President, Licensing] will provide details of and updated information on patent numbers and patented technologies to [Vice President, Marketing] and [Vice President, Engineering] on a quarterly basis.

   9. Outside contractors will be required to sign an agreement stating that any patent rights arising from development work done under contract with [Company] will be assigned to [Company].

(Continued)

Exhibit 2.6 *(Continued)*

B. Copyright Policy
   1. Copyright registration will be used to protect [Company]'s computer programs and product manuals. [Vice President, Licensing] will be responsible for arranging the appropriate registration.
   2. It is the responsibility of every engineer and project leader to mark all copies of all copyrightable materials, including program listings, net lists, disks containing programs, data sheets, evaluation boards, and other product literature with the correct copyright notice. [Vice President, Licensing] will be responsible for providing information on the correct marking of copyrighted materials and for checking and confirming that copyrightable materials are handled as directed in this policy.
   3. Two copies of all finished copyrightable materials intended for registration (three of published works) will be sent to [Vice President, Licensing], one for registration with the U.S. Copyright Office (two for published works) and the other to be kept for reference. Copies of all granted copyrights will be kept in the [Corporate] office in a protected location.
C. Know-How Policy
   1. All proprietary know-how (trade secrets) should be dated, marked "confidential," and only released outside the company if a confidential disclosure or license agreement has been signed. Any trade secrets disclosed orally must be put in writing, stamped "confidential," and sent to the recipient within 30 days of disclosure. Access to trade secrets should be limited to those who need to know and, if possible, copies should be monitored by requiring sign-out.
   2. Nonproprietary know-how should not be provided to competitors, but can be supplied to licensees during joint development activities or consultations. We cannot expect or require such information to be held confidential after the contract terminates.
D. Mask Work Policy
   1. A mask work notice will be applied to all proprietary mask works, both to each mask and to the packaging of related products.
   2. Mask works will be registered.
   3. Two copies of all finished mask work materials will be sent to [Vice President, Licensing], one for registration with the U.S. Copyright Office, and the other to be kept for reference. Copies of all granted mask work registrations will be kept in the [Corporate] office in a protected location.

Mask Works

Policies similar to those for copyrighted works should be developed, implemented, and applied to existing mask works.

Proprietary Know-How

Policies for the handling and protection of know-how should be developed and instituted. All personnel dealing with proprietary know-how should be trained in the policies, and their conformance to those policies should be reviewed regularly.

In addition to instituting or refining policies for intellectual property, IP management includes ensuring that all employees are covered by a suitable employment contract; ensuring that all proprietary information supplied to outside contacts is protected by a non-disclosure or license agreement; establishing and monitoring procedures for documenting the invention process and for disclosing and reviewing inventions; and ensuring that outside contractor agreements provide for intellectual property protection and, if desired, assignment. All IP policies must be communicated effectively to affected employees if the IP management program is to be successful. This includes initial training for all relevant employees and for new hires and should also include continued review of the process.

IP Maintenance

Maintenance is an essential part of IP protection and requires close interaction with legal counsel and licensees. Many of the legal requirements for maintenance were listed earlier in this chapter in the sections on patents, trademarks, and copyrighted works. Other issues of interest include timely payment of maintenance fees for patents, renewal of trademark registrations (including providing proof of use as needed), response to notices of infringement, and preventing infringement by others.

Whenever more than a few patents are managed or whenever trademarks are registered widely, careful administration is required to ensure that all necessary maintenance is performed. The organizational requirements for IP maintenance are listed in Chapter 8.

3

Researching the Market

Accurate and reliable market information is perhaps the single most important component of a successful licensing strategy. Only a thorough understanding of the size, growth, technologies, products, and companies active in the markets of interest will allow the prospective licensor or licensee to estimate its products' potential. In addition, market information is used to develop both the intellectual property and licensing strategies that form the cornerstones of a licensing program.

Market research is generally conducted in several phases. First, there is an initial period during which informal research occurs as part of the normal daily activities of those involved with the technology. This phase may include reading trade magazines and scientific papers, attending trade shows, and having discussions with customers and associates. Some useful information is generally garnered during the initial period, but a complete picture of the technologies, products, and markets of interest is still lacking.

The second phase is the formal process of conducting comprehensive market research, as described in this chapter. In this phase the goal is to obtain all information needed to adequately describe the markets of interest at the current moment and assist in the determination of a technology's prospects in those markets. Depending on the technologies and markets being researched, the second phase may require several months or more to complete. The basic research component of this second phase can be considered completed when analyzing large amounts of new information results in the generation of only a small amount of useful new data. At this point the raw data can be prepared and used, as described in the last two sections of this chapter.

Research should continue after phase two on a permanent but possibly less intensive basis. Resources identified and used in phase two should be continuously monitored for updated and new information of interest, and researchers should constantly be searching for new relevant resources and information. It is usually safe to assume that, if a potentially lucrative market segment has been identified by one party, others will also have recognized the opportunity. Current information on new competitive products and technologies being offered or developed is critical to implement a successful business strategy. Even if the formal research indicates there is insufficient opportunity to proceed, subsequent developments could result in improved prospects.

There is a wealth of information available from a number of sources that makes researching the market, although time-consuming, a relatively straightforward exercise. This chapter outlines what information is needed, where to find it, and how to prepare and use it.

INFORMATION NEEDED

The information needed falls into four main categories: general information about the market of interest; companies currently active in the market and their product lines; existing technologies used in the market and ongoing research and unexploited technologies that may be used in future products; and current licensing practices in the market.

General Information

General information includes the overall market size and compound annual growth rate (CAGR) and similar information for all identifiable market segments. The types of products currently being sold in the market should be identified and their prices, relative strengths, weaknesses, and market positions should be determined. To the extent possible, worldwide markets should be investigated (it can be more difficult to obtain information on foreign markets and products).

Exhibit 3.1 shows a typical presentation of market research data, listing total sales of imaginary "widgets" from 1998 through 2003, with projected 2002 and estimated 2003 data. Compound annual growth rate (CAGR) data is included to show whether the market being examined is growing and, if so, if growth is accelerating, decelerating, or constant. Total sales data can be used together with market penetration estimates to estimate sales of licensed products.

Our imaginary market for widgets can be further broken down into market segments, showing the relative rank of each segment in total sales and the

Exhibit 3.1.   Total Widget Sales and CAGR

Year	Total Sales ($MM)	CAGR (%)
1998	900	20
1999	1,100	22
2000	1,400	27
2001	1,800	28
2002 (proj.)	2,300	28
2003 (est.)	3,000	30

growth rate of each segment. Exhibit 3.2 shows a typical market segment breakdown. Widget manufacturers or companies considering entering the market could learn from Exhibit 3.2 that the sales potential for widgets is much greater in the communications and medical markets than in the industrial market, and could use this information to refine their marketing and distribution strategies.

Finally, widgets themselves should be examined and categorized. For example, some widgets might be used widely and sold in department stores, hardware stores, and other mass merchandising outlets, whereas others might be used for specific (e.g., military) applications and might be subject to special requirements and distribution. Exhibit 3.3 shows typical data on types of widgets and the market share enjoyed by each. This information can also be developed for each market segment and used again to determine the best opportunity and the optimum strategy to exploit the targeted markets.

Companies and Products in the Market

Much useful information can be obtained by studying other companies active in the market and their products. General business information of interest includes location, structure, history, finances, overall corporate strategy, and so on. In addition, detailed descriptions of all products should be obtained. Any proprietary technologies incorporated in the products should also be identified and studied.

In addition to learning technical details of products, attention should be paid to the vendor's marketing strategy. Finally, key personnel in engineering, marketing, and top management should be identified.

For each market segment and product of interest, a list of competing products and their market shares should be prepared. Going back to widgets, if the manufacture of general purpose widgets is being contemplated, and Acme, Ashtabula, and Widgey have been found to be the major vendors of general purpose widgets in the market segment of interest, information similar to that found in Exhibit 3.4

Exhibit 3.2.   Market Segments

Segment	Percent of Total	CAGR (%)
Communications	47	28
Automotive	17	32
Medical	27	29
Industrial	5	28
Other	4	—

Exhibit 3.3.   Types of Widgets Sold

Type of Widget	Market Share (%)
General Purpose	30
A	45
C	10
Other	15

**Exhibit 3.4.   General Purpose Widget Manufacturers
and Product Lines**

Manufacturer	Product (Type)	Market Share (%)
Acme	AC770	50
Ashtabula	545DX	30
Widgey	Zoomer	5
Other		15

can be obtained to rank the various competitors and their products. More de-tailed information on competitive products must also be obtained; instructions for doing so are given later in this chapter.

Technologies Available

Technologies used in competitive products should be carefully analyzed. Often, products incorporating the technologies can be purchased and tested or reverse-engineered. First, the performance of each technology should be compared. Per-formance parameters of interest include cost, efficiency, speed, resource requirements, and so on. Next, the availability of each technology should be as-sessed. Some technologies can be licensed, while others are held closely to pre-serve their owners' competitive advantage. Finally, the intellectual property employed to protect each technology should be examined. This includes publicly available patent information, trademark registrations, and copyright and mask work registrations.

Efforts should also be made to identify ongoing research related to the tech-nologies and products being conducted at other companies, universities, and by individual inventors. Sources for information on existing and potential future technologies are listed later in the next section of this chapter and in Appendix B.

Licensing Practices

Determining licensing practices and learning the terms of existing agreements in a given market can be challenging. Often the information desired is confidential or disclosed only on a need-to-know basis.

Information desired includes the following:

- Licensing strategies used in the market of interest. Is technology freely available (e.g., open source software) and, if so, are there any restrictions on its use?
- Details of negotiated terms of actual agreements. Are licensing terms stan-dardized or must each licensee negotiate terms separately? Is cross-licens-ing a common strategy?
- Revenues generated from licensing.

Again, information sources are listed in the next section of this chapter and in Appendix B.

SOURCES OF INFORMATION

The Internet has greatly improved access to all types of information and will be used extensively by most market researchers. In addition to visiting the sites listed in the following sections, you can conduct key word searches using the various search engines to uncover vast amounts of relevant data. Information obtained via the Internet from unknown sources should be carefully checked for accuracy.

Internal

When initiating market research, start by consulting with internal marketing and engineering personnel. They are usually aware of at least some other companies active in the market, and they can identify information resources and offer valuable assistance in analyzing data. Their leads can be used to identify still more sources of information, and so on.

Targeted Companies

General information on publicly traded companies is available from their annual reports and 10-K filings. 10-K filings may also include copies of license agreements entered into by the company. The easiest way to obtain this information is from the online Edgar and FreeEdgar databases. Another way to obtain annual reports and 10-K filings, as well as other publicity about the company, is to call a company's "investor relations" department and request an investor information package. Privately held companies, while not required to publish annual reports or make 10-K filings, often provide information via their public relations departments. Most firms also include a so-called backgrounder, which discusses company history and key personnel, in their product information packages.

Product information can also be obtained directly from the vendor, often on its Web site. Although such information will obviously present the product in its best light, analyzing several such data packages from different vendors will illuminate key issues that apply to all competitive products. The information should include the standard marketing literature provided to prospective customers, as well as any detailed technical descriptions (e.g., white papers and technical papers prepared for scientific journals) available. Copies of any patents listed on products or in the literature should be obtained, and so should any other relevant information (e.g., prior art or references cited in papers).

Online and Subscription Services

Other sources of general information include independently prepared company analyses, such as those from Dun & Bradstreet, online services, such as

CompuServe, MSN, and America Online, and CD-ROM databases. Online listings of technologies available for license can be searched for technologies of interest, and technologies available for licensing can be listed. Several publishers and independent consulting firms produce and sell books, newsletters, and technology and market analyses. Sources of online and subscription information can be found in Appendix B.

Trade Publications

Another excellent source of information is trade magazines. In addition to containing advertising from vendors of interest, such magazines also frequently publish product analyses and comparisons and directories of products and vendors, all of which can be very helpful. The large number of such magazines and the associated difficulty in finding all articles of interest makes the use of a computer-based archive that allows the user to search by key words helpful. Many libraries also offer the ability to search databases for relevant publications. A list of some trade publications of interest appears in Appendix B.

Trade Associations and Shows

Many industries have formed associations that are dedicated to furthering the interests of their members, disseminating information, and providing a forum for discussion of relevant industry issues. These associations often publish journals that can be valuable sources of technical information. Membership and product directories can also be obtained and used to identify products of interest and key technical personnel. A listing of some associations of interest appears in Appendix B.

Trade shows provide an efficient forum for gathering information, as representatives of vendors, trade magazines, and trade associations are usually present. This allows a large quantity of useful information to be obtained relatively quickly. The trade show business has mushroomed in recent years, and it is often possible to find a trade show dedicated to the subject of interest at a convenient time and location. Directories published by the show promoters also contain useful information on vendors and key personnel. Finally, trade shows often include product demonstrations by vendors and educational seminars, which are conducted by either consultants, academicians, or representatives of vendors. Details of trade shows are published in trade magazines and, in areas where related industries are concentrated, in newspapers. Those who attend trade shows are placed on mailing lists and usually made aware of all future related shows.

Special technology transfer conferences are held regularly where personnel from universities, industry, and various governmental agencies meet to discuss opportunities.

Patent Searches

You can search the United States patent database online either at the United States Patent and Trademark Office (USPTO) Web site (*www.uspto.gov*) or at *www.delphion.com.* Both sites provide the capability to search the database in various ways. The USPTO site also provides the ability to search the federal trademark registry.

The *Official Gazette* publishes summaries of all recent patents issued in the U.S., and similar publications can be found in most other countries. Subscriptions can often be purchased for copies of all patents in a particular area of interest. In addition, many trade publications and even newspapers regularly publish details of patents of interest to their readers. Most patent applications are now published 18 months after their application date.

Universities

Universities are vast repositories of information that can be accessed in a number of ways. Many university researchers are exceedingly well-informed about technological developments in their area of interest, and they can be retained as consultants to assist in finding and evaluating technologies or they can be funded to conduct research in a given technical area. Universities often hold informational meetings on various topics that are open to the public or to affiliates (partners who contribute to research efforts).

Government Agencies

Various governmental agencies can also provide useful information. The Standard Industrial Classification (SIC) codes can be used to identify companies active in the markets of interest. SIC codes can be found in the "Standard Industrial Classifications Manual," available from the Office of Management and Budget.

The U.S. Department of Commerce can supply information on companies, products, technologies, and markets; other federal agencies provide information on government-sponsored technologies that are available for licensing. Regulatory agencies such as the Food & Drug Administration and the Environmental Protection Agency will often supply useful information if requested. The Federal Laboratory Consortium for Technology Transfer, 317 Madison Avenue, Suite 921, New York, NY 10017-5391, promotes the transfer of federal technologies into the private sector and publishes "NewsLink," a newsletter listing technologies available for license from various federal laboratories and research centers. Chambers of Commerce (including those of foreign countries) can also be tapped for information.

Licensing Programs

Information on licensing programs can be more difficult to obtain. One good way to obtain information is to join and actively participate in the activities of the Licensing Executives Society (LES) and the Association of University Technology Managers (AUTM). The membership of both organizations includes many professionals actively involved in licensing. In addition, the LES journal *les Nouvelles* often publishes articles that outline licensing practices and typical terms in various industries. *Licensing Economics Review*, a monthly publication, includes royalty rates negotiated for various intellectual property licenses. *Technology Transfer Business* magazine also provides information related to licensing. Several books, including *Technology Licensing* by Parr and Sullivan (listed in the bibliography), include information on license terms and royalty rates. In addition, some licensing programs that offer standardized rates will provide information on terms to prospective licensees or other interested parties.

PREPARING THE DATA

To effectively use the raw data assembled using the methods outlined in the previous section, it must be handled in a manner that allows management and others involved in the licensing program to extract and summarize for review all pertinent information. The process of handling and preparing data can be thought of as resulting in three levels of information: the organized raw data, prepared documentation based on analysis of the raw data, and distilled synopses prepared for meetings and other review.

Organizing the Raw Data

Raw data should be arranged to allow quick and easy access when needed. Many filing systems are commonly used. One simple yet effective system places all information from a given company in one file, with subfiles as needed for general information, marketing information, technical information, correspondence, and other data. Meeting notes (including those from telephone conversations) should

Exhibit 3.5.   Typical Competitive Product Analysis Matrix

Network Security Competitive Product Comparison

| Product | Operating Systems Supported | Assessment | | | |
		Permissions	Passwords	Suspicious Files	Network
A	System V, SunOS, HP-UX, AIX, other	Good	Good	Good	Good
B	Ultrix, other in some cases	None	Good	Fair	Fair
C	SunOS, Solaris, HP-UX, AIX, Ultrix, other	Fair	Fair	Fair	None
D	SunOS	Poor	Fair	Good	Poor
E	SunOS, HP-UX,	Fair	Good	Good	Good
F	SunOS, Solaris, HP-UX, Ultrix, AIX	Good	Fair	Good	Good
G	SunOS, Solaris, SVR4, NEXTSTEP, UNICOS	Good	Fair	Good	Fair

be prepared and filed appropriately, as should Web site addresses, copies of all magazine articles (which should be placed in multiple files as needed), press releases, papers, and other information received.

Documentation

Notes from a meeting or telephone conversation should be summarized (preferably soon after the event) in a Memoranda of Discussion. If several similar products or technologies are being compared, prepare an analysis matrix, which includes all features and areas of interest and which is used to analyze all products. An accurate and complete matrix is required. Often, preparing the matrix is a useful exercise in itself because technical personnel must understand and explain these important issues. Once there is a relatively complete understanding of a company's product or technology, a case study can be prepared, which outlines all important details. Several typical case studies can be found in Appendix A.

Synopses

The final level of data preparation involves distillation of only the most important and relevant data into a format, often graphical, which can be easily presented and understood by everyone involved. Often overhead slides or computer-based presentation systems are used. Examples appear throughout this book. Exhibit 3.5 (derived from data obtained using an analysis matrix) is a typical competitive-product-analysis synopsis, which was developed to compare various network security software products (the vendors' names have been deleted).

Exhibit 3.5. *(Continued)*

Network Security Competitive Product Comparison

Administration			Monitoring	Analysis	Pricing and Licensing
Identification and Authentication	Access Control	Auditing			
Good	Good	Good	Good	Good	Min. $ (5 servers) + $/client
Fair	Poor	Good	Fair	Good	See Appendix A
Good	Good	Good	Good	Good	typical system of 128 nodes:$
None	None	None	None	Fair	$ for server + all clients
None	None	None	None	Good	$
None	None	None	None	Good	base license $ + $ per client
None	Filter only	Basic	External connections only	Some	Free

USES FOR MARKET INFORMATION

The information obtained by researching the market is used in several ways.

Market Overview

First, a complete overview of the market is obtained, showing how the company's product or technology compares to other products either currently being marketed or soon to be marketed. No matter how well informed, potential licensors and licensees can benefit from a well-prepared and comprehensive summary. By fully understanding the target product's strengths and weaknesses compared to competitive products, a well-reasoned estimate of its prospects in the markets of interest can be projected.

Revenue Projections

By combining market penetration estimates with overall market data, revenues can be projected under a number of licensing scenarios. This information is invaluable in determining the viability of the licensing program and developing a licensing strategy (see Chapter 5). Using a computer-based spreadsheet program, variables such as royalty rates, initial payments, and market penetration can be easily changed to note their effect on revenues. A typical royalty revenue spreadsheet is shown in Exhibit 3.6.

Strategy Development

Based on market research and projected revenues, and with a minimal investment up to this point, licensing plans can be modified or even abandoned if necessary. The data can also be added to the overall business plan and used to justify the licensing program to company executives and directors and outside investors and to assure them that due diligence has been exercised in formulating the program.

Internal and External Contacts

A useful side benefit of researching the market is that contacts are made between internal personnel in marketing, engineering, and administration, often among those who will form the core of the licensing program once it begins. Teambuilding can begin at an early stage, which can result in widespread support for the program later on. In addition, lines of communication will have been established with other companies active in the target market, some of which may become target licensees or licensors.

Determining Value

In addition to market size and penetration estimates, royalty models must be developed to accurately estimate licensing revenues. Reasonable royalty rates can

Exhibit 3-6   Typical Revenue Projection Spreadsheet

Scenario 1—Sliding Scale, $2k Initial Payment, Low Estimate

Year	No. New Licensees	Initial Payments $	No. Products	Avg. Royalty Per Product $	Royalty Income $	Total Revenues $
2002	16	32000	4000	1.5	6000	38000
2003	20	40000	600000	1.5	900000	940000
2004	20	60000	3100000	1.26	3906000	3966000
2005	20	40000	9300000	0.97	9021000	9061000

Scenario 2—Sliding Scale, $2k Initial Payment, High Estimate

Year	No. New Licensees	Initial Payments $	No. Products	Avg. Royalty Per Product $	Royalty Income $	Total Revenues $
2002	16	32000	4000	1.5	6000	38000
2003	20	40000	1200000	1.5	1800000	1840000
2004	20	60000	5580000	1.19	6640200	6700200
2005	20	40000	18600000	0.81	15066000	15106000

Scenario 3 —Sliding Scale, $10k Initial Payment, Low Estimate

Year	No. New Licensees	Initial Payments $	No. Products	Avg. Royalty Per Product $	Royalty Income $	Total Revenues $
2002	16	160000	4000	1.5	6000	166000
2003	20	200000	600000	1.5	900000	1100000
2004	20	300000	3100000	1.26	3906000	4206000
2005	20	200000	9300000	0.97	9021000	9221000

Scenario 4—Sliding Scale, $10k Initial Payment, High Estimate

Year	No. New Licensees	Initial Payments $	No. Products	Avg. Royalty Per Product $	Royalty Income $	Total Revenues $
2002	16	160000	4000	1.5	6000	166000
2003	20	200000	1200000	1.5	1800000	2000000
2004	20	300000	5580000	1.19	6640200	6940200
2005	20	200000	18600000	0.81	15066000	15266000

be determined by valuing the technology of interest and then dividing the incremental benefits associated with using the technology in a particular market between the licensor and licensee.

Market forces have a strong influence on determining the value of a technology, and once the markets of interest have been researched sufficiently, the information gathered can be used to estimate the technology's value under a number of different scenarios.

Other approaches are also commonly used to value technology. The various valuation methods and their strengths and weaknesses are described in Chapter 4.

4

Technology Valuation

Understanding and quantifying the value of technology is an essential step in determining an appropriate licensing strategy. Accurate technology valuation provides the foundation for the development of a logical and defensible royalty structure and can ameliorate many royalty-related problems encountered in license negotiations.

There are many other reasons to value technology: to obtain financing, for use in infringement or bankruptcy proceedings, to obtain tax advantages, and so on. However, this chapter will concentrate on technology valuation for purposes of developing and implementing a licensing strategy.

In most cases, both the licensor and licensee should value the technology to the best of their abilities. If both sides arrive at similar valuations, acceptable royalty rates should be easily determined. If there is a wide discrepancy in valuation, the methods used by both sides should be examined and corrected, if necessary, or license negotiations should be terminated. Even when the license terms are standardized and non-negotiable, the prospective licensee should determine the technology's value to confirm that the decision to obtain a license is indeed correct.

Valuing technology has, in the past, been as much an art as a science. Recently, however, methods have been developed or adapted from tools used to value tangible property, and these methods apply more objective principles to valuation. Several management consulting and accounting firms have experts in technology valuation on staff, some of whom have written books on the subject.

Some of the methods described in this chapter will be useful in certain situations, whereas others will not be. The most accurate valuation would make use of several or all of the techniques outlined in this chapter, using the best features of each to arrive at the most logical and well-reasoned estimate.

SHARING PROFITS

All of the valuation methods outlined theoretically result in an estimate of the total value of the technology. When licensing, profits associated with the technology must be divided between the licensor and licensee in a fair and reasonable manner.

The split of profits depends at least partly on the stage of development of the technology being licensed. A fully developed, commercially proven technology could justify a profit share of up to 50% for the licensor, while for a less-proven technology (e.g., one that has been technically but not commercially proven), the licensor's share might be 25% to 35%. A license for unproven technology that has not been fully developed might specify a profit share of 20% or less for the licensor to compensate for the higher risk shifted to the licensee.

The markets in which licensed products will be sold should also be considered when determining a fair split of the profits. Products targeted at high-profit markets, where little selling is required, can justify a larger portion of the profits being paid to the licensor than can products targeted at low-profit markets with high selling costs.

After licensor and licensee have agreed to a fair division of profit, they must next agree on how profit will be calculated. Determining the appropriate measure of profit used for purposes of calculating royalties can be difficult. Gross profit is probably too broad a measure because it includes overhead, marketing, and other legitimate costs. On the other hand, disagreements may arise between the licensor and licensee regarding the adjustments made to determine net profit. Sales costs can also affect profitability.

To overcome potential difficulties in determining profits, the agreement may specify the royalties due as a percentage of net sales or as some other more easily quantified measure, even though this may not always represent the exact share of the profits negotiated. Calculating (and auditing) royalties paid based on net sales is much easier than calculating royalties based on some measure of profitability. Conversion of share of profits to percentage of sales can be achieved by estimating the profit margin of the licensed products. For example, if the profit margin is 20%, 25% of the profit would equal 5% of the net sales. Alternatively, profit sharing can be coupled with performance requirements to ensure that the licensor receives minimum payments.

Finally, it is likely that in long-term agreements the economic benefit will change over time and that a different split of profits may be justified. Keeping in mind that it is much easier to lower rates than to raise them, the licensor's share can be reduced by a general reduction in rates, by capping total payments in, say, a calendar year, by providing deeper quantity discounts, by refunding a share of the royalties to the licensee, by adding new technologies to the agreement with no rise in royalties, or by a combination of these approaches. If the licensor anticipates that its profit share should increase, the term of the agreement should be shortened to allow renegotiation of rates at the appropriate time.

COST-BASED VALUATION

Cost-based valuation equates the value of a technology with the cost to replace it, either with identical or equivalent technology. It is assumed that market forces will equalize the economic value of a technology with its price, but studies have shown that often this is not the case. More importantly, a cost-based valuation does not take into account the commercial value, either actual or potential, of the technology being valued. Cost-based valuations can be useful in helping to determine whether to license or develop a technology in-house, as long as the legal issues regarding protection of the technology offered for license are considered. In addition, a cost-based valuation can be used by a licensor to help determine a lower limit on acceptable license terms.

One common cost-based approach bases the valuation on the total expenses associated with developing a technology, converted to their current value. The total investment includes the cost of development, including overhead, and any intellectual property protection costs (e.g., patent filings, trademark and copyright registrations, and so forth) associated with the technology. Another approach estimates the cost of recreating the technology. Depreciation and functional and economic obsolescences should be factored into the final figure. With both approaches, some additional amount should be added to cover licensing costs and other uncertainties.

The opportunity cost of investing in the technology can be factored into the cost-based valuation if desired. Although somewhat imprecise, factoring in the opportunity cost is useful in some instances, particularly when choosing between licensing a technology to others and continuing to manufacture products incorporating the technology. In order to estimate the opportunity cost, factors representing the average value of profit generated from company resources and the probability of successful commercialization must be determined. These factors are then applied to the total direct costs of the technology to determine the value of the resources devoted to the technology had they been applied in a different area.

Example

The XYZ company developed and patented a chemical process. The costs associated with the project are shown in Exhibit 4.1. Business conditions have now

Exhibit 4.1. XYZ Company Process Project Costs

Year	Salaries	Overhead	Materials	Legal and Professional	Pilot Plant	Total
1	100	10	100	10	0	220
2	120	15	50	10	0	195
3	200	25	50	100	0	375
4	300	40	100	50	100	590
5	400	60	200	50	500	1,410

changed, and XYZ has decided to sell the process. Determine its value using a cost-based approach.

The costs associated with developing and patenting the process totaled $2,790. However, these amounts should be converted to current (year 5) dollars by adjusting them to account for inflation, as shown in Exhibit 4.2. The cost-based value of the process in year-five dollars is, therefore, $2,962.

MARKET-BASED VALUATION

In market-based valuation, comparable transactions are analyzed to determine a technology's value. Accurate market-based valuations require that there be an active market in comparable technologies, that these comparable technologies be sold and the sales terms be known, and that all transactions studied be between independent and willing parties.

Unfortunately, these requirements are rarely met, although limited comparable data can be found for licensing in general and for certain industries. In addition, an auction can be used to determine a market-based valuation.

The 3% to 5% Rule

When licensing important technologies (as opposed to minor improvements), royalty rates of from 3% to 5% of the manufacturer's selling price are common in many industries.

There is some historical precedent for this range because judgments in patent infringement cases have often been in this range. However, terms imposed by a judge on the basis of found infringement may be quite different from those established through negotiation. On the other hand, many freely negotiated agreements include additional intellectual property (trademarks, know-how, and/or copyrighted works) as well as support, both of which can justify higher rates.

To this day, a large percentage of agreements specify royalties between 3% and 5% (see the next section on industry standards for more details). Because these rates are ubiquitous, many licensees feel comfortable with 3% to 5% royalties and, in contrast, they may feel uncomfortable if proposed rates are higher.

From the licensor's perspective, proposed rates should be justified by analyzing the economic benefit to the licensee of utilizing the licensed technology (see

Exhibit 4.2. Process Project Costs Adjusted for Inflation

Year	Cost	Inflation	Adjusted Cost (Y5$)
1	220	8%	283
2	195	7%	232
3	375	6%	417
4	590	5%	620
5	1,410	5%	1,410

the section on economic analysis). If the analysis supports rates in the 3% to 5% range, the licensor can take comfort in knowing that prospective licensees will probably find the proposed rates reasonable. If the rates supported are in excess of 5%, it is likely that a compelling argument will have to be presented by the licensor to support its proposal. Finally, if rates below 3% are determined to be appropriate, the licensor can factor this knowledge into its negotiating strategy.

It should be noted that a 3% to 5% royalty will often approximate a reasonable share of profits, as discussed earlier in this chapter.

Industry Standards

Valuing technology (or, more accurately, determining appropriate royalty rates) based on industry standards is one of the most commonly used approaches in licensing. Even when other valuation techniques are utilized, licensees will almost certainly compare the terms offered with other licensing arrangements with which they are familiar. However, appropriate terms in any industry will change over time, along with products, markets, and economic conditions. In addition, other license terms may not accurately reflect the value of the technology offered (or even the value of the technology for which they are being used). Nevertheless, industry standards can have a powerful influence over license negotiations.

As noted in Chapter 3, royalty rate information can be difficult to obtain. Some public information is available, and is listed in Exhibit 4.3 (expressed as percentage of net sales unless otherwise noted). More information on royalty rates can be found in the case studies of Appendix A.

All Industries

Several studies have been made of royalty rates, and most agree with the data listed in Exhibit 4.3.

Exhibit 4.3 shows that most licensing-in agreements carry royalty rates of from 0% to 5%, whereas rates for licensing-out are slightly higher. In both cases rates in excess of 10% are rare.

Computing

Royalty rates for computer hardware generally fall in the range of from 1% to 5%, influenced strongly by IBM's adopting this range in their licensing policy of 1988. Rates for licensing-in are predominantly from 0% to 2%, while licensing-

Exhibit 4.3. Range of Royalty Rates

Rate	Licensing-In	Licensing-Out
	(% of agreements)	(% of agreements)
0–2%	30–40%	10–20%
2–5%	40–50%	40–50%
5–10%	20–30%	30–40%
10–15%	5–10%	5–10%
>15%	<2%	<2%

out rates fall more in the range of 2% to 5%. Some computer hardware manufacturers insist on paid-up licenses to avoid loading the cost of each computer sold with royalty payments. To compare the value of a future revenue stream with a paid-up license, you must calculate the net present value of the revenue stream. A method for calculating the net present value can be found at the end of this chapter.

Software royalty rates differ considerably. Applications software products can justify much higher royalty rates (as much as 25%) because of the inherently greater profit margin. Firmware, which is sold together with computer hardware, is often licensed for as little as $.50 to $1.00 per copy.

Biotechnology

Biotechnology royalty rates are increasingly being negotiated as a share of pretax net profits, often 50/50, rather than as a percentage of net sales. In most such cases responsibilities (product development, marketing, and so on) are also shared.

Large initial payments (up to tens of millions of dollars) are often negotiated to fund product development and are tied to achieving specified milestones.

Royalties on net sales generally fall within the range of 8% to 12%, depending on stage of development, strength of the underlying intellectual property, distribution methods, and so on.

Automotive

In the automotive industry, royalty rates for technologies licensed-in generally fall below 5%, with the majority below 2%. This is also true for licensing-out, although, as in other industries, the average rate is slightly higher, and a small percentage of rates falls between 5% and 10%.

Health Care

Royalty rates in the health care industry are among the highest. Rates for technologies licensed-in for use in health care equipment mostly range from 2% to 10%, while licensing-out rates are overwhelmingly between 5% and 10%.

Consumer Electronics

In the consumer electronics industry, per-unit royalties are often used, sometimes on a sliding scale. Royalty rates are generally low because of the high production volumes and low profit margins associated with consumer electronics equipment.

When expressed as a percentage of the net selling price, average royalties range from well below 1% (for the higher priced units) to around 3% (for lower-priced units).

Royalties for technologies incorporated in software range from 0 (e.g., for the use of the Dolby trademark on compact cassettes) to as much as 50% (for game software). Royalties charged for the manufacture of compact discs (CDs) are on the order of 2 to 3 cents per CD.

Auction

An auction is perhaps the purest method of determining market value. First, the technology is offered and the date and terms of the auction are publicized as widely as possible to all interested parties. Then, prospective buyers are given the opportunity to examine the technology, which on the auction date is sold to the highest bidder. Theoretically, the bids received should directly reflect the technology's value without the need to employ any other valuation models.

However, there are several problems associated with auctioning technology. First, a large number of qualified participants must be found, which can be difficult or impossible if only a few prospective buyers may be interested. Substantial time and effort are required to publicize the auction and assist the bidders in evaluating the technology offered; in some cases this may be difficult if the time available is limited. These factors tend to favor the buyer and can result in discounted selling prices. Finally, after a technology is sold the seller's knowledge and assistance is often needed for its effective utilization, whereas the merchandise bought in most auctions is sold as is and is taken by the buyer with little or no further interaction with the seller.

The valuation obtained by the auction method will be final; after the auction the technology will belong to the winning bidder, regardless of whether (subject to some limits) the seller agrees that the final high bid fairly reflected the actual value. Valuation by auction is, therefore, useful only in special situations, such as when several buyers have already expressed serious interest or when forced liquidation is required, for example because of bankruptcy. The technology offered should be sufficiently proven and of wide enough application to ensure that bids will be placed by a number of buyers. Alternative marketing methods, including those mentioned in Chapter 6, should be considered, as should the risk of being forced to sell at a discount.

Selling unneeded patents is one situation in which an auction is an effective strategy. Patents are public documents, so disclosure of confidential information is not a concern and publicizing the property is simplified. Assuming that the patents cover technologies used in industries addressing large markets, a large number of companies could participate in the auction and their knowledge of the technology could be substantial. Finally, the winning bidder can probably utilize the patents purchased with little help from the seller.

Example

Find a value for company XYZ's chemical-process technology, when licensed to prospective licensee NOP company, using a market-based approach, based on the following information:

1. DEF company recently licensed a patented process similar to XYZ's process for an initial payment of $50,000 and running royalties of 2% of the net selling price of licensed product produced. DEF's licensed patent expires in 2007.

Conducting a Patent Auction

A patent auction is a valuable procedure for selling patents. Although it needs expertise and effort to be successful, it will, in some instances, be the vehicle of choice for optimizing revenue from the sale of patents and, in some instances, such as a sale in bankruptcy or a foreclosure on a lien on a patent, may be the required vehicle to assure fairness in the selling process.

What is a patent auction? It is a sale of patents, patent applications, and any other property to the highest bidder on a legally binding basis. The auction may have two or more bidding processes, with an initial bidding step and a subsequent overbid step.

Why are auctions desirable? They may assure the highest possible bid. In the overbid process, companies may get caught up in the bidding process and the selling price may be optimized.

How important is it to have an experienced firm conduct the auction? Very important if you want to contact the right prospects, stimulate interest, avoid mistakes, and maximize revenue.

Does an auction preclude a preemptive sale (or license) of the patent at an earlier date? No, not if permitted by the published rules of the auction.

What are the elements of a patent auction?

- A set of *rules* governing the terms of the auction such as dates for submitting bids, the form of the bid, dealing with ties, overbids, whether the seller is reserving a non-exclusive license, and so forth.
- An *auction book* including the rules; a list of the patents, patent applications, foreign counterparts, and other assets being sold; descriptions (if you can) of the history of the company and the history of the patents; why the patents are believed to be valuable; licenses granted; whether or not the patents were commercialized (and, if so, whether proper markings were used); and litigation history (if any).
- Advice on whether the patents are being sold in one or more groups of patents (recommended if there is a large number of patents, particularly when they cover different technologies) and a list of the groupings.
- The bid form, leaving as blanks only the offeror, the amount of the offer, and the patents for which the offer is tendered.
- The form of the proposed assignment agreement, so the prospective buyer can see all representations and warranties proposed to be given, the scope of the license being reserved (if any), availability of the seller's applicable records and employees and terms of availability. The agreement should require only the amount of payment, payment date, and buyer information to be completed.

- If possible, a non-confidential disclosure (e.g., on CD-ROM) containing (at least) the applicable U.S. patents and their file histories, copies of all applied prior art (U.S. and foreign), and a list of all cited and disclosed prior art. This will avoid the time wasted in ordering file histories and non-patent prior art.
- A confidentiality agreement covering claim charts, license agreements, applicable financial information, and so on, to be included in a confidential disclosure.
- If possible, another confidential disclosure containing pending application information, claim charts, and licenses granted (suitably redacted when necessary).

How do you publicize the auction to ensure adequate interest? You can advertise in suitable business or industry periodicals and send out mailings to companies that could be interested and to patent attorneys who have clients who could be interested. Then, you can follow up with interested parties with telephone calls and personal meetings to discuss the patents and why they are valuable and the prospective bidders should be interested.

Do you just send out the auction booklet to everybody? It depends on how big your mailing list is and how much money you've got to spend. Certainly you send the booklet to the companies that should be interested because they are in the business. To others you may just send an informative letter, a copy of the auction booklet index, and a fax request form to receive the booklet.

Are follow-ups with interested parties really needed? Can't this be expensive? Yes and yes, but they are necessary if you want to maximize revenues.

How long does an auction take? A minimum of four months from the time the auction booklets are sent out, and usually six to eight months, because companies take time to evaluate patents, make decisions, and follow through.

Is it necessary to use an impartial third party, such as a national accounting firm, to receive the bids and monitor the process? No, but you may get more bidders if confidentiality is preserved this way.

2. DEF's production of the licensed product is estimated to total $2,000,000 in 2002 and will rise 20% per year in future years.
3. XYZ's process reduces the cost of production by 15% more than DEF's process, and NOP company estimates it will produce 40% more licensed product than DEF company. XYZ's patent expires in 2006.
4. Both processes can run on NOP's existing facility.

We begin by assuming that the valuation of DEF's process is reasonable. The approach is to adjust the DEF valuation based on the differences between DEF's conditions and the XYZ/NOP conditions. Exhibit 4.4 lists DEF's sales and payments under its license agreement.

First, the net present value of DEF's process should be calculated using the technique outlined in the "Net Present Value Calculation" section at the end of this chapter. Because the patent will expire in 2007, the net present value will equal the initial payment plus the net present value of the cash flow for the first six years. Using a discount rate of 20% (because the process is proven, it is less risky), the net present value is $250,000.

$$NPV = 50,000 + \frac{(2,000,000 \times .02)}{1.2} + \frac{(2,400,000 \times .02)}{1.44} + \frac{(2,880,000 \times .02)}{1.728}$$
$$+ \frac{(3,456,000 \times .02)}{2.0736} + \frac{(4,147,200 \times .02)}{2.48832} + \frac{(4,976,640 \times .02)}{2.985984} = 250,000$$

Next, this amount should be adjusted to reflect the differences between the two processes. First, XYZ's patent expires one year before DEF's licensed patent. Recalculating the net present value of the cash flow for only the first five years results in an adjusted net present value of $216,666.

The 15% reduction in production cost offered by XYZ's process increases its value, but the excess profits should be shared between XYZ and NOP. Assuming the entire 15% reduction can be recovered as profit and that XYZ and NOP will split the excess profit equally, XYZ's additional royalty revenues due to lowered production cost are shown in Exhibit 4.5. The adjusted net present value (again using a 20% discount rate) then increases to $216,666 + 625,000 = $841,666.

$$NPV = \frac{150,000}{1.2} + \frac{180,000}{1.44} + \frac{216,000}{1.728}$$
$$+ \frac{259,200}{2.0736} + \frac{311,040}{2.48832} = \$625,000$$

Finally, because NOP will produce 40% more licensed product, the net present value of the royalty payments (excluding the initial payment) should again be adjusted upward (by 40%) to reflect the greater projected royalty stream. The final adjusted net present value is then $791,666 \times 1.4 = 1,108,332 + 50,000 = \$1,158,332$.

Exhibit 4.4. DEF Royalty Payments

Year	Sales	Payment to DEF Licensor
2001	$0	$50,000
2002	$2,000,000	$40,000
2003	$2,400,000	$48,000
2004	$2,880,000	$57,600
2005	$3,456,000	$69,120
2006	$4,147,200	$82,944
2007	$4,976,640	$99,532

Exhibit 4.5. Royalty Adjustment Due to 15% Excess Profit Split

Year	Sales	Excess Profits Due to Reduction in Production Cost	XYZ Share
2001	$0	$0	$0
2002	$2,000,000	$300,000	$150,000
2003	$2,400,000	$360,000	$180,000
2004	$2,880,000	$432,000	$216,000
2005	$3,456,000	$518,400	$259,200
2006	$4,147,200	$622,080	$311,040

ECONOMIC ANALYSIS

The preferred way to value technology is to estimate the future income attributable to its use. This is done by economic analysis, a standard business technique and exactly the same method used to value tangible assets. Substantial effort and market knowledge is required to value technology using economic analysis. However, the information and strategies generated can be extremely useful in understanding the potential risks and rewards of both parties and in determining appropriate license terms. Most importantly, the use of economic analysis assures full valuation of the technology. Both the licensor and licensee should conduct the economic analysis from their perspectives, and ideally the results of both analyses will be similar.

The economic benefit provided by a technology can be estimated using several different approaches:

- Determine the excess earnings generated through use of the technology. Projected earnings are compared to required returns on all other tangible and intangible assets, which are based on the risk associated with each asset. The difference between projected earnings and required returns represents the value of the technology.
- Estimate the royalty income that could be earned by licensing the technology. After adjusting the amount to take into account the licensees' shares of profits, the total represents the technology's value.
- Estimate all business assets and subtract the value of all tangible assets and other intangible assets. The remainder represents the value of the technology.
- Combine the above methods or use other techniques developed for specific situations.

An appropriate discount rate is applied to the value estimates to account for risk.

All these methods require a detailed analysis of the technology being valued. The first step is to determine as accurately as possible the benefits offered by the technology. Determination of benefits could include answering the following questions:

- Is the licensed technology an essential and primary feature of the product being considered (e.g., a "standard" technology needed to compete in the market) or a non-essential improvement?
- Does the technology provide improvement in performance? If so, what competitive advantage will be obtained by marketing licensed products (can a higher price be justified, will market share increase or a new market be created, and so forth)?
- Are there other licensees? If so, what has their experience been with the technology?
- Does the technology lower the cost of sales, operating expenses, and so on? If so, by how much?
- What is the useful life of the technology?
- What capital investment would be needed to utilize the technology?
- What alternatives are available? How do they compare to the licensed technology, both technologically and in terms of their potential economic benefit?
- What is the size of the market?
- To what stage has the licensed technology been developed? Basic research represents the first stage of development, where the technology concept is invented and proven. Most university-based licensing occurs at this phase. Next, the technology is developed into a useable form (e.g., a marketable product) and product and market testing is conducted. Then, the pilot production stage proves that the technology can be mass produced while meeting quality, safety, and regulatory requirements. The final stage is when the technology or product has been fully commercialized and proven. The investment in and value of the technology increases as each stage is successfully completed.
- Can the technology be used in other markets? If so, an analysis of the technology's prospects in all other potential markets should be undertaken, including the probability of successful exploitation, size of the opportunity, ability of the licensee to exploit the market, and so on.
- Will use of the licensed technology result in increased revenues from other products? In many cases introducing a new or improved product will increase sales of other products. The economic benefit of these potential related sales should not be overlooked.

Next, the components of the technology being valued should be examined.

- *The patent portfolio.* Are the patents fundamental or improvements? Have patents been applied for or issued in all important markets? Is it possible to engineer around the patents? Have the patents been litigated? Will future patents be included in the license?
- *The trademarks.* How well known are the trademarks in the markets in which licensed products will be sold? Have they been protected and policed adequately? What types of trademark promotion have been done in the past, and what (if anything) is the licensor offering in the agreement?

- *The know-how.* Is the know-how important in manufacturing and selling licensed products? Who will pay for technology transfer? What part of the know-how is trade secrets, and what part is show-how?
- *The copyrighted works.* How easy would it be to rewrite the copyrighted works? If computer software or firmware, how efficient is the code being supplied, and will it work without modification in the application envisioned?

Personnel from manufacturing, finance, R&D, and marketing should work together to develop quantitative answers to these questions. Manufacturing personnel can determine what new equipment, material, and labor costs would be associated with the production of products incorporating the new technology, and whether sufficient capacity exists in current facilities. The finance department can determine what capital expenditures would be required to implement and run the manufacturing facility and what production levels would be required to ensure profitability. R&D personnel can assess the technology and various alternatives and determine what additional development would be required to ready the technology for production. The marketing department can identify competitive products and assess the market prospects and potential selling price of the new product. Product sales estimates are often based on a product life cycle model in which growth is slow during the introduction phase, rapid during an intermediate phase, levels off once the product has achieved maturity, and then declines (see the sidebar entitled "Using the Adoption-Diffusion Curve to Estimate Market Penetration" later in this chapter). The span and timing of the life cycle depends on the market and product. Legal counsel can, if required, research the intellectual property history.

At this point projected cash flow over the life of the technology can be estimated, and one or more of the analysis approaches employed. Cash inflow to the licensor will include initial payments, running royalties, and any other payments stipulated in the agreement. Licensor's cash outflows will include the costs of transferring the technology to the licensee, further technology development, license administration, intellectual property costs, and so forth. Licensee's cash inflows will include revenues from licensed and related-product sales, whereas outflows will consist of royalty payments, product development and marketing expenses, capital investments, and so forth.

In all analyses, certain information and outcomes will not be known. Techniques have been developed to allow the incorporation of unknown outcomes into analyses. One such method is decision tree analysis, where various chains of events are envisioned and their probabilities and potential outcomes determined. Alternatives examined can include licensing or not licensing the technology, different license terms, targeting or not targeting certain markets, capital investment, and so forth. Based on the probabilities of each scenario and the economic outcome, the risk and potential for market success for a number of alternatives can be estimated.

Using the Adoption-Diffusion Curve to Estimate Market Penetration

Estimating market penetration in future years can be the most difficult job in economic analysis. Using the adoption-diffusion curve can simplify part of the job.

The Adoption-Diffusion (A-D) Model was developed by the U.S. Department of Agriculture, and was designed to identify which farmers would adopt new agricultural technologies at what time. The A-D model has been shown to apply to other technologies, and its timing data is particularly useful for estimating market penetration.

The research conducted by the USDA resulted in the adoption-diffusion curve of Exhibit 4.6, which plots number of adopters on the y-axis against time on the x-axis. For economic analysis, the y-axis is used to represent market penetration percentage. While the entire curve can be used in some scenarios, the first half is generally most useful, as it represents the early years, which are of most immediate interest.

The procedure is as follows:

1. Estimate the maximum market penetration that will be achieved by the technology being valued. This could be market penetration by a single licensee or total market penetration for the technology. Place this number on the y-axis opposite the highest point on the curve.

2. Estimate the time frame over which maximum market penetration will be achieved. This will depend on the technology and the market characteristics. Place this number on the x-axis under the highest point on the curve.

3. Mark off both axes from the point opposite the highest point on the curve back to the origin. On the x-axis, mark by year (e.g., if the time frame estimated in 2 is five years, mark off five equal segments from the origin to the mark under the highest point on the curve). On the y-axis, choose a suitable scale related to the maximum percentage chosen.

4. From each mark on the x-axis, draw a vertical line to the curve and then a horizontal line from the curve to the y-axis. The market penetration estimates for each year can then be read off of the y-axis. In the example shown in Exhibit 4.6, the market penetration estimates would be:

Year 1:	4%
Year 2:	6%
Year 3:	8%
Year 4:	13%
Year 5:	25%

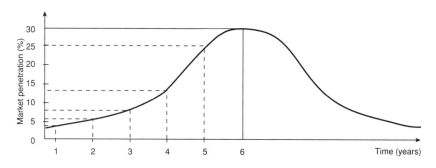

Exhibit 4.6 Adoption-Diffusion Curve

Example

Advanced Memory Technology (AMT) has developed and patented a superior method of designing and manufacturing flash memory integrated circuits. AMT has decided to approach Medium Semiconductor, Inc. (MSI) to offer them a license. MSI currently controls 2% of the global market for flash memory, and, according to its latest annual report, its profit margin averages 30%. Using economic analysis, determine the value of AMT's technology to MSI.

Assumptions for Scenario 1 (see Exhibit 4.7):

1. AMT's technology can be implemented by MSI using its current production process.
2. The technological advantages offered by AMT's technology will allow MSI to capture an additional 2% of the market over five years. From the sixth year on, MSI's additional market share due to its use of AMT's technology will remain at 2% and the total market will grow at the rate of 20% per year.
3. MSI will introduce its first licensed devices in 2002, and market penetration will ramp up linearly from 0.5% in 2002 to 2% in 2005 (alternatively, the adoption-diffusion method could be used to estimate market penetration).

Exhibit 4.7.   Gross Profit Calculation, Scenario 1

Year	Total WW Sales $MM	MSI's AMT Product Share %	MSI's AMT Product Sales $MM	Gross Margin %	Gross Profit $MM
2001	$14,400	0	$0	30	$0
2002	$15,200	0.5	$76	29	$22
2003	$20,800	1.0	$208	28	$58
2004	$27,800	1.5	$417	27	$113
2005	$38,500	2.0	$770	26	$200

4. Due to increased competition from competing technologies, gross margin will linearly decrease from 30% in 2001 to 26% in 2005. It will remain at 26% in subsequent years.
5. The technology has been developed into a useable form, but is not fully proven, so an appropriate discount rate is 30%.

$$V = 0 + \frac{22}{1.3} + \frac{58}{1.69} + \frac{113}{2.2} + \frac{200}{2.86} = \$172\,MM$$

$$T = \frac{(200 \times 1.2)}{(.1 \times 3.72)} = \$645\,MM$$

$$NPV = 172 + 645 = \$817\,MM$$

Additional assumptions for Scenario 2 (see Exhibit 4.8):

1. MSI is currently among the top 15 flash memory producers. In order to reach the top 10, its sales must increase as shown in Exhibit 4.8.
2. Using AMT technology will allow MSI to join the top 10 in five years. Without AMT technology, MSI will remain in the top 15.
3. The "ramping factor" represents the speed at which MSI's sales will increase to top 10 levels due to AMT-licensed products, and is analogous to the market penetration figures of Exhibit 4.7.
4. MSI's AMT Product Sales equals Top 10 sales minus Top 15 sales times the ramping factor.

$$V = 0 + \frac{9.8}{1.3} + \frac{42}{1.69} + \frac{110}{2.2} + \frac{220}{2.86} = \$159\,MM$$

$$T = \frac{(220 \times 1.2)}{(.1 \times 3.72)} = \$710\,MM$$

$$NPV = 159 + 710 = \$869\,MM$$

USING DISCOUNTED CASH FLOW
TO CALCULATE NET PRESENT VALUE

License agreements can require that periodic payments be made or that running royalties be paid on products manufactured or sold in a defined period of time (such as a calendar quarter or year). Other agreements might call for a single up-

Exhibit 4.8. Gross Profit Calculation, Scenario 2

	Total				MSI's AMT		
	WW	Top 10	Top 15		Product	Gross	Gross
	Sales	Sales	Sales	Ramping	Sales	Margin	Profit
Year	$MM	$MM	$MM	Factor	$MM	%	$MM
2001	$14,400	$576	$260	0%	$0	30%	$0
2002	$15,200	$609	$274	10%	$34	29%	$9.8
2003	$20,800	$831	$374	33%	$151	28%	$42
2004	$27,800	$1,110	$500	67%	$409	27%	$110
2005	$38,500	$1,540	$693	100%	$847	26%	$220

front payment. When negotiating terms it is helpful to know the net present value of an anticipated future revenue stream, both to value the overall agreement and to determine the most advantageous strategy. Different strategies can be compared based on their net present values, and the most attractive alternative (the one with the highest net present value) chosen.

Discounting future cash flow to obtain its net present value is the method used to obtain this information. In this calculation, cash flow is defined as net cash flow, that is, the difference between cash inflow and cash outflow. The data required to calculate net present value includes net revenue amounts, timing of payments, and risk.

Net Revenue Amounts

This would include any initial payments made and the estimated future royalty stream, minus the costs associated with administering the agreements, transferring the technology, providing support, and so forth. Projected revenues can be developed using economic analysis, and costs should be estimated based on the terms of the agreement. The accuracy and utility of the net present value calculation will depend greatly on the accuracy of these estimates; market research and the resulting projected sales figures must be of high quality.

Timing of Payments

Initial payments will obviously have a higher net present value than future royalty payments which, projected farther and farther into the future, will have less and less net present value.

Risk

The likelihood of the payments being made must be estimated. From this estimation a discount rate is chosen depending on the degree of risk. Factors affecting risk include the reliability of the cash flow estimates and their underlying assumptions, the viability of the licensee, and so on. Very low-risk investments such as U.S. government treasury bills might carry a discount rate of 6%; the higher the risk the higher the discount rate applied.

Once these three pieces of information are known, calculating the net present value is straightforward.

Net Present Value Calculation

Use the following procedure to calculate the net present value of future cash flow:

1. First, cash flows (revenues less costs) are estimated for, say, the first five years using any of a number of techniques (e.g., a decision tree, as described in Chapter 7).

2. Then, a discount rate is chosen based on the risk associated with the venture. All risks, including opportunity cost, inflation, and venture risk should be included. For high technology start-ups, a discount rate of 35% is often used, while a safer investment would justify a lower rate.

3. The net present value of the cash flow for the first five years is then calculated using the formula:

$$YO + \frac{Y1}{1+D} + \frac{Y2}{(1+D)^2} + \frac{Y3}{(1+D)^3} + \frac{Y4}{(1+D)^4}$$

where V = the value,
   Y0 = cash flow in the first year,
   Y1 = cash flow in the second year,
   Y2 = cash flow in the third year,
   Y3 = cash flow in the fourth year
   Y4 = cash flow in the fifth year, and
   D = the discount rate chosen.

4. Cash flow estimation after the fifth year is much less accurate, so a second method is used to determine the net present value of later cash flow. An annual growth rate G is estimated (say, for example, 10%) for all subsequent years and applied to the estimated cash flow for the fifth year (Y4 above). The terminal value, T, is then calculated using the formula:

$$T = \frac{Y4 \times (1+G)}{(D-G) \times (1+D)^5}$$

Note: D and G are expressed in decimal form in the foregoing equations (e.g., 35% is expressed as 0.35).

5. The net present value NPV is then the sum of the two components, or:

$$NPV = V + T$$

6. Alternatively, if cash flow is estimated to grow at a constant rate, the net present value can be expressed as:

$$NPV = YO \left(\frac{1+G}{D-G} \right)$$

Example

Two royalty structures are being considered by a licensor. The first calls for a $50,000 initial payment and running royalties of $1 per licensed product. The second has a lower initial payment of $10,000 but increases the running royalty to $2 per product.

Licensed product sales estimates are

Year 1:	10,000 units
Year 2:	20,000 units
Year 3:	30,000 units

Year 4:	40,000 units
Year 5:	50,000 units
After year 5:	increasing at 20% per year

Assuming a discount rate of 35% and fixed yearly costs of $5,000, which structure should the licensor propose?

1. First, the cash flow for the first five years should be calculated under both scenarios, as in Exhibit 4.9. Note that the first year's cash flow will include the initial payment.
2. The net present value of the cash flow for the first five years is then

$$V = 55,000 + \frac{15,000}{1.35} + \frac{25,000}{1.35^2} + \frac{35,000}{1.35^3} + \frac{45,000}{1.35^4}$$

$$= 55,000 + 11,111 + 13,717 + 14,225 + 13,548 = \$107,601 \text{ (Scenario 1)}$$

$$V = 25,000 + \frac{35,000}{1.35} + \frac{55,000}{1.35^2} + \frac{75,000}{1.35^3} + \frac{95,000}{1.35^4}$$

$$= 25,000 + 25,925 + 30,178 + 30,483 + 28,601 = \$140,187 \text{ (Scenario 2)}$$

3. The terminal value would be

$$T = \frac{45,000 \times 1.2}{0.15 \times 1.35^5} = \frac{54,000}{0.67} = \$80,597 \text{ (Scenario 1)}$$

$$T = \frac{95,000 \times 1.2}{0.15 \times 1.35^5} = \frac{114,000}{.067} = \$170,149 \text{ (Scenario 2)}$$

4. The net present value is the sum of V + T, or

$$NPV = \$107,601 + 80,597 = \$188,198 \text{ (Scenario 1)}$$

$$NPV = \$140,187 = 170,149 = \$310,336 \text{ (Scenario 2)}$$

It can be seen from this analysis that the net present value of Scenario 2 is greater than the net present value of Scenario 1. Therefore, unless short-term cash flow is badly needed, the licensor should propose royalty structure 2 to the prospective licensee.

Exhibit 4.9. Cash Flow for First Five Years

| Year | Cash Flow | |
	Scenario 1	Scenario 2
Y0	$55,000	$25,000
Y1	$15,000	$35,000
Y2	$25,000	$55,000
Y3	$35,000	$75,000
Y4	$45,000	$95,000

5

Licensing Strategies

The next step in implementing a licensing program is to determine how the technology will be licensed. The strategies, analyses, and information related to intellectual property, markets, and valuation discussed in Chapters 2, 3, and 4 will all be used in developing a licensing strategy.

This chapter will begin with a discussion of factors that should be considered when developing a comprehensive licensing strategy. Then, several key issues that relate to those factors are listed. Special considerations when licensing from universities and the U.S. government are also discussed. Finally, the use of corporate or brand licensing to leverage trademark notoriety and protect trademarks in other markets is explored.

Companies contemplating licensing-out will find these discussions directly applicable, while those seeking products or technologies to license-in should use this information to understand the licensor's strategies and which terms might be negotiable.

DEVELOPING A LICENSING STRATEGY

Once the decision to license has been made, a suitable strategy must be developed. Basic strategic issues will have been considered while comparing licensing to other approaches, but a more detailed and comprehensive examination should now be made from a number of perspectives. First, any strategy chosen should support the overall business plan. Second, projected revenues from the planned licensing activity must be adequate to support the effort and provide a reasonable return on any investments made. Third, the terms should reflect whether the licensing strategy is short or long term and the nature of the technology being licensed and the markets being exploited. Finally, if a long-term strategy is chosen, the licensor's relationship with its licensees must have a long-term perspective; this should be reflected in the strategy, especially with respect to granting rights to improvements and new technologies.

Strategic Fit

The first consideration in developing a licensing strategy is how the licensing program will fit into the overall company business plan, from both short- and long-term perspectives. A well-reasoned strategy will complement and enhance a firm's product line and assist in positioning the firm favorably in the markets in which it is active. Licensing strategies that will negatively affect product manufacturing and sales should be avoided if possible.

One way to ensure that licensed products will not compete with a licensor's product sales is to license only for markets or territories in which the licensor is not active. For example, a technology used in refining petrochemical products could be licensed for use in the production of pharmaceutical products, or an American firm not active in Europe could license a technology to a European competitor but restrict sales of the licensed products to Europe.

If a standardized technology is being licensed, the licensor may consciously decide not to compete with its licensees by avoiding manufacturing and selling products in the markets in which the technology is licensed. An example of this approach is outlined in the Dolby Laboratories case study, which can be found in Appendix A1.1.

If competitors will be licensed, the strategy must be developed carefully to minimize the potential problems inherent in such an approach. Territorial and market restrictions (discussed later in this chapter) can limit the licensee's ability to compete, or the license can be limited to older, less useful technology. Rights to the licensee's technologies can be transferred to the licensor as part of the agreement (cross-licensing). If the license is negotiated as part of the settlement of a legal action (e.g., a patent infringement suit), it must be carefully drafted to ensure that the terms precisely reflect the agreement between the parties. If not, future misunderstandings are likely to arise.

Revenues

The revenues and other benefits of the licensing effort must be sufficient to justify the effort and expense associated with implementing and maintaining the program. Although seemingly obvious, it is quite common (and natural) for a prospective licensor to overestimate revenues and underestimate expenses and time when planning a licensing strategy.

It is not uncommon for 18 months to pass between the decision to implement a licensing program and the consummation of the first license agreement. During that time substantial effort is required to market and promote the technology, which usually includes preparing materials necessary to explain and demonstrate the technology, visiting prospective licensees, and negotiating licenses. Inadequate allocation of resources to these efforts can delay or even prevent the program's success.

After the agreement is signed it must be administered, the technology must be transferred and, if trademarks are licensed, a quality control program must be implemented. Steven S. Szczepanski, a shareholder with Willian Brinks Olds Hofer Gilson & Lione and author of *Eckstrom's Licensing in Foreign and Domestic Operations*, estimated some time ago that as much as $25,000 per year should be budgeted to administer each agreement.

Therefore, accurate estimations must be made of both projected revenues and of the expenses associated with each strategy being considered. Revenues should be estimated conservatively and extra expense assumed. If the strategy being examined can produce positive cash flow under such a scenario, it may be viable.

Financial Terms

The financial terms chosen must make sense for both parties. For example, the licensor cannot expect to be paid royalties that exceed the added value that the licensed technology is bringing to the licensee's products. If the licensor's strategy requires such payments to be viable, it must be changed or abandoned. Requiring large initial payments from small, cash-poor prospective licensees is another example of an incompatible strategy.

Long-term strategies generally require a relatively modest initial payment and running royalties, based on the number or value of licensed products sold. Should the product or technology be very successful, this strategy, although inherently riskier for the licensor than a paid-up license (a license agreement in which all royalties are paid over a short period of time), has the potential to provide a much larger revenue stream over the life of the agreement. Long-term strategies are generally most effective with cooperative licensees; uncooperative licensees (such as infringers) are often issued paid-up licenses because of the difficulties in maintaining an ongoing relationship and insuring payments are made.

On the other hand, there are times when short-term revenues are required by the licensor. One example of such a situation would be the liquidation of a firm's assets. In this case, the licensor may need to negotiate a paid-up license. Because it is difficult to estimate the market potential of a product or technology, especially early in its life cycle, the licensor runs the risk of earning substantially less revenues from a paid-up license than from a longer-term arrangement.

Licensees might also desire paid-up licenses. From the licensee's perspective, if it is capable of making a large enough payment to obtain a paid-up license and is convinced that the technology's prospects are good, a one-time payment may represent a substantial discount over the long term. Furthermore, there are markets in which paid-up licenses are commonly negotiated. For example, computer manufacturers commonly seek paid-up licenses to avoid loading the cost of each product sold with several royalty payments for the various hardware and software technologies incorporated in the device.

When developing financial terms, licensors should compare each strategy to determine which will produce higher revenues and still meet all other requirements. Licensees can compare offers from different licensors or a smorgasbord of offers from a single licensor. Terms can be compared by calculating their net present value, as explained and demonstrated in Chapter 4.

Improvements and Continuity

If the licensing program is long-term, it should address the use of future developments by both the licensor and licensee. If the licensor will continue developing new technologies after the initial agreement has been consummated, the licensee will be interested in learning about and possibly utilizing them. Because of the potential competitive and strategic importance of these improvements, their handling should be considered when the initial licensing strategy is developed. For example, if a technology is licensed to increase the density of data on magnetic media, and the licensor subsequently develops new technology that will double the density provided by the licensed technology, this will greatly affect the existing licensee's business. To promote and maintain a long-term relationship with its licensee, the licensor could include rights to improvements of this type in the original agreement, with or without time, market, or territorial restrictions and additional payments. On the other hand, to protect its core business, a licensor may consciously exclude existing technology or technology under development from licensed technology. For example, technology licensed for use in integrated circuits could be restricted to current or perhaps next-generation manufacturing processes, excluding future processes to give its owner more flexibility in its utilization.

Likewise, it is possible that the licensees will improve on the licensed technology. The handling and use of these improvements can be of great concern to the licensor, particularly when the technology is standardized. Some licensees have developed strategies to license technology and then develop and protect improvements in the technology to wrest control of the technology from its original developer. For example, Microsoft licensed the Java software language from Sun, then made changes to the technology to restrict its use to other Microsoft products. Sun eventually terminated Microsoft's Java license, and Microsoft has since introduced a competing technology. Other licensees develop improvements to standardized technologies and then attempt to have their improvement adopted as part of the standard. In this way, they gain leverage and control over the standard and other companies that provide technology used in the standard. One way to handle improvements made by licensees is with an improvements pool (discussed in Appendix C), where all improvements are made available to all licensees. Another way is for the licensor to share or buy rights to related improvements from its licensees. Both situations can be handled in the original agreement.

If trademarks are being licensed, their use in conjunction with products incorporating improvements should be considered and a strategy should be developed that maximizes their utility. One way to do this is to license a trademark that can be easily modified for use with a number of technologies (e.g., "ABC," "ABC Pro," and "ABC Gold"). By continuing to use the original mark, its market recognition and value will be maintained and enhanced.

STRATEGY CONSIDERATIONS

This section will list and discuss several considerations related to developing an overall licensing strategy. It is recommended that the topics be considered in the order listed, as later considerations are often dependent on those that are discussed earlier.

Exclusivity

Unless there is a compelling reason to do otherwise, nonexclusive licensing should be the first choice of most licensors. There are several advantages to nonexclusive licensing:

- *The risk to both licensor and licensee is minimized.* The licensor is free to license other firms, and is thus not entirely dependent on the success of one licensee. The licensor's need to verify the ability of the licensee to exploit the market is also reduced (but not eliminated). Licensee's risks are lowered because the higher initial and royalty payments generally associated with exclusive agreements are avoided.
- *The licensor retains more control over its product or technology.* By retaining the right to manufacture and sell products in the market and to license other companies in the same and other markets, the licensor can more actively participate in the promotion and marketing of the product or technology, and can prevent a single exclusive licensee from controlling but purposely not commercializing the technology for competitive reasons. One very effective way to do this is to establish the technology as a standard (e.g., through one of the various standard-setting bodies), and license all companies active in the market (usually under standard terms). Licensors can also prohibit the granting of sublicenses if desired.
- *The desirability of the product or technology can be enhanced.* Wider usage can support a licensing model with lower royalties, which in turn can expand the market. Multiple licensees will use the technology in different markets and products, and will increase the probability of improvements being developed, which will enhance the technology still further.

A number of important issues should be considered when determining whether an exclusive license is appropriate. First, the licensor must feel that limiting the use of its product or technology to one licensee is the best way to exploit its potential. The competitive advantage given by the exclusive license must be sufficient to make the licensed products clearly superior to other non-licensed products in the market, so that a large market share can be taken by the licensee. The licensee must have the manufacturing and marketing resources (and commit them) to selling licensed products. The product or technology licensed should not be one that depends on standardization for market acceptance. Exclusive licenses can rationally be granted to dominant vendors in markets with relatively few competitors, where the barriers to entry for the licensor are high.

Second, the degree of exclusivity should be considered. Even where long-term exclusivity is not warranted, some exclusivity can be considered (e.g., for a limited period of time to early licensees to reward them for the risks associated with licensing unproven technology). Similar techniques are discussed in the later sections of this chapter, "Market and Territorial Limitations" and "Royalties."

Third, the exclusivity granted should be supported by a commensurately higher royalty rate, which can be developed based on a percentage of the increased value given to the licensee's products by the licensed technology. The initial payment can be substantially higher than for nonexclusive use, and often there are more technical obligations agreed to by the licensor, including training the licensee's engineers, conducting further technology development, and even designing the licensee's products. Licensees are often required to make guaranteed minimum yearly royalty payments under an exclusive license. The amount of such minimum payments should be a significant percentage (say, 50% to 60%) of the royalties that would be due under licensee's sales projections.

Finally, granting an exclusive license implies granting the right to sublicense. See the section on anti-trust considerations for more details.

Cross-Licensing

If the prospective licensee owns intellectual property that is of interest to the licensor, cross-licensing can be used to grant both parties access to the technologies or products of interest. License terms are adjusted to take into account the value of the licensee's technology. Cross-licensing can also be used to settle IP disputes, and is a primary motivation to obtain defensive patents, as described in Chapter 2.

Large corporations in certain industries commonly cross-license their competitors to avoid litigation and to obtain rights to IP needed in their business. An excellent discussion of cross-licensing in the semiconductor and telecommunications industries can be found in "Managing Intellectual Capital: Licensing and Cross-Licensing in Semiconductors and Electronics," by Grindley and Teece, listed in the bibliography.

Additional Licenses Required

In some cases a prospective licensee may be required to obtain a separate license from another licensor (or several others) in order to utilize the technology or product being offered. The cost of both licensing and implementing the other technology must be considered. The licensor should determine the incremental economic benefit offered by its technology, independent of the additional technology required, in determining an appropriate royalty structure. Equally important, the additional technology required must be available at a fair and reasonable rate to all prospective licensees.

The licensing of multiple technologies, known as stacking, can quickly result in a licensee being required to pay a total royalty so high that its licensed products will be priced out of the market. In many cases it is more sensible for the various licensors to join together, either directly or through a standards-setting organization, and license all required technologies using one agreement for one price. However, agreeing on an equitable split of royalties among the various technology providers, and even agreeing on what technology should be included in the package, can be difficult.

Market and Territorial Restrictions

It is possible to limit both the markets and territories in which licensed products may be sold. Such restrictions can often allow the licensing of a product or technology where licensing would otherwise present difficulties.

Consider first the common situation in which proprietary intellectual property is incorporated in a manufacturer's products that are being sold in a particular market. It is quite possible that those technologies could be used in other products sold in a different market. Since the manufacturer is focused on its own market (and rightly so), an effective way to utilize the technology in other markets (and generate revenues from those markets) is to license manufacturers active in those markets. Likewise, a product designed for a particular market is often useful in other markets, and a similar strategy can be employed. Licensing consultants are often used to identify markets and companies that may find a technology or product useful and to assist in their licensing.

In a similar manner, the territories in which licensed products may be sold can be restricted. The most common example is the separation of foreign and domestic markets: The licensor remains active in its local market but licenses its technology or product to other firms active and experienced in the various foreign markets. The barriers to entry in foreign markets are often high, and using foreign partners is often the most effective way to enter their markets. In addition, protecting intellectual property in some foreign markets can be problematic; by partnering with local firms you can often avoid their opposition to patent applications, unlicensed use of copyrighted works, filing of similar or equivalent trademark applications, and other similar problems.

Exclusivity can be combined with market and/or territorial restrictions when necessary. For example, a licensee can be granted the exclusive right to sell licensed products in certain territories or markets and the nonexclusive right in others.

Other Restrictions

Historically it has been acceptable for licensors to fix the price of products incorporating their licensed technologies. However, this right has become restricted due to anti-trust considerations. For example, one court found that several patent owners cannot combine their patents, license the combination, and fix the price of the licensed products. Several other cases resulted in the finding that a licensor cannot license several companies active in the same industry under terms that fix prices. Because of the changing laws and general confusion surrounding this issue, it is best to avoid fixing prices in license agreements.

In some situations, the licensor can control the quantities of licensed products produced, although in other situations such control could be construed as price fixing. For example, if a small manufacturer of pumps licenses its technology to a large pump producer, it would seem to be reasonable to allow quantity restrictions in the agreement to ensure that the licensor can continue to compete in the market.

Future Developments

In short-term licensing arrangements (e.g., paid-up licenses to settle infringement), the handling of improvements is rarely addressed. In a successful long-term licensing relationship, it is likely that improvements to the product or technology licensed will be made by either the licensor or licensee. The use and disposition of improvements is an important aspect of the licensing strategy.

From the licensor's perspective, it is often advantageous to obtain rights to any improvements developed by its licensees, preferably including the right to sublicense the improvements to other licensees. This is particularly important when the core licensed technology is a standard, because improvements are of little value unless they can be incorporated in the standard. However, unless there is some leverage to induce such grants, licensees are often reluctant to grant back rights without compensation. Reasonable compensation might constitute a share of any additional licensing revenues generated as a result of licensing the improvement to others, and royalty credits or payments, if the improvement is used by the licensor.

It is also in the licensor's interest to continue development of licensed technologies and products and, in most cases, to make the improvements available to its licensees. This is obviously required if the technology is standardized. However, even if the technology is not standardized, as long as the licensee is not competing directly with the licensor, allowing the licensee to use improvements should result in increased sales of licensed products and licensing revenues. In some cases additional royalties may be justified; in others, the licensor may license improvements at no additional charge to maintain its position as a technology supplier and to maintain control of the market. The incremental costs of licensing improvements to existing licensees are modest.

The licensee, when choosing a product or technology to license, would like assurances that the licensed goods will not quickly become obsolete. Access to licensor-developed improvements is an important means of ensuring the continued viability of the licensed product or technology. However, since neither the life of the technology nor the technology's improvement potential are known at the time the license is negotiated, some creativity must be employed in determining appropriate royalty rates and other terms. As a practical matter it is the licensor who ultimately controls the disposition of its improvements, and prospective licensees would be wise to examine the licensor's past practices in this area for clues as to how future improvements will be handled.

Improvements made by a licensee to licensed technology may be of little use unless the licensee has rights to the underlying intellectual property. However, improvements can be used to provide a competitive advantage over licensed products made by another licensee. Often this is the best way to use improvements, especially when their scope is narrow or when they are process-related.

If the licensee's improvement is fundamental, the licensor can in some cases (such as with standardized technology) make the improvement worthless by refusing to include it in the licensed technology's specifications. To avoid this, the licensee can work together with the licensor to ensure the improvement will be utilized, even if a share of the benefits associated with the improvement must go to the licensor. On the other hand, the licensee can use a fundamental improvement or extensive new development to attempt to gain control of the licensor's core technology. Pursuing a competitive strategy may sour the licensor/licensee relationship and result in, at the minimum, an end to cooperation between the licensor and licensee and, possibly, termination of the license agreement.

Technical Assistance

The majority of long-term licensing arrangements require substantial technical assistance on the part of the licensor. When technologies are licensed, frequently tooling, samples, and documentation and other technical data must be transferred, and personnel must be assigned to assist the licensee in ramping up production.

If trademarks are licensed, the licensor must provide the required quality control for licensed products throughout the life of the agreement. This will include developing technical specifications and test procedures for licensed products, testing the licensed products, inspecting licensees' production facilities, and so on.

Initial payments and royalty rates should reflect the type and scope of technical assistance that will be provided.

Royalties

All of the considerations mentioned up to this point should be factored into the development of a suitable royalty structure. This section will outline several royalty schemes that are in common use, and provide some guidelines for determining appropriate rates.

In general, the licensor has the right to charge any acceptable royalty, although charging different royalty rates to different licensees where all other factors are identical has been viewed by the courts as restraint of trade. There are, however, no restrictions on negotiating agreements where different royalty rates are charged for different rights granted and obligations incurred by the licensor and licensee, which is a situation that occurs frequently.

Royalty payments can be structured in a number of ways, but generally consist of an initial payment and subsequent payments over the life of the agreement.

The initial payment is usually paid when the agreement is signed. Agreements intended to provide short-term revenues generally specify higher initial payments than long-term agreements. A paid-up patent-only agreement negotiated to license an infringer could specify a payment to cover past infringement and additional paid-up royalties to cover future use of the patent(s). The total payment can be very high (e.g., Kodak paid damages and interest of over $900 million to Polaroid for infringing various instant color film patents). Lump-sum payments can be paid in several installments over a period of time or upon achievement of specified milestones (transfer of technology, further development, and so on).

Initial payments for long-term agreements with running royalties can be as low as $5,000 to $10,000. When agreements involve substantial effort on the part of the licensor to transfer technology, the initial payment can reflect the cost of these efforts.

In many agreements, running royalties are paid based on the number or value of licensed products made or sold in a specified time period. There are several variations:

- Paying a fixed royalty for each licensed product (e.g., $1 per product). The royalty can be assessed on each product manufactured, or each product sold.
- Paying a percentage (*n* percent) of the value of each licensed product (the value can be defined as the wholesale price, the retail price, or some other mutually acceptable price).
- Paying a percentage of the value of the part of the licensed product in which the licensed technology is incorporated. If the licensed technology is used in only part of a product (e.g., an integrated circuit used in a computer), it is often more reasonable to tie the royalty payment to that part of the product rather than to the whole product.
- Paying a percentage of profits earned from the sale of licensed products.
- Paying a percentage of any cost savings realized by the licensee through utilizing the licensed technology. This approach would be useful, for example, when a manufacturing process was licensed that resulted in, say, a 10% decrease in the cost of producing stainless steel. If the licensee made $10 million dollars worth of stainless steel a month, the savings would amount to $1 million/month. Of this $1 million, an agreed percentage would be paid to the licensor as a royalty.

A sliding scale, where royalty rates decrease as quantities increase, is commonly combined with one of the above approaches. The rates can reset (i.e., return to the highest rate) each reporting period or they can continue to slide based on the cumulative total of licensed products sold. Scales that slide up are also used in certain circumstances, such as when an unproven technology whose prospects are uncertain is licensed. In this case royalty rates are kept low at first, but they increase as the technology becomes more successful.

The shape of a sliding scale should be chosen based on the characteristics of the market in which licensed products will be sold and the number of licensees anticipated. The break points at which the royalty rates change should take into account the number of products a typical licensee will produce in the payment period chosen. Sliding scales for mass-produced products will feature break points at higher quantities than sliding scales for niche market products. The highest royalty rate and the amount royalties decrease from one break point to the next depend on the types of licensees to which the scale will apply. If a mix of licensees is anticipated, with some producing relatively small quantities of high-margin products and others producing large quantities of commodity products, the scale should feature a high initial rate followed by fairly steep reductions at each break point. Under this scheme, smaller licensees will pay higher average per-unit royalties, which will help to compensate the licensor for the proportionally higher administrative costs associated with the smaller licensees.

Payments can be made annually, biannually, or quarterly. Generally, more frequent payments are to be preferred by the licensor, as payments are received sooner and more control can be exerted over the licensee. However, administrative overhead must be balanced against the time value of money. Some agreements specify that rates are to be adjusted periodically (e.g., each year) to compensate for changes in the cost of living. Agreements that specify royalties as a percentage of the licensed product cost generally do not include cost of living factors, as the price of the licensed product will generally increase with inflation, automatically raising the royalty amount.

Sublicensing

Unless specifically prohibited in the agreement, the licensee usually can sublicense to others. Although this is not necessarily bad, the licensor should understand the following:

- If trademarks are licensed, sublicensing must be prohibited or the licensor may lose its trademark protection.
- If the licensor intends to actively pursue licensing its products or technologies to others, licensees' sublicensing could cause confusion and loss of control over the licensing activities.
- If sublicensing is allowed, the terms and conditions should be explicitly stated in the agreement. In particular, the division of sublicensing royalties and responsibilities for administration of sublicenses should be clearly delineated.

In general, unless there are good reasons to do so, granting sublicensing rights should be avoided when the licensor is actively promoting its technology. However, sublicensing can be used strategically when resources are not available to fully exploit a technology. In this case, the licensor can grant an exclusive license to a partner, who in turn sublicenses other companies. This master licensee will develop collateral materials (e.g., demonstration units and marketing materials) and be responsible for all technology marketing activities. If further development is required, the master licensee may also provide engineering services. In general, the licensor and the master licensee each contribute resources to the venture and agree to accept certain responsibilities in return for a split of the licensing revenues based on their contributions to the commercialization effort. The master licensee may or may not manufacture and sell licensed products; competition in the marketplace between the master licensee and sublicensees could adversely affect the licensing effort. Responsibilities for license administration and IP protection are assigned in the master-license agreement, as are acceptance of liability and warranty provision.

Warranties, Indemnification, and Liability

Most license agreements include language addressing the representations and responsibilities of the licensor with respect to its licensed IP and the responsibilities of the licensee with respect to products incorporating the licensed IP. The licensor may or may not warrant that its IP is valid, and may or may not indemnify the licensee for any expenses the licensee may incur as a result of infringement or other actions related to the licensed IP. The licensee will generally accept liability for any damages related to the licensed products.

The licensor generally wants to avoid warranting that any of its IP is valid, and also does not want to indemnify the licensee for any damages related to the licensed IP. If the IP is well known (e.g., if the licensed patents have been litigated and found to be valid) and the IP has been widely licensed, the licensee may accept an agreement with no warranties or indemnification. However, if the IP (and, perhaps, the licensor) is unproven, it is reasonable for a licensee to ask for assurances that the IP is valid and covers the technology being licensed. Unfortunately, it is practically impossible for the licensor (or anyone else) to know that all of its IP is valid. Unknown prior art can surface at any time, invalidating patents despite efforts to ensure their novelty. IP protected as trade secrets can be invalidated at any time through independent invention and patenting by another party. Trademarks, copyrighted works, and mask works are somewhat less vulnerable in this respect. Therefore, it is dangerous for a licensor to offer warranties, particularly with respect to patents and know-how. A conscientious licensor will have expended considerable effort to ensure that its IP is valid, and should be willing to warrant that, to the best of its knowledge, its patents are valid and its know-how can be used without infringing on others' patents. If the licensor has an aggressive trademark protection and enforcement program in effect, warranting that its trademarks are valid in the countries in which they are registered may also be possible. Finally, if the licensor is certain that its copyrighted works have been developed independently, it can warrant their validity as well.

If the licensor is willing to warrant that its IP is valid, it may also be willing to indemnify the licensee to some degree against damages related to the warranted IP. Total indemnification can result in a high level of financial exposure for the licensor, which can be dangerous if the licensor does not have adequate financial resources. Small licensors providing technology to large licensees is a particularly dangerous situation, as large companies are often targets for infringement actions. Lesser degrees of indemnification include allowing the licensee to stop paying royalties and use the royalty payments to cover legal expenses if an infringement suit is filed or indemnifying the licensee up to the amount paid to the licensor under the agreement. The licensee can also be indemnified with respect to certain elements of the IP, and not with respect to others. For example, the licensor could indemnify the licensee against claims of copyright infringement, but not against claims of patent infringement, or could indemnify against claims of copyright infringement related to, say, video content, but not against claims of copyright infringement related to licensed firmware.

There are several types of liability related to the manufacture and sale of licensed products, including liability for property damage and personal injury. As already mentioned, the licensor should generally insist that the licensee indemnify the licensor against this liability, and the licensee should agree to do so. The sample license agreements in Appendix C include language related to warranties, indemnification, and liability.

Anti-trust/Restraint of Trade

Owners of intellectual property generally have no obligation to utilize or license their property in any way. However, if they choose to enter into license agreements, these contracts are subject to legal requirements governing restraint of trade.

The federal Sherman Act and Clayton Act are the foundations of law governing restraint of trade in the United States, and their provisions reflect many related state and foreign laws as well. The Sherman Act declares that any contract which restrains trade affecting interstate or foreign commerce is illegal. It also prohibits any act, whether or not contractual, which either monopolizes or attempts to monopolize trade. The Clayton Act, as amended by the Robinson-Patman Act, forbids specific trade restraints like price discrimination (charging different prices for the same commodity in order to reduce competition), exclusive dealing arrangements that force customers not to buy from competitors, acquisitions of other companies that lessen competition, and other unfair or deceptive acts.

Of course, many contracts can be said to restrain trade in some sense, so the law applies a *Rule of Reason* analysis. That analysis examines the circumstances of each contract, such as the overall effect of the contract on competition and whether or not one party has substantial market power over one of the affected products, in order to determine whether or not a particular agreement or act imposes an unreasonable restraint. Franchising, for example, is a modern business practice that generally is not an unreasonable restraint of trade. Some restraints, however, like price-fixing among competitors, are considered to be anti-competitive in any context and so are per se, or automatically, illegal.

In addition, *misuse* of intellectual property is forbidden. For example, patents that are obtained fraudulently (e.g., by refusing to disclose known prior art when applying) cannot be enforced and should not be licensed. Similarly, if the license of a patent is conditioned on paying royalties for products that do not incorporate the licensed technology, patent misuse may be claimed.

All these forbidden practices must be avoided when developing license agreement terms. If agreements are consummated that include terms constituting restraints of trade or IP misuse, the agreement can be terminated, IP protection can be voided, and/or antitrust liability involving treble damages can be imposed.

Antitrust, IP misuse, and restraint of trade are complex subjects, and it is recommended that all licensing arrangements contemplated be checked by legal counsel to ensure compliance with the law. Although far from exhaustive, the following list notes several areas that must be approached with care:

1. It may be unlawful to *tie* or *bundle* the license of a product, technology, service, or process that a customer or licensee wants to the purchase or license of something else that is unwanted. For example, if an IP owner conditions the grant of a patent license on the licensee also purchasing from the licensor the materials to be used in manufacturing the licensed product, or if the licensor insists that the customer also license another unrelated patent, the courts may find that unlawful tying has occurred. This risk is increased if "the . . . owner has market power in the . . . market for the . . . product on which the license . . . is conditioned" (Subsection 5, 35 U.S.C. Section 271(d)). Although many IP owners may doubt that they enjoy such market power, the potential for a court deciding otherwise is substantial where IP rights are involved. Because IP rights by definition grant a form of limited legal monopoly that the IP owner believes has value, it is not difficult for an enterprising opponent to argue that some relevant economic market corresponds to the scope of that legal monopoly. In any event, determining what tying is allowed is tricky and, unless absolutely necessary and undertaken with full knowledge of the risks involved, licenses that tie are not recommended.

2. Licensors generally cannot prohibit licensees from dealing with competitors. For example, Company A probably cannot license its manufacturing process to Company B with the requirement that Company B not buy raw materials from Company C, a competitor of Company A.

3. Royalties for patent licensing cannot be collected after the patent has expired. Hybrid agreements, where patents, trademarks, know-how, copyrighted works, and/or mask works are licensed together, must address this issue (usually by separating patent royalties from royalties for other licensed intellectual property) if it is desired that the agreement survive beyond the expiration dates of the licensed patents.

4. The licensor of a patent can only control the manufacture, use, and sale of licensed products until they are sold for the first time (the *Exhaustion* or *First Sale Doctrine*). Once a licensed product has been sold by the licensee, it can generally be resold or used as the buyer sees fit. For example, if a technology is licensed with the restriction that the licensed products only be sold in the consumer electronics market, once the licensee sells the licensed products (through normal consumer-electronic-product marketing channels) the licensor cannot prevent the buyer from using the product in a professional recording studio. In addition, royalties can only be collected once.

   One technique that allows more than one licensee to pay royalties for technology covered by a single patent is known as "claim splitting." Consider the situation where a technology is incorporated in an integrated circuit that is eventually used in a game system. In this case, the licensor can license the IC manufacturer or the game system manufacturer, but not both without potentially violating the First Sale Doctrine. Each choice is problematic, and either would probably reduce the benefits to the licensor as compared to licensing both companies. In order to avoid this conundrum, the licensor can draft the claims of the patent in such a way that certain claims cover the implementation of the technology in an IC, and others cover its use in a finished game system. Since patent claims can be licensed individually, the implementation claims are then licensed to the IC manufacturer and the system claims are licensed to the game system manufacturer. Other IP can be included as needed in both agreements, and royalties can be collected from both companies. Successfully exploiting this strategy requires that the patent attorney drafting the patent application be aware of and sensitive to the licensing strategy (always a good idea).

5. As with large mergers, the lawfulness of licensing arrangements between companies having substantial market shares is more likely to come under scrutiny and challenge, which can result in time-consuming and expensive regulatory processes and litigation. However, in order to mitigate these concerns in smaller transactions involving Rule of Reason analysis, the U.S. Department of Justice has promulgated a set of guidelines that include a safe harbor provision for license agreements in which the licensor and licensee together account for less than 20% of the market being addressed in the agreement. In such cases, unless the terms of the agreement constitute a per se restraint, the federal government will not challenge the agreements as anti-competitive restraints of trade.

6. Computer software and e-business licenses increasingly present interesting issues for anti-trust and copyright misuse analysis. For example, it may constitute an anti-trust violation for a software copyright holder to impose more restrictive license terms on customers in order to prevent independent computer consultants and service organizations from accessing the customer's computer-resident software as part of service offerings in competition with the copyright holder. Such anti-trust and infringement analyses are made particularly difficult by uncertainties in how to apply—and sometimes in the wisdom of applying at all—old rules to new or hybrid technologies.

Taxes

United States and foreign tax regulations can have a significant impact on income derived from licensing. In addition to issues affecting all licensing transactions, special tax rules apply to transactions between related parties (corporate parents, affiliates, and subsidiaries, both foreign and domestic).

The following are tax issues affecting all licensing transactions:

- Is the transaction a license or a sale of assets? Income from the sale of intellectual property can be treated (generally more favorably) as a capital gain, whereas income from licensing must be declared as ordinary income. Income from non-exclusive licenses must be treated as ordinary income, while income from exclusive licenses can be either ordinary income or a capital gain, depending on the terms of the agreement.
- Initial payments for patent licenses must be amortized over the life of the patent. Licensed know-how generally cannot be amortized. Patents and know-how acquired as part of the purchase of a business must be amortized over 15 years.
- Are there foreign tax considerations? When technology is licensed internationally, initial payments are generally taxed in the licensor's country of residence, whereas running royalties are taxed in the place where the technology is used (the licensee's country of residence). Foreign taxes paid on royalties can usually be offset against the licensor's domestic tax liability, subject to certain limitations.
- If tangibles are transferred as part of a license agreement, the entire transaction may be subject to sales tax. Even including a simple demonstration board can attract attention from tax authorities. Agreements that require the licensor to deliver tangible property as a condition of the agreement should be reviewed by a tax attorney to avoid unanticipated sales tax liability.

The terms of license agreements consummated with related parties must be the same as if they had been negotiated with unrelated parties to avoid tax consequences. This so-called arm's-length standard is easy to apply in some cases (e.g., when nonexclusive agreements with standard terms are used or when the products and markets are well known), but it is more difficult to quantify if unproven technology is licensed exclusively.

In addition, tax rules require that when technology is licensed (defined broadly as the transfer of any intangible assets) to foreign related parties, the royalties charged must "be commensurate with the income attributable to the technology." This is generally interpreted to mean that all excess profits generated by the licensed technology must be paid as royalties. However, entering into a joint venture to share the costs of R&D can release the related party from any royalty obligations. Tax implications should be carefully considered and factored into licensing strategies and agreement terms.

LICENSING FROM UNIVERSITIES

Researchers associated with universities conduct much of the basic research performed in the U.S. and abroad. Thousands of commercially viable inventions (many protected by patents) are developed every year in the U.S. alone and, as their owners are generally precluded from commercializing them, available for licensing. However, licensing technologies from universities can be quite different from licensing in the commercial sector. This section will discuss some of the important issues that should be considered when contemplating licensing from universities.

Background

Prior to the Second World War, there was very little support of university research and little licensing by universities. However, in the late 1940s, U.S. government support of university research expanded significantly. It was believed the results of such research would yield benefit to military as well as commercial competitiveness. This was in regard both to research results that could be applied to practical use and the supply to the economy of university graduates trained in cutting edge research.

In the following years, the developed world has moved from an industrial economy to an information economy to today's knowledge economy. The benefit of the U.S. national policy determination to support university research is evident in U.S. industrial competitiveness in the information and knowledge economies.

The first government funding agencies were military, with the Office of Naval Research in a lead role. Later, the National Science Foundation was established, not to conduct research, but to fund university research. Today, over 20 U.S. government agencies support university research. Other countries were slower in understanding the benefits to their economies of university research, but beginning in the 90s other developed countries began increasing their support of university research.

Prior to the 1970s few U.S., and fewer non-U.S., universities had active technology licensing programs. Most universities used the services of a national research development organization (NRDO). Research Corporation filled that role in the U.S., while the most successful non-U.S. NRDO has been the British Technology Group of the United Kingdom.

Before 1980, the U.S. agencies that supported university research had varied policies regarding intellectual property and licensing. Many agencies took title for the government to intellectual property rights to inventions arising from their funding. Universities were able to demonstrate that they licensed about 50% of patents to which they held title, while only about 2% of patents held by the government were licensed.

With support of universities and the patent counsels of the NSF and the precursor to today's National Institutes of Health, Public Law 96-517 was signed into law in 1980. This law provides that a university has first option to take title to an invention arising under support of any government agency, with a requirement to be diligent in seeking commercialization through partnership with industry. Any exclusive license of a U.S. patent must be to a company that will manufacture in the United States.

The passage of PL96-517 led to a sharp growth in campus-based university technology licensing programs in the U.S. Policies and laws in other developed countries to enhance university licensing began to be enacted in the 1990s. As campus licensing programs grew, licensing by NRDOs began to wane.

In 1991, the Association of University Technology Managers (AUTM) began a comprehensive, annual survey of its university members in the U.S. and Canada (including teaching hospitals). This survey collects data in a number of areas, and also provides information on start-up companies spinning out of universities and on important inventions that have brought significant benefits to the public. Exhibit 5.1 shows the growth since 1991 in three areas: patents filed, licenses granted, and royalty income.

In the year most recently surveyed (1999), the total sales of university licensed products was calculated as $40 billion, creating several hundred thousand new jobs and over $5 billion in incremental tax revenues. Thus, by almost any measure, the passage of Public Law 96-517 achieved the intended results: to encourage the disclosure and protection of innovation from publicly supported research; and to see the commercial development of products from such innovation for public benefit.

The growth of membership in the Association of University Technology Managers (AUTM) has been steep since 1980, with membership primarily from U.S. and Canadian universities and other non-profit research organizations. However, there has been a significant growth in membership from other countries, with foreign membership in 2001 equaling approximately 10% of the total membership of around 3,000.

AUTM publishes an annual survey report of its membership. Key findings (U.S. and Canadian organizations only) from the report of data for the year 1999 were:

- Over 417 new products were introduced.
- Over 344 new companies were formed based on an academic discovery.
- 82% of the new companies were in the state/province of the licensing university.
- Economic impact models showed $40.9 billion of economic activity can be attributed to results of academic partnering with industry, supporting 270,900 jobs (97% U.S. economy, 3% Canadian economy).

Exhibit 5.1.   AUTM Survey Results 1991–1999

Year	Patents Filed	Licenses Granted	Royalty Income (US$ millions)
1991	1643	1278	186
1992	1951	1741	248
1993	2433	2227	323
1994	2429	2484	360
1995	2872	2616	424
1996	3261	2741	514
1997	4267	3328	611
1998	4808	3668	725
1999	5545	3914	862

Source: AUTM

- 62% of new licenses and options were to startup or existing small companies.
- 50% of new licenses and options were exclusive and 50% were non-exclusive.

More information about AUTM and its services can be found in Appendix B.

Technology from Stanford University alone formed the commercial base for new companies such as Cisco, Sun, Silicon Graphics, Yahoo!, Google, Collagen, Excite, Genentech (with the University of California, San Francisco), and older companies such as Varian and Hewlett-Packard.

Characteristics of University Licensing

University technology is rarely ready for the marketplace and a university licensee must undertake significant development at risk. Hence, most university licenses are exclusive, at least for a period of time, to encourage that development. The AUTM data above (showing 50-50 exclusive to non-exclusive license proportion) is distorted by a few basic technologies such as recombinant DNA, where over 400 non-exclusive licenses were granted for that single technology.

While exclusive licenses are offered in many cases, university licenses often include fairly stringent performance requirements (e.g., significant minimum yearly royalties) to ensure that the licensee will devote itself to commercializing the technology. In addition, it should be noted that, by law, the government must be issued a license to all government-funded research. Universities will often insist on indemnification from their licensees to protect themselves from product liability lawsuits, and will often ask licensees to assume responsibility for protection (and sometimes even prosecution) of the licensed patents. When licensing small companies, equity is sometimes accepted in lieu of cash license payments.

Most university technologies pertain to a small market and cases yielding over $200,000 are few, on the order of 1 to 3 of 100 technology disclosures received by a university licensing office. Absent those few higher yielding cases, a university will find its licensing program not economically viable. Hence, for most technology disclosures, a university licensing officer seeks to focus on key potential licensees, make the deal with a responsible and qualified licensee, typically an exclusive license, and move on to the next case. For the few big hit cases, however, the expenditure of significant effort and financial resources is a prerequisite to successful licensing programs.

Because of the uncertainty associated with licensing basic research, there are often several steps, starting with the signing of a non-disclosure agreement (NDA), which allows the university to disclose the invention while still ensuring that intellectual property rights can be protected. If the licensee is still interested, a letter-of-intent is sometimes negotiated to allow further evaluation of the invention by the licensee while the university agrees to suspend marketing efforts. In some cases an option agreement is then negotiated before the final license agreement is signed. Payments by the prospective licensee may be required in one or both of the above two additional steps.

It is often the case that a company may wish to engage the university scientist as a consultant, or hire the graduate student involved with the technology, or support additional research at the university. A faculty member is typically permitted to consult one day in seven. So as not to divert the graduate student from his or her studies, the hiring would not take place until after completing requirements for the degree, including (if required) the thesis.

All research performed at a university has to be of thesis quality. That is, the research must be suitable for Ph.D. candidates, directed toward increasing human knowledge rather than commercial development. A university accepts no restrictions on publication of research results. However, most universities will agree to a notification period, typically 90 days, so that intellectual property protection can be sought before publication.

A university retains title to intellectual property developed under external funding, but will provide the industrial research sponsor an option to an exclusive license to commercialize research results when the sponsor has fully funded the research. Fully funded means that the sponsor pays both the direct costs of the research and indirect costs. The indirect cost rate for U.S. universities averages around 50%.

Research at a university is typically funded by external research sponsors, under discrete grants or contracts, with each project under the direction of a faculty principal investigator. This environment, and the fact that a university does not have corporate control over its faculty and students, often requires some learning for a company that has not previously dealt with a university.

For example, a company will want rights to improvements in the technology conceived after the license or after the research. However, unless the company fully funds the research, such rights cannot be provided as they will be subject to the terms of another research sponsor.

As another example, the lack of corporate control means an agreement cannot extend beyond the individuals involved in the license or research agreement. It is indeed possible that another professor or graduate student will conceive an improvement or new invention in the field of the license or research agreement, but the university cannot grant rights in their conception without their agreement.

University technology can be hard to find, although progress has been made in recent years in publicizing university intellectual property available for license. Many university researchers publish their results in scientific and association publications, and the universities themselves often provide listings of opportunities and publish reports and newsletters. Industry affiliate programs and associated presentations and conferences are used to introduce newly developed technologies to selected audiences. Other sources of information can be found in Chapter 3 and Appendix B.

Despite these peculiarities of dealings with universities, the rate of university-industry interactions continues to grow. The restructuring of the world's economy is observed to have arisen in part from the rapid adaptation of new discoveries into commercial products and processes. Few technology-based companies today do not maintain close awareness of university technologies.

LICENSING FROM THE U.S. GOVERNMENT

Over 100,000 engineers and scientists work in the 700 federal laboratories, with a combined annual budget of over $25 billion. Research is conducted and important discoveries are made in nearly every imaginable discipline. It is the policy and desire of the government to facilitate the transfer of technology developed in the federal laboratories to the private sector for commercialization. Although the process is similar in many ways to university licensing methods (both universities and federal laboratories largely license government-funded research results at early stages of development), a few important differences should be noted:

- Each government laboratory is responsible for licensing its own technologies, and most of the revenues generated stay with the licensing laboratory. Most laboratories have set up licensing organizations to assist in technology transfer. However, as with universities, this decentralized approach can make it difficult to locate suitable technologies.
- The intellectual property available for licensing consists primarily of patents and patent applications. Copyright protection is generally not available for government works.
- As with most university technology, the government retains a royalty-free license to the technology for its own use.
- Prospective licensees must submit an application outlining their plans to develop and market the technology. If the license sought is an exclusive one, the application must be published in the Federal Register to allow objections to be filed.
- Unpatented technology from government laboratories is transferred using Cooperative Research and Development Agreements (CRADAs). Usually, partners in the private sector provide funding, materials, and/or personnel resources for further development of the technology, in return for which they obtain the right to license any patents granted or patent applications filed as a result of the CRADA. The government laboratory supplies personnel and facilities but in most cases cannot provide funding. The non-government partner retains its ownership in any patents developed by its personnel as part of the CRADA. The government retains its royalty-free license.

ADVANCED TECHNIQUES—CORPORATE LICENSING

Up to now this chapter has focused on developing strategies for licensing technologies, whose IP components might include patents, trademarks, copyrighted works, mask works, and/or know-how. Once a strategy that includes the licensing of trademarks has been successfully implemented, the value of the licensed trademarks will increase through their use on licensed products. If the trademarks achieve enough notoriety, they can be used alone (without their accompanying technology) in other markets.

The practice of licensing a corporate name or trademark for use on consumer products generally unrelated to a company's main line of business will be referred to as corporate licensing. Corporate licensing (sometimes called brand licensing) is a means to leverage the value of trademarks that have been established through a technology licensing program through their use in other markets. Advantages to the licensor include increased recognition of the trademarks, improved protection of the trademarks, and the generation of additional revenues.

For the rest of this section *licensing* will refer to corporate licensing (not technology licensing) and *licensed product* will refer to products bearing the licensed trademark but not incorporating licensed technology.

There is an active industry today that licenses names and images to manufacturers of consumer products. The total revenues generated through the retail sale of licensed products (i.e., products bearing licensed trademarks) is in excess of $100 billion in the United States alone. Several web sites and publications, including "The Licensing Letter," document developments in the industry.

Half the licensed products sold fall in the category of clothing and fashion accessories or playthings, with most of the rest being stationery and publishing products, gifts and novelties, and home furnishings and housewares. While licensed names come from a variety of sources, including cartoon characters, sports figures, and designers, the largest and most rapidly growing source is corporate names.

Benefits

Once a trademark has been established, whether through a technology-licensing program, the manufacture and sale of products, or a combination of the two, corporate licensing should be considered. Benefits include:

- Increased public awareness of the licensed name.
- A new source of potential revenues.
- Expanded legal protection and better control of the name or trademark.

Increasing brand awareness through corporate licensing is a good strategy when the company's business success depends to any degree on consumer identification. The use of the licensed trademark on products and in related advertising and promotional activities can increase its value and quality image, in much the same way as when licensed as part of a technology licensing strategy (as discussed in Chapter 2). However, if the same trademark or name is licensed under a corporate licensing program and as part of a technology licensing strategy, care must be taken to ensure that its value is not diminished in the eyes of the technology licensees. The products chosen for the corporate licensing effort should ideally complement, but certainly not conflict with, the products being sold by the technology licensees.

Revenues generated from corporate licensing can be substantial, depending on the industry in which the trademarks are licensed. Traditionally, royalties are based on a percentage of the sales revenues. In industries where corporate licensing is well established, such as the fashion/apparel industry, there are cases where the majority of a company's income is derived from licensing. In other industries, however, including many of those where technology licensing is common, revenues generated can be modest. Starting a program of corporate licensing can be a costly and time-consuming exercise. Revenue streams can develop slowly, and resources must be devoted to promoting the program; therefore, technology licensors should look to other benefits (increased public awareness of the trademark and improved protection) in the short and medium term.

Protecting and using the name or trademark in areas unrelated to the licensor's main activity can be beneficial, particularly if it is close to attaining famous-mark status in any country. As noted in Chapter 2, if a trademark becomes so well known that consumers confuse the trademark with the goods bearing the trademark ("Formica," for example), it becomes generic, and protection is lost. Corporate licensing is a good way to protect and strengthen a name or trademark in classes of goods not covered by the original mark registrations.

Types of Products

Products that are candidates for corporate licensing generally fall into three categories:

1. Novelty items
2. Design products
3. Brand extension products

Novelty items are key chains, coffee mugs, and similar products, which generally have little or no association with the trademark being licensed. Sales of novelty items can generate significant revenues and can result in some additional recognition of the trademark.

Design products use the trademark as part of the licensed product's concept or design. Also known as lifestyle products because the trademark is used to represent a style, design products must reflect fashion trends of their targeted markets.

Brand extension, the most important category for corporate licensing, uses a trademark that has become well known in one market to establish a presence in another, sometimes related, market. Snickers ice cream bars is an example of brand extension, where the Snickers trademark, well known in candy bars, was used to sell ice cream snacks. Using an established trademark can be more cost-effective than developing a new trademark from several perspectives. The investment in establishing an existing brand in a new market is often much less than that of developing and establishing a new trademark. In addition, the time required to establish an existing mark can be less, resulting in a faster increase of sales. The use of an existing trademark in a new market can also symbiotically result in increased sales in the original market.

As always, any corporate-licensing strategy, particularly one in which a trademark will be licensed for use in related markets, should be examined carefully to ensure no conflicts with the overall business strategy.

Implementing a Corporate-Licensing Program

Corporate licensing is a specialized field that is, in most cases, outside the realm of normal corporate activities. Developing a suitable strategy, or even understanding the important issues, can require knowledge and skills not normally found in the corporate setting. Finding and assessing prospective licensees, who are usually in industries quite different from the corporate licensor, can be difficult, as can estimating the costs and revenues associated with a corporate licensing program.

For all these reasons, seek outside help when considering a corporate licensing strategy. Several consulting firms offer services related to developing and implementing corporate licensing strategies, and any of them can be retained early on in the process. Alternatively, someone with the required expertise can be hired as an employee, once the decision to proceed has been made.

6

Technology Marketing

M arketing technology can be more difficult than marketing conventional products because of the intangible nature of intellectual property. A product comprised of patents, trademarks, copyrighted works, mask works, and/or know-how is simply more difficult to explain and grasp than, say, an automobile, whose features, form, functions, and value can be quickly understood.

This chapter begins with a general discussion of factors affecting the marketability of technology. Insight gained through understanding the marketability of a technology can be used to develop business and marketing strategies and to determine where resources can be used to the greatest benefit. Using this knowledge to position a technology favorably can maximize the probability of successful licensing.

First, the marketing techniques chosen for a particular situation should take into account the marketability of the technology and the markets and companies that will be targeted. Then, the best ways to approach and appeal to the targeted companies should be determined, and collateral materials that will be used in the marketing effort should be prepared. Once all the elements are in place, the strategy is implemented. Sources of information used to identify prospective licensees are detailed in Chapter 3 and Appendix B.

Chapter 7 discusses license negotiations and agreement drafting, stages of the licensing process that occur after the marketing stage, once a targeted company has defined a need for a technology and a desire to obtain a license. Although somewhat arbitrary, the chapters have been arranged this way based on the observations that first, the targeted licensee must be convinced of the viability, desirability, and applicability of the technology from a technical perspective before value can be established and terms can be negotiated, and second, that the technology marketing stage generally requires different skills and activities from the negotiating and agreement drafting stages, which, therefore, should be treated separately.

FACTORS AFFECTING MARKETABILITY

Several factors affecting a technology's marketability are discussed in the following sections. It should be clear that marketability considerations are inextricably intertwined with IP strategy, licensing strategy, and technology valuation. Further discussion can be found in Chapter 2 (deciding whether to patent an invention), Chapter 4 (valuing a technology), and Chapter 5 (developing a licensing strategy).

Economic Viability

First and foremost, the technology must provide a demonstrable economic benefit to the licensee. The greater the benefit, the more desirable (and marketable) the technology. If, for example, a process for manufacturing styrene plastic is licensed, the overall cost of production when using the process must be shown to be substantially lower, after taking into account all costs associated with its use (including royalties). The cost of any special machinery needed for the process, its efficiency, energy requirements, and throughput (the amount of material put through a process in a given time) are some of the factors that should be considered when determining the overall cost of production. All relevant factors should be compared to the current process and to other possible solutions, either licensed or developed in-house.

The cost of implementing the technology must be reasonable (and preferably low) for the markets and products envisioned. In mass markets, where price sensitivity is high, any technology that adds significantly to the final product price can greatly reduce sales volumes. A technology improvement to television electronics, for example, should ideally be implemented in a low-cost integrated circuit and should add a few dollars at most to the final cost of the unit. In more specialized niche markets (Formula 1 racing cars, for example), improved performance may be pursued at almost any cost, in which case expensive technologies (like magnesium and carbon-fiber parts) will be practical.

Finally, the benefits of using the technology must be well defined and obvious. A technology that lowers production costs can be used either to lower the product's price (to increase market share) or to raise the product's gross margin. Using a technology to improve performance can increase competitiveness and thus increase market share or it can provide entry into new markets. Licensing a technology can also benefit the licensee by reducing the time required to bring products to market by eliminating the need to develop the technology independently.

Utility

There must be an identified need for the technology in the target markets. Either the technology must allow the commercial exploitation of a totally new market (a good example would be encryption technology that allows secure commercial transactions to take place on the Internet), or an existing market must be identified in which using the technology will result in a cost advantage, a competitive advantage, or some other advantage.

Utility and economic viability are related in that, for a technology to be useful, its use must make sense economically. However, there are cases where economic viability does not make a technology useful (e.g., an improvement to televisions that makes them incompatible with existing standards). Technologies related to obsolete products (improvements to slide rules, for example)—no matter how excellent—will be difficult to market because products that could incorporate the technologies are either disappearing or already gone.

Stage of Development

The more advanced a technology's stage of development, the more marketable it will be. The most advanced stage is when a product incorporating the technology has been mass produced and successfully marketed. Economic viability and utility are proved and valuation is straightforward. Products incorporating the technology can be obtained and analyzed freely. In fact, the prospective licensee can often judge its interest in the technology with no marketing effort at all by the licensor.

In the pilot production stage, the technology has been proved, both functionally and in terms of manufacturability, but not in the market. The licensor will generally have sample units and finished documentation that can be shown to the prospective licensee at this stage. In this case the risks associated with using the technology are greater, but so are the potential rewards, since market potential can only be estimated.

In the prototype development stage the technology has been functionally proved, but manufacturability and market viability have not yet been demonstrated. Again, demonstration units are generally available, but documentation is often preliminary. Technologies in this stage whose manufacture involves well known and understood techniques, such as consumer-electronic products or automobiles, can be considered nearly to the pilot production stage, whereas technologies whose mass production can be problematic, such as certain chemical processes, cannot be so considered.

The lowest stage of development is basic research results. At this stage considerable investment is required by the licensee to complete the technology's development, and economic and market viability have not been proved and are difficult to estimate. Often only fellow researchers can understand the technology and its commercial implications, which can make marketing efforts difficult. However, the greater risk associated with licensing research results is often mitigated by lower royalty rates.

In general, it is much easier to market a technology developed to at least the prototype stage. Not only are economic viability and market success easier to estimate, but in addition the technology can be effectively demonstrated and understood by the targeted licensees' marketing and technical personnel.

Proven Performance

The technology offered must function as advertised. Incompletely developed
technologies, as evidenced by inoperable prototypes, unsuccessful demonstrations, black box implementations (i.e., where only input and output are shown
without any details of the technology being visible), and delays in providing
supporting documentation and data are difficult to market. They raise suspi-
cions in prospective licensees, and thereby reduce the perceived value of the
technology.

When marketing technologies at an early stage of development, make sure
that targeted licensees understand and accept this fact. Be diligent in preparing
demonstrations, but if something goes wrong admit it; don't try to cover it up.
Most marketing and engineering personnel have been through similar circumstances and will empathize. Obtaining and providing an independent evaluation
by a respected outside expert can also assist in establishing the technology's viability and the viability of its supporting IP.

Understanding the Market

Prospective licensees will initially evaluate the technology being offered on the
basis of economic benefit, competitive advantage, products and markets in
which the technology will be used, technology life, and financial considerations.
In order to be able to address these non-technical concerns, the licensor must
have a thorough understanding of the targeted licensees' products, markets, and
overall business strategy. Methods for obtaining such information can be found
in Chapter 3, and sources of information are listed in Appendix B. Any regulatory requirements (e.g., FDA approval) should be fully understood and factored
into the marketing strategy. In general, if the licensor can provide compelling answers to all the prospective licensee's non-technical concerns, the licensing
process will proceed more smoothly.

Once the prospective licensee's non-technical concerns have been addressed, the relationship can move on to a more technical level. This will usually include a thorough evaluation of the technology and its underlying
intellectual property.

DEVELOPING A MARKETING STRATEGY

Armed with an understanding of the markets of interest and a list of companies
active in those markets (see Chapter 3), and a licensing strategy (see Chapter 5),
the next step for licensors is to develop a marketing strategy. The elements of a
marketing strategy include identifying which companies should be contacted
and when, defining the marketing process (what steps will be taken), developing the collateral materials that will be used, establishing follow-up procedures,
setting responsibilities, and planning for periodic review and adjustment of the
plan as needed.

Targeting Prospective Partners

Several factors should be considered when selecting prospective licensing partners. The licensor looks for a partner that has the desire and ability to effectively exploit its invention in the appropriate markets. The licensee is interested in finding the best technology for its application and in dealing with a licensor that can fulfill its obligations under the license agreement. In long-term agreements, the licensee is looking for a technology supplier who will continue to add value to the partnership, for example, by developing and supplying new technologies or assisting the licensee in developing and marketing licensed products.

When a licensor selects prospective licensees, the first (and obvious) requirement is that the targeted company be interested in and have an application for the technology being offered. In addition, the licensee must be capable of fully exploiting the licensed technology by possessing the following qualities:

- *Technical capability.* The licensee should demonstrate sufficient technical capability to fully understand the technology and effectively develop and manufacture licensed products. The licensor should examine the prospective licensee's product development process and method for allocating development resources, and should evaluate examples of recent successful product development efforts. To further judge the prospective licensee's capabilities and level of interest, the licensor can request that the licensee prepare a licensed product development plan; it should include resource commitments, a development schedule, and required investment. Based on an analysis of the plan, the licensor can determine whether the licensee's resources and level of commitment are adequate to exploit the technology sufficiently to warrant granting a license.
- *Commitment.* The licensee should demonstrate commitment to and success in commercializing products similar to those that will incorporate the licensed technology, and the financial resources necessary to implement an effective business plan for licensed products. The product development plan already mentioned should detail the licensee's financial investment in the project and performance benchmarks. Because several years may be required before substantial revenues will be generated by the licensed technology, the licensee's stability and long-term commitment will be important to the success of the partnership.
- *Good fit.* The licensee should be a good fit with the licensor in corporate culture and goals, at least vis-à-vis the technology and the markets in which the licensee will be active. The two cultures do not need to be the same; in fact, in many cases large corporations with well-entrenched and inflexible systems will license technology from a smaller start-up firm to take advantage of their creative, entrepreneurial spirit. It is important, however, that each side understands and appreciates the other's contribution to the partnership. It is helpful to have one key contact well placed in the licensee's organization to champion the technology and the licensor to his or her colleagues both during and after the initial negotiation phase.

Those responsible on both sides for implementing and maintaining the agreement must stay in personal contact to ensure that all parties understand and will support the development and marketing of licensed products. Long-term licensing arrangements can go on for many years, with dozens of communications and several meetings each year required to administer and promote the partnership.

- *Marketing and distribution capability.* The licensee should demonstrate marketing and distribution capabilities with products and markets similar to those contemplated. The licensor should examine the licensee's marketing and sales organizations, including market segments and customers currently being served. In addition, the licensor should analyze recent and similar product introductions. A marketing and sales plan for the licensed product can then be developed by the licensee, including marketing strategy, timing, resource allocation, projected market penetration, and initial sales targets. This exercise will help the licensee to better understand the value of the technology and will help both sides in justifying and, if needed, modifying agreement terms.

By going through an extensive evaluation process, the licensor will help ensure the ultimate success of the licensing partnership by clearly identifying how the technology will benefit the licensee. In addition, the licensor will better understand the licensee's business methods and plans for the technology, which will allow the licensor to more accurately estimate the revenues that will be generated by the licensee and the resources that will be required to transfer the technology and fulfill the licensor's other obligations under the agreement.

The prospective licensee's concerns are similar. Again, the first requirement is that the technology being offered must fulfill a perceived need and offer some benefit. In all cases, the technology itself should be thoroughly examined and valued as outlined in Chapters 3 and 4. Equally important, the licensor must be able to fulfill all of its other obligations, such as the following:

- *Technical resources and commitment.* The licensor should demonstrate both the technical resources required and the commitment to assist the licensee in effectively exploiting the licensed technology. The extent of such assistance depends on the terms of the agreement. A simple, paid-up patent license would require far less assistance from the licensor than a more complex and long-term agreement with, for example, technology development by the licensor. Some licensing arrangements require the licensor to provide long-term support that is vital to the licensee's successful exploitation of the licensed technology. In this case, the long-term viability of the licensor (or at least the support) is critical to the licensee. The section on escrow in Chapter 7 discusses one way agreements can be structured to mitigate this concern.
- *Experience and prior success.* It can be reassuring to the licensee to know that the licensor has considerable experience and success in technology licensing. The technology and terms offered by an organized, well-known li-

censing organization that has consummated agreements covering a variety of technologies with a number of licensees may be seen by the licensee as inherently more reasonable than those offered by an unknown licensor with little or no licensing experience. Likewise, a standard technology offered under standard terms, which has already been licensed to several companies, will also be viewed favorably by a prospective licensee.

- *Good fit.* The corporate culture of the licensor must fit well with that of the licensee, as already mentioned, at least with regard to the licensed technology. The licensor should assign technical, business development, marketing, legal, and other personnel to close and maintain the agreement, and all assigned personnel should initiate and maintain close relations with their counterparts in the licensee's organization.

Defining the Process

The marketing process includes several stages. The first stage involves identifying and contacting targeted companies and providing them with information of gradually increasing levels of detail. At each level, the licensor must judge the licensee's level of interest, whether contact has been made with the proper people, and, assuming continuing interest, what next steps will be required.

When the stage has been reached at which proprietary information must be disclosed, a suitable nondisclosure agreement is often used to protect both parties. At some point in the process the licensor and licensee will want to begin a series of meetings for discussion, demonstration, establishing personal relationships, and generally sizing each other up. Negotiating and closing agreements are discussed in Chapter 7.

Personnel resources required to implement the marketing plan can vary from a single marketing person supported by management and technical personnel to a team whose responsibilities are divided by market, territory, or both. All marketers benefit from ideas and support provided by their colleagues and associates. In the early stages, a single skilled marketer can usually handle up to a hundred or so targeted companies in a few related markets. Depending on the response, additional help may be required later in the process.

On the other hand, if the targeted markets vary widely, the licensor may decide to divide the marketing effort among several people, each with expertise in one of the markets. If this approach is used, provision should be made to assign responsibility and credit for the inevitable overlap that will occur (say, if someone responsible for one market finds a licensee in another market). Dividing the market by territory is a good idea when foreign licensees are sought because marketers familiar with foreign markets, customs, and languages will generally be most effective. Company employees, preferably from the home office, should retain control of all foreign marketing activities when foreign consultants are used to ensure that the company's best interests are represented in all situations. If several technologies are being marketed to different markets, assigning individuals to each market makes sense, again taking into account the potential for overlap. When the marketing involves several people (or more), efforts should be coordinated and directed by a technology marketing manager, who should also handle liaison with other departments involved in the process. All technology marketing strategies must support the firm's overall business strategy.

When possible, targeted companies should be ranked by their suitability and the probability of closing an agreement (as best as can be determined), and contact should be made first with the best prospects. In some cases the largest and highest volume target will not be the first choice; the second or third largest producer might be more interested in the competitive advantage offered by the technology. When suitability cannot be determined, all targeted companies can be contacted simultaneously or the target list can be approached randomly.

In some cases, companies may make unsolicited inquiries to licensors. A somewhat different marketing plan may be needed in this case; techniques for the handling of such inquiries are discussed later in this section.

Every marketing plan must be flexible to allow changes to be made in response to what is learned in the course of implementing the plan. Feedback should be solicited (and may be provided unsolicited) from targeted licensees to learn which aspects of the marketing plan are effective and which need to be improved or changed. Performance benchmarks, such as contacts made or agreements closed in a certain time period, should be set and, if not met, new approaches should be investigated to improve performance or goals should be modified to reflect the new understanding of the marketing program. In setting performance benchmarks, the difficulties and challenges associated with marketing technology, particularly technology at an early stage of development, should be understood and reflected in the goals set. Periodic reviews of the overall program should be held to measure its success, set new goals, and generally guide the process.

CONTACTING THE TARGETED LICENSEE

Targeted prospective licensees can be first contacted by telephone, fax, or electronic or regular mail. Contact can also be made at trade shows and conferences, either by conducting meetings at a booth or hotel suite at the show or by visiting targets' booths. Contact should be initiated with high-level management in marketing and engineering. Often it is necessary to telephone companies to obtain the name of the appropriate contact, at which time a brief discussion can be held if the contact is available. If the contact is known, it may be preferable to send information by e-mail first, and then follow up by telephone. Although in many cases the contact will not have reviewed the information provided prior to the follow-up call, at least it will be on hand for review during and after the call.

The licensor should supply information in stages and only as needed by the prospective licensee. A typical initial package of information could be a computer-based presentation that introduces the company and describes the technology and its competitive advantages, or a mailed package that includes an introductory letter and a high-level technical description, often in the form of a leaflet or brochure. The whole package should take no longer than 5 to 10 minutes to review, but it should contain enough details to clearly differentiate the technology offered from competing products. The purpose of the initial contact is to convince the targeted licensee to continue to the next step in the marketing process and, if possible, to get initial feedback from the target on issues related to the technology that are of concern.

An example of a typical cover letter appears in Exhibit 6.1, and a sample leaflet appears in Exhibit 6.2.

Keep records of all contacts with targeted companies, including the date of contact, the name of the person contacted, what was discussed, and what materials (if any) were sent. Several computer programs (including ACT) are available to track marketing efforts, or simpler systems using various filing methods can be used.

Follow up the initial package with a telephone call a few days after it has been received by the targeted licensee. When following up, the licensor should confirm that the initial package was received, determine whether the person to whom the package was addressed is the correct contact, answer questions, and

Exhibit 6.1.   Typical Initial Contact Cover Letter

[Date]

Mr. _____
_____ Inc.
50 Stamford Street, Suite 800
Boston, MA 02114

Dear Mr._____,

Adaptive Differential Entropy Compression (ADEX) is a powerful yet simple digital audio compression technology. Its low implementation cost and flexibility make ADEX ideal for use in computer audio and multimedia applications. ADEX is the most powerful currently available algorithm not requiring a digital signal processor, and can also be implemented in software if desired.

ADEX was originally developed at SRI International; subsequently, Digideck was formed to further develop and commercialize the invention. We are now seeking to license ADEX to companies active in digital audio processing, and we believe that your company is a potential candidate.

The enclosed brochure contains more detailed information. Please take a few minutes to read it, or pass it along to the person in your organization responsible for technology review. I will call you in a few days to discuss this matter further.

Yours sincerely,

Robert Megantz

enc: brochure

Digideck

ADEX

Digital Audio Compression Technology

Digideck

Digideck is a privately-held company formed to develop and commercialize digital audio compression technologies derived from research originally performed at SRI International.

Ongoing development activities include system optimization for various applications, integration of the ADEX algorithm in firmware and software, and joint overall system development and planning.

Applications

- Multimedia Computer Systems
- Digital Recorders and Editing Systems
- Cable and Wireless Cable Systems
- Direct-Broadcast Satellite Transmission Systems
- Video Games
- Digital Signal Distribution Systems

For more information please contact:

Robert Megantz
Digideck, Incorporated
1503 Grant Road, Suite 210
Mountain View, CA 94040

Tel: 415-961-6955
Fax: 415-961-7316

Digideck is a trademark of Digideck, Incorporated.

Exhibit 6.2 Typical Technology Marketing Leaflet

Technical Description

Adaptive Differential Entropy Compression (ADEX) uses a combination of entropy codes and digital compression filters to achieve high fidelity at a data rate of 4-6 bits per sample with very low computational complexity.

As shown in the block diagram, the encoder consists of an A/D converter, a least-significant-bit (LSB) truncator which can include noise shaping, a linear compression filter, a variable-rate entropy-based encoder (Huffman-type), a formatter which can include error detection and correction and a bit stream buffer to smooth instantaneous variations to match the data rate to the communications channel. The decoder consists of another buffer, a deformatter/decoder, an expansion filter and the D/A converter. Error detection and masking circuitry, if used, form a second control path.

The differential entropy compression filter uses difference equations to predict the bit rate of an entropy code, optimizing itself among a set of filters. Only a small number of simple first or second-order integer-based filters need be cascaded to form the set that minimizes the entropy of virtually all voice and music signals. Further, the filter primitives all have exact inverses, allowing exact (bit-for-bit) reproduction by the decoder.

Unlike logarithmic companders and other techniques, the entropy coder that follows also allows exact reproduction of its compressed input after decoding. ADEX additionally adapts the entropy coder to optimize the code to each music segment while keeping the size of stored tables to a total of just 32 words.

Combining differential entropy filtering, entropy coding and smoothing achieves exact inversion of 16-bit high fidelity audio at 7-10 bits per sample, depending on the program material.

Further compression is achieved by truncating input LSBs. For each input LSB truncated, the entropy of the compressed signal is reduced approximately one bit per sample. Thus, by temporarily reducing a 16-bit input signal to 14 bit resolution, a compressed signal that might require 8 bits for exact reproduction can be reduced to 6 bits per sample, a 25% reduction in the compressed bit rate. The noise produced by this process can be hidden using appropriate noise shaping techniques during encoding.

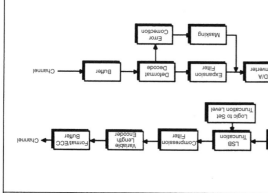

BLOCK DIAGRAM – ADEX SYSTEM

Features

- Very Low Cost

- Simple to Implement (12k gates for complete processor including error correction)

- Variable Compression (high quality performance at 3:1 ratio, can be increased to 6:1)

- Lossless Mode with 2:1 Compression

- Low Power Consumption (no multiplication)

- Capable of High Speed Processing

- Software-Only Implementation Available

- Very Robust with Simple Error Correction

Exhibit 6.2 *(Continued)*

determine the level of interest in the product or technology being offered. Often, the person receiving the package will specify a different contact and a new package must be sent and the process started anew.

The licensor must be conscientious about following up all contacts and supplying information and other materials in a timely manner. The actions and responsiveness demonstrated by both the licensor and the licensee in the initial stages of the marketing process will set an example for future relations and can have a big effect on the success of the licensing process. A typical license negotiation can take months or even years from the date of first contact to final execution of the agreement, so long-term commitment of personnel and other resources is required.

If the prospective licensee expresses interest in the offered product or technology, secondary materials should be provided as needed. This may include more detailed technical information, such as published technical or white papers, copies of patents, engineering drawings, schematic diagrams, test data, and market research data; and licensing materials, including a simple licensing term sheet (as shown in Exhibit 6.3) or a draft license agreement (a sample annotated agreement can be found in Appendix C).

Use of a Non-Disclosure Agreement (NDA)

Information disclosed in secondary licensing discussions is often confidential in nature. To protect both parties, if confidential information will be disclosed by either party, a suitable non-disclosure agreement (NDA) should be executed before any confidential information is discussed.

In some industries, especially those with short product life cycles, it is common to sign an NDA before any substantive discussion occurs. In others, NDAs are rarely signed at all, and licensing discussions often begin later, after patents have issued or products incorporating the technology are available on the open market. A typical NDA is shown in Exhibit 6.4.

The NDA of Exhibit 6.4 is one-way, that is, proprietary information of the licensor is being shared with the licensee, but the licensee is not disclosing any of its proprietary information. Two-way NDAs are used when disclosure by both parties is required.

Intellectual property that should not be discussed without first signing an NDA includes patent applications (which have not yet been published), unpublished copyrighted works, and both know-how and (generally) show-how. In practice it may be necessary to bend these rules at times to stimulate interest, but any bending should be done with full knowledge of the potential consequences. Further information on IP rights and protection can be found in Chapter 2.

To protect their own internal development efforts, many large corporations have a policy of refusing to sign NDAs (or, often, to even accept unsolicited disclosures of inventions or technologies). In this case, prospective licensors must decide to what extent they are willing to disclose information without legal protection. Ideally, materials can be prepared that give an adequate description of the product or technology without disclosing any confidential information. If

Exhibit 6.3.   Sample Licensing Term Sheet

[Date]

Preliminary Proposal

For Internet Appliance OEM Manufacturing License Agreement
and Joint Development
Between Company A and Company B

Property:	U.S. and International Patent Applications. Trademarks. Copyrighted Works (object code for client software, design data). Know-How.
License:	Worldwide, to make and sell Internet appliances, to distribute the client software, and to use the Trademarks and Know-How. Non-exclusive.
Term:	Life of the patents.
License Fee:	$_____ (includes client and service integration).
Royalties:	Unit quantities on a yearly basis 0 – 100,000: $_____/unit 100,000 – 300,000: $_____/unit 300,000 – 500,000: $_____/unit 500,000 – 1,000,000: $_____/unit 1,000,000 and up: $_____/unit
Joint Development:	Company A and Company B will work together to develop the first Licensed Product. Company B will provide the hardware reference design, TCP/IP stack, and operating system license together with the processor. Company A will provide the client software for the processor and will assist in integrating and testing the client software and will deliver a full software build for Company B's use. Company A will also provide usage tracking, content profile, user management, auto update, quality control, and other services for the Licensed Products. This work will be done as part of the basic licensing fee according to a mutually agreed upon schedule.
Revenue Sharing:	Company A will pay Company B _____% of the net revenues generated by end-users using Licensed Products made and sold by Company B.
Marking:	Company B agrees to mark the Licensed Products with Company A's trademarks according to Company A guidelines.

not, it may be best to wait until enough public information is available to allow the prospective licensee to analyze the technology without disclosing any proprietary information. Such decisions, as well as the wording of an appropriate NDA, are best made with the advice of legal counsel. *Any discussion of proprietary information without first signing an NDA can constitute legal disclosure, and important intellectual property rights can be lost.*

Exhibit 6.4   Typical Non-Disclosure Agreement

Supertech, Inc.

ONE-WAY CORPORATE NON-DISCLOSURE

Agreement ID: _____ Effective Date: _____

In order to protect certain confidential information, Supertech, Inc., ("STI"), and the "Recipient" identified below, agree that:

1. Disclosing and Receiving Party: The party disclosing confidential information ("Discloser") is STI. The party receiving confidential information ("Recipient") is: _____.

2. Primary Representative: Each party's representative for coordinating disclosure or receipt of confidential information is:

STI: _____

Recipient: _____

3. Description of Confidential Information: The confidential information disclosed under this Agreement is described as: _____

_____

_____

   Use of Confidential Information : The party receiving confidential information ("Recipient") shall make use of the confidential information only for the following _____

_____

4. Confidentiality Period: Recipient's duty to hold confidential information in confidence expires three (3) years from the date of actual disclosure by STI to Recipient. (Note: This is the period of protection of confidential information.)

5. Disclosure Period: This Agreement pertains to confidential information that is disclosed between the Effective Date and one (1) year from the Effective Date. (Note: This is the period during which confidential information is going to be disclosed.)

6. Standard of Care: Recipient shall protect the disclosed Confidential Information by using the same degree of care that Recipient uses to protect its own Confidential Information of a like nature, but no less than a reasonable degree of care, to prevent the unauthorized use, dissemination, or publication of the Confidential Information as required under this Agreement. Recipient must inform and similarly obligate all relevant parties including employees, and third parties of their obligations under this Agreement. In no event shall Confidential Information be shared with any third parties including, but not limited to, joint ventures or any other entity in which Recipient has a debt or equity interest that is a direct competitor of STI and its affiliates or subsidiaries unless authorized by STI in writing and receiving party is similarly obligated under confidentiality/non disclosure agreement with STI.

7. Marking: Recipient's obligations shall only extend to confidential information that is described in paragraph 3, and that: (a) comprises specific materials individually listed in paragraph 3; or, (b) is marked as confidential at the time of disclosure; or (c) is unmarked at the time of disclosure, but is subsequently designated as confidential in a written notice sent to Recipient's primary representative within thirty (30) days of such disclosure, summarizing the confidential information sufficiently for identification.

(Continued)

Exhibit 6.4   *(Continued)*

8. Exclusions: This Agreement imposes no obligation upon Recipient with respect to information that: (a) was in Recipient's possession before receipt from Discloser; (b) is or becomes a matter of public knowledge through no fault of Recipient; (c) is lawfully received by Recipient from a third party; (d) is disclosed by STI to a third party without a duty of confidentiality owed by third party to STI; (e) is independently developed by Recipient; (f) is disclosed by Recipient with STI's prior written approval; or (g) is requested by governmental body and Recipient provides reasonable prior written notice to STI.

9. Warranty: STI warrants that it has the right to make the disclosures under this Agreement. NO OTHER WARRANTIES ARE MADE BY EITHER PARTY UNDER THIS AGREEMENT. ANY INFORMATION EXCHANGED UNDER THIS AGREEMENT IS PROVIDED "AS IS".

10. Rights: Neither party acquires any intellectual property rights under this Agreement except the limited rights necessary to carry out the purposes set forth in paragraph 4.

11. Marketing: In no event shall Recipient mention the existence of this business relationship to any third party unless necessary to carry out the purpose of this contract.

12. Recipient shall adhere to all applicable laws, regulations, and rules relating to the export of technical data, and shall not export or reexport any technical data, any products received from STI, or the direct product of such technical data to any proscribed country listed in such applicable laws, regulations, and rules unless properly authorized.

13. This Agreement does not create any agency or partnership relationship.

14. All additions or modifications to this Agreement must be made in writing and must be signed by both parties.

15. This Agreement is made under, and shall be construed according to, the laws of the State of California, U.S.A. (excluding California's Conflict or Choice of Law Provisions).

16. Recipient agrees that STI will suffer irreparable harm if Recipient fails to comply with the obligations set forth herein, and further agrees that monetary damages will be inadequate to compensate STI for any such breach. Accordingly, Recipient agrees that STI will, in addition to any other remedies available to it at law or in equity, be entitled to the issuance of injunctive relief to enforce the Agreement.

Agreed to and Accepted by:

>Supertech, Inc.
>1299 St. Regis Ave.
>Mountain Glen, CA 96093

By: _____
                                     (Signature)

Name: _____

Title: _____

Date: _____

Recipient:_____

Address:_____

_____

By: _____
                                     (Signature)

Name: _____
                                   (Please Print)

Title:_____

Date: _____

Exploratory Meeting

All initial and secondary materials should attempt to stimulate sufficient interest in the product or technology being offered to convince the targeted licensee to arrange for a meeting and demonstration. The importance of personal contact in successfully consummating license agreements cannot be overemphasized. The targeted licensee must meet and establish relationships with the licensor's personnel who will be involved in negotiations, technology transfer, and other aspects of the licensing arrangement, and receive a positive overall impression of the licensor as a company. This will reassure them that the licensor is in fact a viable concern, capable of meeting its obligations under the proposed agreement. At the same time, the licensor must examine and analyze the targeted licensee as a potential partner and make sure that it is capable of manufacturing and selling sufficient quantities of licensed products to warrant attention and is also capable of maintaining a long-term licensing arrangement. Tours of both the licensor's and licensee's facilities should be arranged when possible.

Unsolicited Inquiries

In some situations, for example, when a well-known licensing program is in place, licensing standard technology to a market, the licensor will receive unsolicited inquiries from companies wishing to license its product or technology. In this case, it is often in the licensor's interest to institute some kind of preliminary screening of the prospective licensee before providing information, arranging meetings, and incurring the costs associated with establishing a relationship. This can be particularly important when the inquiry comes from a foreign firm, where information can be difficult to obtain and marketing costs are relatively high.

An effective strategy for dealing with these inquiries is to request qualification information from the prospective licensee before proceeding with further licensing activities. After the inquiry is received, a questionnaire (such as the one shown in Exhibit 6.5) would be sent to the prospective licensee requesting general, financial, marketing, and technical information.

Note the similarities between the information requested in the Prospective Licensee Questionnaire and market research information collected for the target licensees (as described in Chapter 3). In fact, most of the items in the questionnaire could be readily obtained by the licensor if desired. Asking the prospective licensee to collect and provide the information is a way to ascertain its level of interest, based on the depth and quality of its response to the request.

The licensor should analyze the response as if performing market research, that is, licensing personnel should carry out a general and overall analysis with assistance from the finance, marketing, and engineering departments as needed. If the information provided appears to be satisfactory, the licensor can then send the originally requested information and begin the normal licensing process (probably skipping the initial package stage) described earlier in this chapter.

Exhibit 6.5   Prospective Licensee Questionnaire

PROSPECTIVE LICENSEE QUESTIONNAIRE

In order to better understand how you would use our technology, we would like you to send us information about your company and products. Please include the following:

1. General company information—Details of the organization, location, and size of your company, as well as the names, addresses, and telephone and fax numbers of key personnel who will be involved in the licensing and use of our technology. If your company's shares are publicly traded, please include a copy of the latest annual report and 10-K filing.
2. Financial information—If the annual report or 10-K filing is not available (for example, if your company is privately-held), please provide audited financial statements for the last three years. In addition, please include a banker's reference.
3. Marketing information—Please provide details of markets in which your company is active, current marketing activities, and details (to the extent known) of your market strategies envisioned for products incorporating our technology. Please also provide us with typical marketing materials for your current products.
4. Technical information—Please send us specifications and schematics for your current products that are similar to those in which you intend to implement our technology. Providing us with a sample of a typical current product will help us better understand your current market position and allow us to better recommend how utilizing our technology can benefit your company.

PUBLIC RELATIONS

In addition to marketing the licensed technology directly to targeted companies, public relations techniques can be used to publicize a technology and its licensing program to targeted industries.

Trade Shows

Trade shows can be fertile ground for finding both prospective licensees and providers of licensable products and technologies. The prospective licensor can rent space in the exhibition hall and demonstrate its non-confidential products and technologies to targeted licensees and, at the same time, can often obtain additional publicity via press coverage. If a lower profile is desired, a hotel suite can be utilized for demonstrations to selected companies, and invitations can be sent out to targeted companies for private discussions and demonstrations in the suite.

Technical and marketing personnel can participate in workshops, panels, and paper sessions, which are attended by those interested in similar products and technologies. This is often done in conjunction with renting space on the exhibition floor or a hotel suite.

Licensor's representatives can also visit exhibits from other companies active in the market of interest and can distribute information about the licensable products and technologies, as well as obtain information about competitive products. In practice, targeted company personnel at exhibit hall booths are often unavailable for discussions because of their booth duties and other activities, but contact names and company information are usually available. In general, a successful trade show contact would include meeting the proper person, having a brief discussion about the technology, and providing some supporting written materials; the initial contact is then followed up after the show.

Those looking for products or technologies to license-in can attend trade show functions related to the product of interest and visit exhibitors marketing related products. Again, contact names and some details can be obtained, but detailed discussions are usually held after the show.

Publications and Trade Organizations

Licensor's technical and marketing personnel should actively and on an ongoing basis contribute articles related to licensable technical developments to trade magazines and academic journals. Not only will this publicize the licensable products and technologies, but it will also enhance the career development of the authors. Similarly, technical and marketing personnel should be active in trade organizations, attending meetings and presenting non-confidential research results and product developments.

Press releases publicizing new technologies and developments should be provided to newspapers and magazines; many unsolicited inquiries are generated through articles in the press. The articles can also be used in subsequent marketing activities. Many trade magazines and organizations offer awards for significant achievements. Nominations for the technology or products incorporating the technology should be submitted and any awards granted should be publicized.

Other

Other marketing techniques, including direct marketing, can also be employed. However, the nature of technology marketing generally requires a more directed and labor-intensive approach.

There are a number of organizations that, for a fee or a share of revenues generated, will market inventions and technologies. The quality of the services offered varies, but generally, if using outside help is contemplated, a business-oriented firm with expertise in licensing and the technology and markets of interest should be retained. Firms and consultants that offer marketing services for a wide variety of technologies and markets will often follow a set procedure, using market research techniques and a marketing strategy that may or may not be appropriate. Many of these firms are active in professional organizations such as the Licensing Executives Society (LES), which maintain databases of the firms and their specialties. A list of licensing-related professional organizations can be found in Appendix B.

7

Negotiating and Drafting Agreements

Once a match has been found between a technology offered for license and a prospective licensee's needs, license terms must be negotiated and a suitable agreement drafted.

The negotiation of terms is a sensitive stage in the licensing process. When licensing-out, the licensor's expectations and strategies should be well known before any negotiations begin (see Chapter 5). The prospective licensee may have quite a different view of the technology and its prospects, and may also have internal restrictions on allowable licensing arrangements. When licensing-in, the opposite may be true. Flexibility, open-mindedness, and receptiveness to the other side's perspectives and needs are required. The successful completion of the negotiating process depends on the ability of both sides to match the licensor's strategy, including its notion of the value of the licensed technology, with the prospective licensee's needs and willingness to pay. The first section of this chapter discusses the concepts and techniques used in successful negotiations.

Once all terms have been agreed upon, a formal license agreement must be drafted. Many books have been written on drafting agreements (some are listed in the Bibliography), and a detailed discussion is outside the scope of this book. However, a brief discussion of the structure of a typical agreement can be found in the second section of this chapter, and two annotated sample agreements can be found in Appendix C, one targeted for licensing technology used in hardware and the other for software.

Because of the unique nature of its development, protection, distribution, and use, software licenses are often somewhat different than licenses used for other technologies. The third section of this chapter discusses types of software commonly licensed, models currently used to license software, and future trends in software licensing.

As discussed in Chapter 1, licensing can be used to legitimize infringement.

The last section of this chapter discusses various techniques that can be used to deal with infringers.

NEGOTIATION IN THE 21ST CENTURY

During the first 80 to 90 years of the 20th century the objective of most business negotiations was to win at any cost. Purchasing personnel in industrial companies (there were few service companies at that time) were told by top management to wring the last penny out of all negotiations with their suppliers. There was no consideration of an ongoing relationship with any company. On the other side of the table, sellers were expected to use every available strategy (fair or not so fair) to get orders at the highest price possible. Both sides seldom looked beyond the current negotiation.

The results of these win/lose negotiation philosophies were contracts that produced definite winners and losers, and bad feelings on both sides of the negotiating table. As you would expect, after most such negotiations, this win/lose attitude resulted in lose/lose relationships, as the side that lost at the table was determined to get even before the contract was completed.

Almost all negotiations result in a relationship after the negotiation is finished. This is particularly true for long-term licensing arrangements. For example, the licensor often must transfer technology to the licensee and provide support and/or trademark quality control services during the life of the agreement. The licensee generally must provide statements and pay royalties due, and may be required to provide product samples for evaluation by the licensor. If one side feels they were taken advantage of during the negotiations, they may try to get even during the term of the agreement. For example, a licensee can delay sending royalty statements and payments if he or she feels that the royalty terms are unfair.

In the past 10 to 20 years there have been major changes in the business world regarding negotiations. Most businesses today have concentrated on their core businesses and are no longer vertically integrated and, as a result, depend almost completely on outside sources for key components, including technology. Some companies just develop technology and all products incorporating their technologies are made under license.

The key to success in the 21st century is to remember that the purpose of the negotiation process is to set the ground rules for a future relationship. Your negotiation results will *not* be judged by what you accomplish at the negotiating table, but by the final outcome of the relationship, months or even years later. Licensing negotiations must be win/win. This objective *must* be fully incorporated into all aspects of your licensing strategy.

Negotiation Concepts

When negotiating, both the licensor and prospective licensee must attune themselves to the needs of the other to ensure a satisfactory conclusion. The single most important concept that must be recognized is that for a long-term licensing arrangement to be successful, both the licensor and licensee must have their needs fulfilled. Thus, the interests of both parties should be understood and prioritized as much as possible prior to the commencement of negotiations.

In addition to strategic considerations, traditional negotiating techniques must be addressed to assure a successful outcome. Exhibit 7.1 illustrates graphically the relationship between the licensor's and licensee's range of acceptable values for a given negotiated term (e.g., the royalty rate).

Point A is the licensor's initial quote, and usually starts the negotiation process. Point B is the licensor's minimum price. Point C is the licensee's initial offer (or counteroffer to the licensor's initial quote), and may be given verbally or in writing. Point D is the licensee's maximum allowable price. From Exhibit 7.1, you can see that the limits of a possible agreement are B and D. If E is the licensor's desired price and F is the licensee's desired price, the negotiated price will probably fall between E and F.

The following are other traditional negotiating techniques that must be considered:

- Planning is the key to success. Most negotiators do not spend enough time *before* the negotiation. It has been proven that the side that does the best planning job will do better in obtaining its objectives. In *The Pre Negotiation Planning Book* (listed in the Bibliography), a 25-point checklist details all of the activities that must be completed before the negotiation starts.
- Negotiations should not be affected by the personalities of the negotiators. Battles of will can slow and even kill a negotiation and should be avoided. Negotiators should exhibit courtesy, sensitivity, and a generally positive attitude.
- A common mistake that technical people make in a negotiation situation is to believe that, if the facts are in their favor, they will win the negotiation.

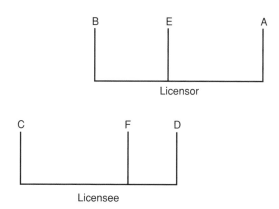

Exhibit 7.1   The Negotiation Process

Facts do not negotiate—people negotiate. Negotiation is a people process, and strong people skills are needed to obtain your objectives. Facts will support your position. The way facts are presented and used are the keys to success.

- In negotiations your objectives determine your results. Studies prove that negotiators with tougher objectives obtain better results.
- Negotiations are not zero sum events. The side that is creative and is able to add value to the process is the side that will do the best. If one side wants 60% of the pie and the other side wants 60%, the only way to succeed is to make the pie 120%.
- The side that asks the most questions during the negotiation process will do the best because they are receiving information. Many technical people believe that it is a sign of weakness to ask a question. They think the other side will believe they are ignorant. This egotistical belief must be avoided to be a successful negotiator.
- The side that listens the most will do the best. When a person is talking, he is providing information. When a person is listening, he is receiving information.
- It should be recognized that both sides have multiple, hierarchical interests. Both shared and conflicting interests will lie behind opposing positions. Negotiations should focus on shared rather than conflicting interests. Successful negotiators know they must attack positions, not people.
- Negotiators should be flexible and creative in developing and discussing options. Multiple approaches, based on shared interests, must be considered. There will always be more than one way to reach a win/win solution.
- Negotiations should be based on logic and objective criteria. Proposals should be supported by facts and compelling reasoning, as should responses to proposals from the other side.
- Each negotiation has many issues to be negotiated, and the successful negotiator is the one who is able to negotiate a large number of issues at one time. For example, in most licensing negotiations the most obvious term to be negotiated is the royalty structure, but other strategic considerations, such as market and territorial restrictions, length of the agreement, payment schedules, handling of improvements, and so on, must also be part of the negotiation. A good negotiator will understand that changes in other terms can affect the required royalty rates.
- Responsiveness is a key to success. Negotiations should proceed as efficiently as possible. The chief negotiators for both the licensor and the licensee need to coordinate the negotiations and be responsible for internal communications with all key personnel. Proposals and requests for additional information advanced by either side should be considered and responded to in a timely manner. Meetings between licensor and licensee should be held on a regular basis to discuss progress and how to overcome any problems that may arise during the negotiating process. Complete preparation, sensitivity to the other side's needs and desires, and a clear understanding of the technologies and markets of interest are the best means of ensuring that negotiations will stay on track.

- Concessions are among the most powerful tools that can be employed to advance negotiations. However, the granting of concessions must be managed in such a way as to further the parties' sensitivities to each others' needs; that is, the problem leading to the need for a concession must be understood and framed in the context of both parties' needs. Concessions should only be considered as a means to achieve an acceptable agreement, and not as a goal in and of themselves. Generally a concession from one side is matched (not always value for value) with a concession from the other side.

  When the licensor discusses any changes in terms, the effect of such changes on the licensor should be clearly communicated to the licensee. At the same time, the licensor should fully understand their effect on its overall strategy and not agree to any terms that contradict the goals of the licensing program. Any legal issues arising during negotiations, including anti-trust and restraint of trade, must be reviewed and cleared by counsel before negotiations are completed.

  One special type of concession used in licensing is the granting of so-called *pioneer licenses*. When beginning a licensing program, a licensor may offer special terms to more rapidly establish the program and promote the manufacture and marketing of licensed products. Enticements include the waiving of some or all of the initial payment, reduced royalties for a period of time, and limited exclusivity. Dolby Laboratories, for example, granted KLH, their first licensee, exclusive rights to the B-type noise reduction technology for two years.

  The effect of such preferences must be carefully considered, especially if widespread licensing is desired under standard terms. Many prospective licensees desire most-favored-nation status, where their terms are equal to the best terms granted to any other licensee, to avoid being placed at a competitive disadvantage in the licensed markets. Therefore, granting pioneer preferences can affect licensing to others while such preferences are in effect. One way to avoid conflicts between pioneer preferences and most-favored-nation clauses is to make the most-favored-nation clause apply only to agreements executed after the pioneer license.
- Usually, a technology can be used by more than one target licensee. Pursuing several opportunities simultaneously can increase the probability of success. Concentrating all efforts on what seems to be the most likely candidate is a mistake; negotiating with all interested parties will not only increase the chances of consummating other agreements, it will also strengthen the negotiating position with the most probable candidate.
- The relative positions of the licensor and licensee can affect negotiations. Large and small entities often have different corporate cultures, which can cause delays or misunderstandings. For example, individual inventors or small companies who have developed and patented technologies often have a difficult time convincing large corporations who they feel are infringing to take them seriously. Anyone considering an infringement action should make sure that sufficient resources are in place to support a long negotiating

Using Escrow to Reduce Risk in Licensing Technology

Companies developing and commercializing technology are often admired as rapidly growing, innovative enterprises, yet many are smaller operations fighting to remain competitive in highly volatile industries. The risk of failure, and the resulting inability to fulfill obligations to partners, is of great concern to prospective licensees of these technology vendors. In many cases, particularly those where computer software is licensed, an escrow arrangement can help safeguard the interests of both the licensor and licensee. In 1988, the United States Bankruptcy Code § 365 N was modified to provide protection to companies licensing technology. This provision excludes deposits on escrow arrangements from the protection awarded to companies filing for bankruptcy.

Escrow is used when the licensor owns an intellectual asset that is not provided to the licensee under the agreement, but that is critical to the licensee being able to fully utilize the licensed technology. For example, if software is licensed in the form of object (machine) code, the licensee may require that the source code be placed in escrow so that, if the licensor fails to fulfill its obligations under the agreement or ceases operation, the licensee will be given access to the source code. This situation often occurs when large companies license technology from small licensors with uncertain prospects.

Each licensee should evaluate its technology providers to determine the risks involved in licensing technology. The typical factors for determining the need for escrow are cost of the product, replacement cost of the product, uniqueness of the product in the marketplace, training cost for the product, service reputation of the vendor, and the dependency the company has on the functions of the particular technology.

THE ESCROW AGREEMENT

The foundation of any escrow arrangement is the agreement. A professional escrow agent is often used to establish and implement the escrow agreement, and can be helpful in providing solutions, offering sample contract language, and, once the agreement has been executed, in providing a secure environment for the escrow deposit to be held. Although the escrow agent may offer a form contract, the licensor and licensee may both profit by having their own terms to present to one another when beginning the escrow discussions.

The conditions under which the materials placed in escrow will be released should cover typical concerns with the product service, including maintenance, support, and upgrades. The rules and procedures under which materials will be released must be clear; vague release requirements benefit no one and often invite extended legal battles.

Escrow requirements should be submitted prior to the execution of the license agreement. This provides the licensee with significantly more leverage in its request and allows portions of the escrow agreement to be referenced in the license agreement.

THE DEPOSIT MATERIALS

It is important to ensure that the materials placed in escrow are adequate to provide the required protection. Communication between the parties will go a long way toward the creation of a reliable escrow deposit.

The following is a partial list of typical recommended deposit materials:

- Two copies of the source code for each version of the licensed software on magnetic media
- Any relevant manuals not provided to the licensee
- Maintenance tools and third-party systems needed to use the escrowed materials
- Names and addresses of key technical employees that the licensee may hire as subcontractors in the event that the licensor ceases to exist
- Compilation instructions in written format or recorded on video

The escrow deposit materials should be shipped to the escrow agent electronically or via a traceable courier. Upon receipt of the materials, the escrow agent should contact both the licensor and the licensee to confirm receipt, and provide an inventory report of the submitted materials.

STORAGE OF THE DEPOSIT MATERIALS

Fluctuating temperatures and humidity can damage magnetic media. Therefore, the escrow agent should provide a *media vault* facility with the following features to secure the deposit materials:

- Minimum four-hour fire rated walls
- FM-200 gas or other gas-based fire extinguishing system
- A controlled storage environment that maintains constant temperature and humidity
- Extensive security systems within the facility

(Continued)

If the licensed technology is upgraded, it is critical that the revised source code be sent to the escrow agent, so that the escrow deposit corresponds to the software version being used by the licensee.

VERIFICATION OF THE DEPOSIT

Many licensees are concerned about the accuracy and reliability of the escrow deposit. Escrow agents can often provide a testing option in-house or recommend a professional software-testing agency to check the deposit. The best test will compile the software using the escrow materials and then test the resulting code. If any deficiencies are discovered, the escrow agent will report the test results to the licensee and work with the developer to upgrade and correct the deposit.

RELEASE OF ESCROWED MATERIALS

Most requests for a release are initiated by the licensee because the developer has either ceased operations or failed to support the product. To initiate most releases, the licensee contacts the escrow agent and provides the documentation that is required by the escrow contract to support the request. The licensor is then given the opportunity to rectify the problem, after which the materials are released to the licensee based upon the directives of the escrow contract.

CONCLUSIONS

- Escrow should be considered by licensees that need to secure long-term support for licensed software, particularly if there are concerns about the viability of the licensor.
- The escrow terms must be carefully developed by both the licensor and the licensee, and established under the premise that escrow will eventually be used.
- A strong escrow contract forms the necessary foundation for the service.
- Parties considering using escrow may want to contract with a professional, impartial escrow agent to assist in developing and implementing the service.

process and, possibly, litigation. On the other hand, when contemplating long-term licensing, large corporations often see small technology providers as having a high risk of failure and a low probability of being able to fulfill the terms of a long-term agreement. Small licensors must work hard to convince prospective licensees of their viability.

In summary, a successful negotiation is one where an agreement is consummated and where both parties feel that their goals and interests have been advanced through the negotiation process. Concentrating exclusively on agreement details (even important details such as royalty rates) without keeping the big picture in mind can be counterproductive. Both sides should carefully consider all alternatives to licensing prior to entering into negotiations, so that a clear understanding of the benefits and drawbacks of both licensing and failing to license is in place. Concerns of both parties must be taken seriously by all, and both parties must remember they are establishing the ground rules for their future relationship.

DRAFTING AGREEMENTS

Use of a Memorandum of Understanding (MOU)

In some situations the licensor and licensee may execute an interim document that is more complete than the term sheet discussed in Chapter 6, but something less than a complete, formal license agreement. This may be required to avoid development delays associated with lengthy negotiations of the terms of the license agreement, before publicly announcing the relationship, to establish a higher level of commitment on both sides, to obtain funding, or for a number of other reasons. In this case, a memorandum of understanding (also sometimes referred to as a letter of intent, or LOI) can be used. The MOU includes the business terms of the proposed license agreement and some, but not all, of the legal boilerplate, and is executed by both parties. Alternatively, the term sheet can be expanded as needed and signed by both parties. A typical MOU is shown in Exhibit 7.2.

Agreement Structure

Most license agreements are structured similarly. A typical agreement usually contains the following sections:

Cover Page and Table of Contents
The cover page identifies the parties entering into the agreement, gives the date the agreement is effective, and provides other information as needed or specified in the body of the agreement. Signatures can appear either on the cover page or the last page of the agreement.

Exhibit 7.2. Typical Memorandum of Understanding

MEMORANDUM of UNDERSTANDING BETWEEN

Company A and Company B

Dated: _____

Company A ("Licensee"), a Delaware corporation having its headquarters at 55 High Street, Burbank, CA 91911, and Company B ("Licensor"), a California corporation having a place of business at 1669 Portage Street, Palo Alto, CA 93411 (collectively "the parties") wish to confirm certain understandings with respect to a proposed License Agreement between the parties.

BACKGROUND

The purpose of this Memorandum of Understanding ("MOU") is to set down the business terms of a License Agreement between the parties to allow Licensee to manufacture and sell products that provide the capability to access Licensor's service.

Licensed Products incorporate Licensor's software and reference designs to allow users to access content, such as movies, on a local area network. Licensor aggregates the content through agreements with streaming content providers and provides the infrastructure to connect users with the streams and provide other interactive services. Licensee manufactures consumer electronic products to which they want to add the ability to access the content.

This MOU sets forth the mutual intentions of the parties with respect to its subject matter. However, the parties acknowledge that many details of the License Agreement have not been discussed or finalized and, therefore, except for the obligations set forth in Sections 3 and 5, entitled "Confidentiality" and "General Provisions," respectively, this MOU and other communications or discussions on this subject do not give rise to any liability or obligation binding on any party (other than the obligation to proceed in good faith). In furtherance of the foregoing, either party may unilaterally withdraw, with or without cause, at any time without liability.

1. **AGREED TERMS OF THE PROPOSED LICENSE AGREEMENT**
    A. **License Grant**—Licensor will grant Licensee a non-exclusive, worldwide license to make and sell hardware products, to distribute the client software, and to use the Trademarks and Know-How in association with the products.
    B. **Term**—Life of the patents.
    C. **Initial Payment**—U.S. $10,000.
    D. **Royalties**—Licensee will pay Licensor a royalty for each unit that is sold according to the following schedule:

Number of units sold on a yearly basis	Royalty
0–100,000:	$2/unit
100,000–300,000:	$0.75/unit
300,000–500,000:	$0.50/unit
500,000–1,000,000:	$0.25/unit
1,000,000 and up:	$0.20/unit

    E. **Revenue Sharing**—Licensor will pay Licensee 1% of the net revenues generated by end-users using Licensed Products made and sold by Licensee. Net means after payments to content providers and other commissions but before any of Licensor's overhead expense.

2. **RESPONSIBILITIES OF THE PARTIES**
    A. **Client Software Port**—Licensor will provide client software for the platform of Licensee's choice. Licensor will retain rights to the client software. Licensee will pay Licensor U.S. $200,000 for the client software port.

(Continued)

Exhibit 7.2   *(Continued)*

    B. NREs—Licensor will work together with Licensee to develop a module that implements Licensor's technology. This will include designing the module, implementing the design in hardware, incorporating the chip set of choice, and testing the implementation. The cost of this work will be based on the time spent and expense incurred by Licensor, and will be payable based on a detailed scope of work and schedule of deliverables to be agreed to between the parties. However, based on similar work done previously, it is estimated that the cost will be approximately U.S. $300,000.

    C. Marking—Licensee agrees to mark the Licensed Products with Licensor's trademarks according to Licensor's guidelines.

3. CONFIDENTIALITY

The existing Mutual Non-Disclosure Agreement effective between Licensee and Licensor dated September 5th, 2001, is hereby incorporated by reference and will govern the disclosure of confidential information by and between the parties.

4. AGREEMENTS

Licensor and Licensee agree to work expeditiously to develop one or more definitive License Agreements, based on this Memorandum of Understanding, containing terms and conditions acceptable to the parties involved.

5. GENERAL PROVISIONS

    A. Limitation of Liability—No party shall make a claim against, nor be liable to, any other for any consequential, special, incidental, or punitive damages, including, but not limited to, lost profits suffered by it because of the negotiations under this Memorandum of Understanding or any performance or failure to perform under this Memorandum of Understanding, or for the failure of any negotiations with respect to any definitive agreement.

    B. Public Announcement—The existence and contents of this memorandum shall remain confidential until the parties mutually agree to make a public announcement.

Licensee ACCEPTANCE   *Licensor ACCEPTANCE*

By:_____   **By:**_____
         [Name and title]   [Name and title]

Recitals

Commonly referred to as *whereas clauses*, the recitals give background information on the licensor and licensee and the agreement. Recitals are not essential, but are usually included.

Definitions

Terms basic to the agreement are often defined at the beginning so that their meaning will immediately be clear to the reader. In a simple agreement, definitions can be included in the text. Accurately defining key terms such as *licensed patents, sales price*, and *licensed product* is important to clearly show the scope of the agreement and avoid misunderstandings between licensor and licensee.

License Grant

The intellectual property licensed and the scope of the license (exclusivity, territorial or market restrictions, and so forth) are stated. In addition, any limitations to the license granted are listed. Licenses can be granted for individual patents (or even certain claims of a patent), portfolios of patents, individual or groups of trademarks, single copyrighted works (or specific rights for a single work), collections of copyrighted works, and various combinations. In many cases, however, the licensing of a technology or product requires rights to patents, trademarks, copyrighted works, and know-how, and a hybrid license is granted, which licenses rights to all necessary intellectual property in one license. Further discussion of hybrid and separate licenses can be found later in this chapter and in Appendix C.

Payments

The payment section includes the royalty structure and details of when and how royalty and other payments will be made. In addition, this section specifies the information that must be included in statements that accompany the payments, records the licensee is required to keep, licensor's access to those records, and which party is responsible for any taxes due on the payments.

Other Obligations

There are often other obligations associated with the license that are spelled out in the agreement. They may include transfer of technology, further product development by the licensor, proper use of licensed trademarks and marking of licensed products, protection and maintenance of licensed intellectual property, confidentiality, and handling of improvements and updates.

Termination

In addition to stating when the agreement will expire (e.g., when the last licensed patent expires), reasons and procedures are given for termination for cause (due to breach of the agreement by either the licensor or licensee). Before the agreement is terminated for cause, the breaching party is usually given the opportunity to cure the breach, in which case the agreement remains in effect.

Warranties, Indemnification, Liability, and Authority

Both the licensor and the licensee may provide warranties in the agreement. The licensor may warrant that some or all of its IP is valid (or valid to the best of its knowledge), and both parties may warrant that nothing prevents them from entering into and fulfilling their obligations under the agreement. The licensee often indemnifies the licensor against any product liability damages associated with licensed products, and in some agreements the licensor will provide limited indemnification against infringement actions related to the licensed IP. The licensee may be given the right to assign the agreement (e.g., if it merges with or is acquired by another company). Finally, the licensee is usually required to comply with governmental restrictions (e.g., on the export of sensitive data).

Miscellaneous Provisions
Where and how to send notices, restrictions on public announcements, how disputes will be resolved, applicable law, and other boilerplate topics are included in this section.

LICENSING COMPUTER SOFTWARE

Software is usually protected as a copyrighted work, although it can also incorporate other intellectual property rights. For this reason, most software licenses grant rights to some or all of the bundle of rights associated with copyrighted works. As explained in Chapter 2, the bundle of rights includes the rights to use, copy, distribute, and prepare derivative works of the work. These rights are separable and can be licensed separately as appropriate to a given situation.

There are a variety of scenarios under which software is licensed. First, software can be licensed to manufacturers for use in products ranging from automobiles to medical devices. This type of software, also referred to as *firmware*, can be supplied as *object code*, in which case the licensee uses the software with no modifications, or as *source code*, in which case the licensee can modify the software and produce new object code for use in its products. In the first case, the license would most likely allow the licensee to use, copy, and distribute the software in its products, while in the second case the right to prepare derivative works could be added. Other intellectual property included in the license could include trademarks, patents covering inventions implemented in the software, and know-how. Further development by the licensor is also frequently a part of the deal. In a similar manner, software can be licensed, as either source code or object code, to a manufacturer for inclusion in another software product intended for sale to end-users for either personal or commercial use. The valuation methods and licensing strategies discussed in Chapters 4 and 5 can be used in these scenarios.

The right to distribute a ready-to-use software application can also be licensed. This situation would arise if, for example, an Internet browser program were to be included on a CD-ROM and distributed, together with other software, in a computer-related magazine. In this case, the licensor would supply executable code (not source code), and the license would include the right to use, copy, and distribute the software. A sample license agreement for this scenario can be found in Appendix C.

Software can also be licensed directly to end-users. In this case, familiar to most users of personal computers, the license generally grants the licensee the right to use the software and, in some cases, to make a limited number of copies for archival purposes. The rights to make large numbers of copies, to distribute the software, and to prepare derivative works are generally not included in end-user licenses. Grants for other, related intellectual properties are generally not needed, as the licensee is only granted the right to use the software.

For these reasons, end-user licensing of software is somewhat different from the licensing discussed up to this point. The remainder of this section will discuss some of the methods used in licensing software to end-users.

Background

Before the advent of networking, software packages were sold for use in individual computers. Shrink-wrap licenses, where the breaking of a seal on the packaging constitutes recognition of, and agreement with, the terms of the license agreement (printed on the package), became the rule.

Networks allowed a single software package, installed on the server's hard disk, to be used by everyone connected to the network. A single license (and fee) was obviously unacceptable, so software makers began charging for every computer connected to the network and, in some cases (e.g., Microsoft), requiring every user to carry a hard copy of the license agreement.

The advent of networks has made software licensing far more difficult and the potential for illegal usage much greater. Most of the PCs used in business are connected to networks, yet there is no such thing as a standard network license agreement.

Supervising compliance with several sets of licensing requirements can be difficult. Multi-platform networks make administration even more difficult.

With the growing success in fighting piracy and unauthorized use of computer software has come the realization that standardized and easily implemented licensing schemes are needed. However, while everyone would benefit from standard practice, it is not at all certain that standard terms will be developed, as doing so could be in violation of anti-trust laws, primarily for what could be considered price fixing.

Current Licensing Practices

Most licenses fall into a few broad categories:

- *The site license.* For a flat fee, an unlimited number of users (in a specified site or company) can run the software on an unlimited number of nodes. Users like site licenses for their simplicity, but vendors have largely stopped offering them to all but their largest customers.
- *A license for each machine (Windows).* If licenses are purchased for all machines, this approach is easy to administer, but it can be inflexible (e.g., if users want to use their software at home they may have to remove it from their office machine). If licenses are purchased for only some machines, administration becomes difficult. This kind of license is often used for operating system software, which must be resident on every machine.
- *A license for each user (early Microsoft, Oracle).* Although simpler than machine licensing, in some cases users are allowed to use the software on more than one machine and in others they are not. Home and/or portable use of the software (in addition to its primary use) is often allowed under the "80% rule," which states that the software can be used at home or with

a portable computer as long as this represents less than 20% of the total usage. For this and other reasons, administering user licensing can be awkward in large organizations.

- *A license for each concurrent user (commonly used to ameliorate the problems associated with machine and user licensing).* In this arrangement the total number of users at any given moment is limited to the number of licenses. This method is flexible and generally less expensive for software purchasers but requires more management. Metering software with lockout systems can be used to simplify administration. Much of the industry uses concurrent licensing.

- *A license for each server (Oracle).* If there is a license for each server, either an unlimited number of users can access the server, or users are licensed in blocks (e.g., blocks of 10). In the latter case, the users can be specific individuals or nodes or can be nonspecific. Server licenses are somewhat similar to concurrent licenses but are more difficult to price and, therefore, less popular with vendors. Oracle introduced (and later abandoned) the concept of Universal Power Units, where the license fee for a server was determined by multiplying the processor speed (in MHz) times the number of processors in the server times the UPU price. They replaced the UPU pricing structure with two structures, one based on the number of users and the other a modified server licensing scheme where the license fee is based on the number of processors in the server, with unlimited users.

Software utilities are available to help keep track of licenses and compliance. Some allow network administrators to disable programs executed from local drives and prevent users from running altered or unauthorized files. Some applications supply their own license management capabilities.

The Open-Source License Model

The introduction of the Linux operating system brought widespread attention to the open-source model used in its licensing. The Free Software Foundation licenses Linux (and other software) under its general public licenses, which implement the so-called *copyleft* concept. Licensees can use, copy, distribute, and make derivative works of the licensed software, and have access to the source code. They can charge their customers for copies of the software or derivative works, but they must give their licensees the same rights that they received in their general public license (i.e., the rights to use, copy, distribute, and prepare derivative works of the software, and access to their source code). Further, any patents that are granted to licensees covering the software must be made available for the free use of all or not licensed. No warranties are given for the software.

The effect of these terms is to promote widespread use and development of the software and allow developers to profit from their efforts, but to prevent any developer from controlling the software's use or development by establishing a proprietary position. Opponents of open-source licensing (e.g., software companies whose business models are based on proprietary technology such as Microsoft) point out that the open-source model encourages incompatibility among different versions of the software, and that the limited potential economic benefit from its exploitation results in vendors being unable to devote the resources necessary to fully develop the software or provide adequate support to end-users.

Other examples of open-source licensing include the Berkeley System Distribution license (used, for example, with sendmail and Apache), and the Mozilla Public License, used by Netscape to license Communicator 5. Both licenses are somewhat less restrictive than the GNU license, allowing licensees to develop proprietary derivative works.

Future Trends

The Internet is becoming increasingly important in the licensing of applications software. This trend has manifested itself in several ways. First, software is increasingly being distributed over the Internet. The prospective purchaser finds the appropriate software on a Web site, pays using an online transaction service, and then downloads and installs the software on his or her computer. Updates and patches to fix bugs in the software are also distributed via the Internet. This reduces distribution costs and ensures that the latest version of the software is made available to customers. Tier-one customer support and customer registration are also often handled via the Internet.

So-called *application service providers* rent software on a monthly or usage basis, and host the application on a server that is connected via the Internet to end-user clients. These ASPs are often the same companies that develop the software. Advantages to the licensee include less installation and support effort required (the server software is maintained by the ASP), easier upgrades, and lower initial acquisition cost. The ASP gains a recurring revenue stream (rather than the usual one-time payment), an easier way to upgrade the software, and a closer relationship with its licensees.

DEALING WITH INFRINGERS

When an IP owner suspects infringement, a number of options are available, ranging from doing nothing to mounting an all-out campaign to stop the infringement. Each action (or inaction) has both business and legal consequences that should be considered carefully and, as always, legal issues should be discussed with an attorney before any action is taken.

Determining Infringement

The first step in developing a strategy to deal with infringement is to determine as precisely as possible the nature of the infringement. The ultimate determination of infringement is made in court by a judge or jury. Nevertheless, anyone contemplating pursuing an infringement action should perform a thorough analysis of the suspect product. The output of the analysis is a mapping of features of the product to the IP the product is suspected of infringing. Further, the IP owner should conduct extensive research on related IP (both the IP that is suspected of being infringed and other prior art) to plan a suitable strategy and determine how to address the targeted infringer's possible defenses.

Patents, copyrights, and trademarks are infringed in different ways. The following sections discuss some ways to determine infringement.

Patents

A product infringes a claim of a patent if each element of the claim can be found in the product. In addition to this so-called *literal* infringement, infringement can also be found under the *Doctrine of Equivalents*. The doctrine states that, if the product performs the same function in the same way and achieves the same result as described in the patent claim, it infringes the claim. Proving infringement under the Doctrine of Equivalents is usually more difficult than proving literal infringement.

In Exhibit 7.3, Case 1 is classic direct infringement, where the patent claim contains elements A and B and the suspected infringer, XYZ, makes a product that includes A and B. Case 2 is where XYZ may have improved on A + B (by adding a third element C), but still infringes because all elements of the claim (A + B) appear in the product. Note that infringement exists even if A + B + C is patentable. In Case 3, there is no infringement because only two of the elements of the claim (A + B) appear in the product, while the claim has three elements (A + B + C). In Case 4, there likely would be no direct infringement, so infringement would be decided under the Doctrine of Equivalents (elements C v. C'). In Case 5, each company goes its own way, and even if both sets of elements are patented, neither would infringe on the other.

Copyrights

Copyrights are violated when someone uses copies, distributes, or prepares derivative works without permission. The development of equivalent works, that is, products that perform the same function, is allowed, as is reverse engineering, where copyrighted products are technically analyzed to determine their functionality. Once the functionality has been determined, a new product can be legally developed (often in a so-called clean-room environment, to avoid later claims of infringement).

Therefore, to prevail in a claim of copyright infringement, you must show that

Exhibit 7.3   Patent Claim Chart

CASE	PATENT CLAIMS	XYZ MAKES	INFRINGEMENT?
1	A + B	A + B	YES
2	A + B	A + B + C	YES
3	A + B + C	A + B	NO
4	A + B + C	A + B + C'	?
5	A + B + C + D	A + B + C + E	NO

your copyrighted work was used (usually this means copied) in the offending product. Software developers often intentionally add useless code, special comments, or grammatical errors in their code to be able to show that it has been copied.

Trademarks

If the trademark is a word, and if it has been registered for a certain class of products, it is generally easy to show that anyone who uses the same word for the same type of product is infringing. The alleged infringing user may try to show that use of the word on its products will not confuse users, and therefore should be allowed, or may present some other defense. Often, disputes are resolved by the alleged infringer agreeing to limit its use of the trademark to certain markets that are not of concern to the original trademark owner.

If the trademark is a symbol or a stylized word, proving infringement can be more difficult. The trademark owner must show that use of the two marks will confuse the public as to the origin of the marked goods. This can be expensive and time-consuming. Again, disputes are often resolved by agreement between the parties rather than by litigation.

Several possible strategies related to dealing with IP infringement are outlined in the following sections.

Do Nothing

A technology owner may choose to ignore infringement of its patents or copyrighted works, either because of a lack of resources needed to pursue an infringement action or for strategic reasons. Knowingly allowing someone to infringe a patent for a substantial period of time without taking any action, however, can result in the infringer gaining rights to use the patent. The technology owner should notify the suspected infringer and eventually take further action to avoid inadvertent loss of patent rights.

On the other hand, waiting to confront a suspected infringer can have benefits for the technology owner. For example, if infringement is claimed early in the product development stage, the infringer may decide to reengineer the product to avoid using the patent. If, however, a product is already being mass produced and selling well when infringement is claimed, there may be more incentive to negotiate a settlement (of course, there may also be more incentive to pursue legal action to fight the claim).

Unauthorized use of trademarks should always be stopped, either by forcing the user to stop using the mark or by granting a trademark license. If trademark infringement is allowed to continue, protection can be lost.

Escalating Actions

An effective way to address suspected infringement while initially conserving resources involves a phased, escalating campaign whose goal is to license the infringer. Licensing infringers has some benefits, including legalizing the infringer's use of the involved intellectual property and generating revenues.

However, the decision to license infringers should be made only after fully understanding the effect on the licensor's own business activities. The five basic elements of such a campaign are listed below and in Exhibit 7.4, which outlines a strategy for licensing a technology when some targeted licensees may be infringing while others are not.

1. An initial package of information describing the technology or product, as described in Chapter 6, is prepared and mailed to the suspected infringer.
2. When following-up, the prospective licensor tries to determine if the suspect is an infringer. If infringement is definitely ruled out and the suspect expresses no interest in the technology or product offered for license, no further action is taken.
3. If infringement is suspected, product information, samples, and other data are obtained and analyzed to verify infringement. Again, if infringement is ruled out the effort is abandoned.

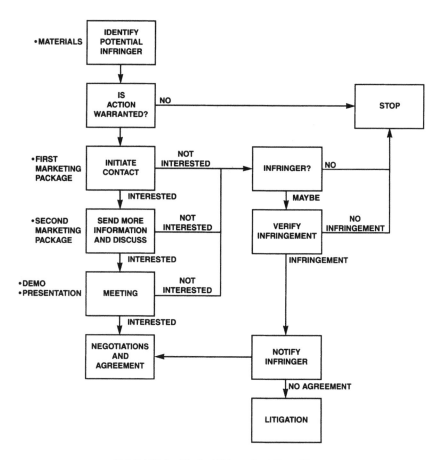

Exhibit 7.4   Typical Licensing Flow Chart

Decision-Tree Analysis

A decision-tree analysis can be used to predict the results and ramifications of various licensing scenarios. Briefly, the possible outcomes of each uncertain event are assigned a probability of occurrence, with the sum of all probabilities for a given event equal to one.

Values are then assigned to each possible outcome. With regard to the escalating actions described previously, from the licensor's point of view doing nothing costs the least but has no reward, whereas taking legal action will incur significant expense but, if successful, may result in a large reward. The prospective licensee faced with the possibility of an infringement action would examine the probability of each outcome and its related cost.

By arranging each event serially, starting with the initial action and ending with each possible outcome, the probability of each outcome and its related reward or cost can be calculated. This information can then be used to decide on an appropriate course of action.

A simple decision-tree-analysis flow chart is shown in Exhibit 7.5. In the example shown, a company accused of infringement uses decision-tree analysis to determine the probability and cost of several alternatives. In this example the cost of a license is $1,000 and the estimated cost of a damage award resulting from litigation is $2,000 with related legal expenses of $500. The probability of the patent being valid is estimated as 80%, and the probability of the product being found to infringe the patent is estimated at 60%.

Four outcomes are possible:

1. The infringer takes a license, at a cost of $1,000.
2. The patent is declared invalid in litigation (20% probable), at a cost of $500.
3. The patent is found to be valid, but the product is found not to infringe (32% probable), at a cost of $500.
4. The patent is found to be valid and the product to infringe (48% probable), at a cost of $2,500.

Based on this analysis, the company accused of infringement can decide to take a license for $1,000 or to risk litigation, in which case there is a 52% probability that the cost will be $500 and a 48% probability that the cost will be $2,500.

Decision-tree analysis is useful in other aspects of technology licensing as well, including technology valuation (see Chapter 4). In practice, decision trees are often much larger than in the example shown. Implementations using computer spreadsheet programs can be used to easily and quickly change various parameters and note the effect on outcomes. Estimating costs and probabilities accurately is the biggest challenge in decision-tree analyses, as in all other forecasting techniques.

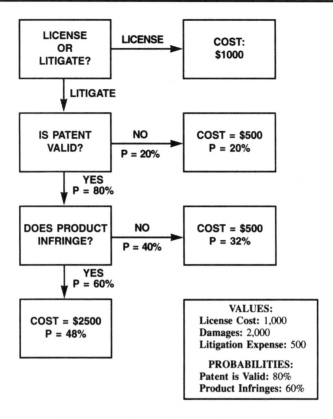

Exhibit 7.5. Sample Decision-Tree Analysis

4. A letter is written and sent to the target infringer detailing the evidence of infringement, and once again a license is offered. If interest is expressed in obtaining a license, a meeting is arranged, details are agreed upon, and a license is issued.
5. If the infringer is still resistant, the licensor must decide what legal action to pursue.

High-Level Response

A high-level response to infringement begins with a reassessment of the value and scope of the intellectual property suspected of being infringed, a complete technical evaluation of the suspected product that infringes, and a reexamination of prior art and other possible defenses the infringer might raise. A report is then prepared showing exactly which parts of the product infringe which patent claims, and a meeting is arranged with the infringer to present and explain the report. The object is to present a court-ready case to the infringer that is so compelling that it would be illogical to refuse to license the technology. Substantial up-front and follow-up resources are needed for both legal and technical services, and the prospective licensor must be prepared to litigate if the targeted infringer refuses to cooperate.

A high-level response is very effective and often results in the infringer agreeing to a license. In many cases, licenses are negotiated with paid-up royalties. Technical consultants can be retained to reverse-engineer suspected products and prepare detailed infringement reports. More details of this type of approach can be found in the SGS-Thomson case study in Appendix A3.2.

This technique can also be effectively utilized by patent holders to discourage litigation or encourage prospective licensees to enter into an agreement. By conducting a detailed analysis of prior art and the scope of the claims, a patent owner can persuasively argue the validity of its patent without resorting to expensive and time-consuming litigation.

Defensive Licensing

When faced with infringement, a technology owner's best option may be to license, even if the infringer is unwilling to pay reasonable royalties. Other advantages that can make such licensing attractive include the following:

- By signing a license agreement, the infringer will agree to use and protect the licensed intellectual property (including, importantly, trademarks) properly, which can be beneficial to the licensor, particularly in foreign countries, where enforcement of IP laws can be difficult and expensive.
- The costs of litigation can be largely avoided.
- The agreement can be publicized and used to induce other companies to become licensed.
- In lieu of royalties, other concessions can be obtained, including access to the licensee's technologies (via cross-licensing).

Selling Infringed Patents

If a patent owner is willing to sell a patent that is infringed, substantial value can sometimes be realized without the time, cost, and uncertainty of licensing the infringer. This approach does not work well in all industries, but does often work in the computer, electronics, and telecommunications industries because of the aggressive activities of TI, Lucent, IBM, Xerox, and others.

The patent owner must first identify patents that are infringed by third parties and establish a convincing case for infringement, as in the high-level response described earlier. The patent will ideally be infringed by one of the aggressors in the market of interest (or one of the growing ranks of would-be aggressors, as those who have been sued and lost seek to exploit the expensive lessons they have learned). Sometimes the target company may also be an infringer, and, if they won't buy the patent, it could be easier to persuade them to license the patent.

Patent Infringement Abatement Insurance

In recent years, at least two insurance companies have begun offering policies to cover the costs of patent infringement lawsuits. Because the average cost of an infringement action is now around $1.5 million, purchasing an infringement abatement policy allows smaller patent holders to enforce their rights and improves their leverage in negotiations with larger targeted licensees.

The basic terms of a typical policy include the following:

- The policy provides $3 million in coverage (the insurer will pay up to $3 million for litigation costs associated with infringement of covered patents).
- The insured must pay 20% of all litigation costs out-of-pocket.
- Prior infringement is not covered.
- If litigation is instituted and is successful, the insurer gets back its costs plus a premium (typically 25%).
- Premiums paid by the insured are on the order of $50,000 per year, depending on the amount of coverage, the number of patents covered, and the payback premium.

In addition, most policies include the following:

- The insurer must approve the legal counsel chosen to handle the litigation.
- An independent expert must determine and provide an opinion letter stating that there is infringement before the insurer will approve instituting any action.
- The insured has the authority to settle the suit. However, if the insured settles the suit for something other than a cash payment (e.g., an injunction preventing the infringer from selling products covered by the patent), the insurer can require that it be paid an amount equal to what it would have been paid under a cash settlement.

You can also sell a piece (legally known as an *undivided interest*) of a patent for assertion in litigation and licensing against a single company. The target purchaser may feel that the price for the entire interest is too high, or they may have cross-license agreements with some of their major competitors, in which case, by buying the patent, their cross-licensed competitors would gain rights to the patent (perhaps without any further payment). The patent owner gets some income from selling an undivided interest in the patent, and would retain all of its rights against other infringers.

ADVANCED LICENSING TECHNIQUES— HYBRID VERSUS SEPARATE LICENSES

Once a licensing program has been established and in place for some time, new issues may arise that were not apparent at the time of inception. Markets can change substantially over a period of years, which can affect the value of intellectual property licensed in those markets. New competitive technologies can appear. The value of licensed trademarks and their share of the total value of the licensed intellectual property can change dramatically.

Strategies that take into account known changes, such as the expiration of licensed patents, can and should be developed and implemented as part of the initial licensing strategy discussed in Chapter 5. Other less predictable changes, such as those in the licensed markets, can be difficult or impossible to anticipate, and may require modifications to an existing licensing strategy.

As explained previously, hybrid agreements are often used to license several types of intellectual property together. However, in some situations hybrid agreements may no longer be the preferred way of doing business for technology licensors. Over long periods of time the relative values of the various IP components can change dramatically. In particular, licensed patents can become obsolete or expire and become worthless, whereas licensed trademarks can greatly increase in value. Using a hybrid agreement structure can make it difficult or impossible to respond to changes in relative value, resulting in agreement terms that no longer fairly represent the value of the license. To avoid these problems, it may be advantageous to use separate agreements covering each licensed IP component. This section discusses the pros and cons of each approach in light of today's fast paced technology development.

Hybrid Agreements

In many markets it has become quite common to license a variety of intellectual property, such as patent rights, trademark rights, software rights, know-how, and trade secrets, in a single, comprehensive agreement. These hybrid agreements are generally used for long-term partnerships, in which access to a technology or system involves extensive interaction between the licensee and the licensor. Frequently such agreements, when used over longer periods of time, become established in the industry as standard agreements. The license agreement used by Dolby Laboratories to license their noise reduction technologies is a good example of an industry-standard hybrid agreement.

The elements of a hybrid agreement are shown in Exhibit 7.6. In this case, patents, trademarks, know-how, and software (usually in the form of copyrighted works) are licensed together using a single agreement. A single royalty may be

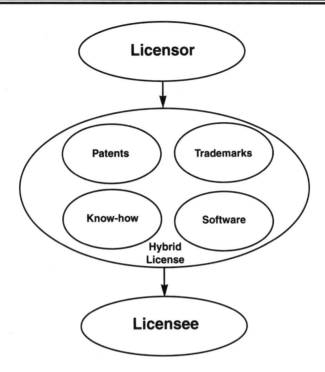

Exhibit 7.6.   Hybrid License Agreements

charged for all the components, although it can be beneficial to stipulate separate royalties for the licensed patents and other licensed intellectual property. If a single royalty is charged for the patents, trademarks, copyrighted works, and know-how, and if at some future time the patents are invalidated, the entire agreement could be invalidated as well. If royalties for the patents are specified separately, only the patent license may be invalidated. The hybrid agreement may end when the last-to-expire patent expires, or the part of the agreement covering trademarks, know-how, and software may continue after patent expiration.

When a license granting rights to just patents and know-how is required, the license can be drafted to grant rights only to the know-how, but it can also provide immunity from suit under any related patents. This can allow the license to continue as long as the licensee uses the technology, rather than only for the life of the patents.

Hybrid agreements offer advantages to both parties. For the licensee, a hybrid agreement provides access to the entire technology, or system, with a single, comprehensive document. If the agreement is to be reviewed by counsel (always a good practice), all aspects of the arrangement can be examined together, and the time and expense associated with the review is minimized. If the agreement is an industry standard (i.e., it is known to have been signed by a large number of the target licensee group in substantially unaltered form), even further reduction of review time and expense is possible. This is of particular advantage to smaller licensees, who may not yet have the resources for comprehensive legal advice.

For the licensor, the advantages are similar. Well-known and established hybrid agreements take less legal review time. Fewer demands for changes occur, and it becomes easier and less costly over time to activate new licensees for a given system or technology. If identical standard royalty rates are used in all agreements issued for a given technology (i.e., by means of a most favored nation clause), the target licensee audience develops a certain familiarity and feeling of security with the license, which also leads to better long-term relationships between licensees and licensors.

Another advantage from the licensor's perspective is that the life of the license (if properly drafted) can exceed the life of the patent rights, as long as the licensee wants to continue to use the licensed trademarks, copyrighted works, and/or know-how after patent expiration. In addition, the licensor can include its trademarks in the agreement even if the licensee does not necessarily want to use them. There are several important advantages to doing this. First, the licensee can be discouraged from developing and using a competitive trademark. Second, the inclusion of the trademarks can be used to help justify the royalties charged. Finally, if the trademarks are used and acquire value over the life of the license, the licensor's royalty income stream can continue indefinitely based on the use of the trademarks.

There are also a few disadvantages to the hybrid licensing approach. If the licensee's application does not require all the intellectual property included in the hybrid agreement, it may not justify payment of the full standard royalty. For example, if the agreement includes patent and know-how rights, the licensee may wish to be licensed under the patent rights only and then to develop the required know-how in-house.

With many modern technologies, software, which is often protected as a copyrighted work, frequently becomes an important ingredient in an overall system. The licensee, however, may wish to develop its own software and not be saddled with any restrictive clauses covering software, which may be part of such hybrid agreements. For example, agreement provisions related to copyrighted works often cover derivative works (see Chapter 2), and it may be difficult to determine exactly what is or is not a derivative work if the licensee develops its own software but has had access to the licensor's source code as part of the technology transfer.

The disadvantages of hybrid agreements can be greater, however, from the licensor's point of view. As already mentioned, in hybrid agreements that are intended to extend beyond the life of the patent rights, the portion of the royalties attributable to the patents should be separated from the portion for all other licensed intellectual property. This can result in a decrease in total royalties when the patents expire, which will in turn reduce the long-term value of the agreement to the licensor. In the early years of the agreement, the underlying patents may well be the most important asset being licensed, and a royalty reduction, once that asset no longer exists, would seem reasonable. Over time, however, other components of the license may increase in value and even exceed the value of the whole package of intellectual property originally licensed. Trademarks, for example, can acquire substantial value of their own if associated with popular technologies. In fact, the value of a trademark near the end of a technology's life can exceed that of the underlying technology itself. In this case an increase in royalties may be justifiable, while under the terms of the hybrid agreement an increase may be impossible. The rates may, in fact, decrease because of expiration of the licensed patents or because of increases in quantity discounts due to expansion of the market.

The sample hybrid agreement in Appendix C includes several provisions that illustrate this disadvantage. First, as drafted in Article IV (Example 1), the royalty rate decreases as the number of licensed products sold in a quarter increases (4.02). Therefore, as the market increases (and the trademark attains more value), the per-unit royalty rate will decrease rather than increase. However, the fact that the quantity discount resets every quarter tends to mitigate this effect. Second, in Section 4.06 royalty rates are lowered by 50% for products made and sold in countries with no patent protection. This does not take into account the value of the trademarks in non-patent countries, which may in fact be higher than in patent countries. The agreement also expires when the last patent expires (however, once the agreement expires, the licensee can no longer use the trademarks). These provisions, drafted early in the technology's life to reflect the initial situation and to make the agreement palatable to prospective licensees, make it impossible to adjust royalties to reflect changes in the value of the underlying intellectual property, especially the trademarks.

Separate Agreements

To avoid the problems associated with hybrid agreements, separate agreements can be prepared for each major intellectual property component of a system license. The terms of each agreement, including royalties, term, and the rights granted, can be optimized for the particular IP component addressed in the agreement. A patent license can be issued that covers only the patent rights that are being licensed. Such an agreement would be valid for the life of the patents and could end, for example, on the expiry date of the last-to-expire patent. Royalties for the use of the patents could be determined by valuing the patents as discussed in Chapter 4.

At the same time, a trademark license can be issued for the identical licensed goods, including all the required quality control provisions. Methods for adjusting royalties over time can be defined so that any changes in the value of the trademark can be reflected in the royalty rates. For example, the rates could be adjusted for increases in the cost of living to reflect increased value over time, or the rates could be adjusted for increases in the total number of products sold by all licensees to reflect the exposure value of the trademark. In addition, more relative criteria could be used such as the size of the potential target audience (e.g., all consumers or just members of a certain class of consumers).

Together with the patent and trademark licenses, a separate software license can grant rights to copyrighted works. Know-how and/or trade secrets can be included in the software license as well. Again, royalties charged will reflect the value of the licensed property. Computer software can be licensed in a variety of forms. For example, specific, executable object (machine) code can go along with a license for a single, precisely defined product. Alternatively, high-level source code with the right to generate derivative works can be licensed, in which case royalties can then be based on either the number of derivative works made and distributed, or a lump sum can be paid for the rights granted.

Using separate agreements, the licensee can choose the desired components of the IP package and adjust the package over time as needed. For example, a licensee may wish to develop software in-house and, therefore, forego the software license, or the licensee may not wish to use the licensor's trademark if the application is one where using the licensed trademark would gain little market advantage.

Exhibit 7.7 illustrates the concept of separate agreements. In this case, the licensor's technology consists of know-how, patents, trademarks, and software. Separate licenses are offered for each component, each bearing a royalty based on the individual value of its contribution to the overall package. The licensee then chooses only those components needed. All licensees would presumably be required to take the patent license, but the other three components may or may not be needed.

The licensor can optimize each agreement for the specific IP component being licensed and can adjust the valuation of each component independently over time. For example, there might be a need to frequently renegotiate a software agreement when new software is developed by the licensor that can be used to advantage by the licensee. Also, as mentioned earlier, the market value of a licensed trademark may increase dramatically over time. Having separate, limited life agreements allows a regular renegotiation of terms. By renegotiating each agreement individually as needed, both parties also benefit from not being burdened with examining all aspects of the licensing relationship each time any component needs to be adjusted.

Using separate licenses also allows the licensor to provide assurances more easily to its licensees that the licensed intellectual property is free from third-party claims. Many licensees require such assurance to limit their risks in using the licensed technology. Although indemnification can often be provided regarding some components of the IP package such as trademarks, it can be very difficult to determine with certainty that the granted patent rights do not infringe on other patents or patent applications, or to know that undiscovered prior art invalidating the patent rights will not come to light, particularly in advanced technical fields.

The main disadvantage of using separate license agreements is the increased administrative effort required on the part of both the licensee and licensor. Both parties need to keep track of a greater number of agreements. Independent royalty arrangements may require different data for the compilation of royalty reports and the calculation of royalties due. Potentially different expiration dates of the various agreements require greater attention to determine the schedule for renegotiation.

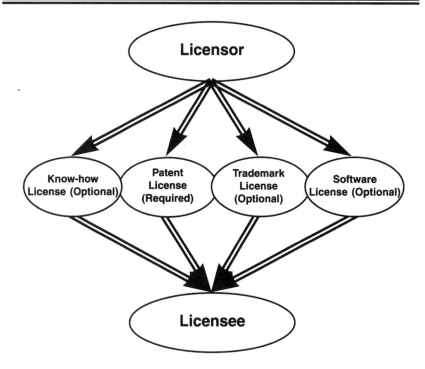

Exhibit 7.7.   Separate License Agreements

For the licensor, separate royalty rates must be developed for each agreement, requiring that valuations be performed for each component of intellectual property licensed. During the introductory phase of a new technology, when both the technology and the licensor are relatively unknown, this may be a difficult if not impossible task, especially when trademarks are being licensed. When a new technology is introduced by an unknown licensor, any associated trademarks may have almost no market value. Even if escalator clauses are built into the agreement, the royalties generated by the trademarks may be far less than adequate if the initial valuation is near zero. Furthermore, the advantages associated with renegotiation of the royalty terms of the trademark license can be offset by the risk of the licensee opting to drop other components of the technology, thus providing lower overall royalty income to the licensor.

Separate Agreement Models
The Patent License. Exhibit 7.8 shows how separate agreements might be structured in a practical way. As explained earlier, all licensees obtain a patent license. Royalties for the patent license are based on a valuation of the patents when used in the licensed products and markets. The license expires when the patents expire. Since the value of a patent often decreases with age, the royalty structure of the patent license may provide for decreasing royalties in the later years of the agreement. However, adding new patents to the license (to cover

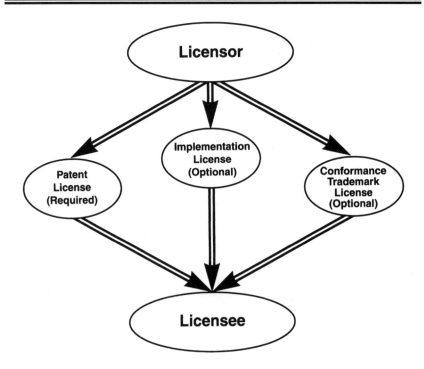

Exhibit 7.8.   Three Components of Modern Technology Licenses

improvements, for example) can increase the value of the patent license and thus justify raising royalty rates.

The Implementation License. The implementation license covers all proprietary elements related to using the technology to build products, including know-how, show-how, and software. The implementation license is tailored to each licensee's needs. Some licensees, preferring to develop all know-how, show-how, and software in-house, may not want the license at all; others who don't have the resources to develop the know-how or software may want to license some or all of the elements. Royalties for the implementation license reflect the scope of the license negotiated and the products and markets licensed, and they may be paid in a lump sum when the agreement is negotiated or in phased payments based on the achievement of agreed milestones. All upgrades, new developments, and other improvements that are offered later by the licensor to its licensees (and not patented) are incorporated in the implementation license, with royalties adjusted accordingly.

The Conformance Trademark License. The conformance trademark license allows the licensee to use the licensor's trademarks on products covered by the patent and implementation licenses. Licensed product quality control provisions are included in the trademark license (as opposed to the patent or implementation licenses), and royalties can be adjusted at agreed-upon intervals, using the various means discussed earlier, to reflect the trademarks' changing value.

CONCLUSION

A hybrid approach may well be preferred by the licensor in the early stages of its technology licensing program, especially until its trademarks have been established. In later stages, when the technology base has expanded and the licensed trademarks have accrued substantial independent value, separate agreements may be preferable. If a hybrid approach is chosen, terms should be chosen, if possible, that will not preclude the use of separate agreements at a later time if desired.

The best approach for the licensee will depend on its size and position in the market. A large, mature licensee may prefer to be offered a menu from which to choose the IP components it wishes to license. The small licensee starting out in the business or a larger licensee with little experience may prefer the comprehensive hybrid approach. Any approach considered should be carefully examined to ensure a good fit with both the licensor's and the licensee's overall business needs.

8

Post-Agreement Activities

Signing a license agreement is just the beginning of what will hopefully be a long and productive relationship between the licensor and licensee. The success of the relationship will depend at least partly on how well the parties execute their responsibilities under the agreement. This chapter will discuss ongoing responsibilities of both the licensor and licensee that are typical in licensing business partnerships.

Agreement-related activities generally fall into two categories: Administrative, which includes the preparation, delivery, and accounting of royalty payments and IP protection and maintenance; and technical, which includes technology transfer, development, and trademark quality control.

Administrative and technical liaison personnel for both licensor and licensee should be chosen and assigned responsibility for communications and all obligations mentioned in the agreement.

Close attention must be paid to post-agreement activities by both the licensor and licensee to ensure a successful licensing partnership. The rewards will be an effective program and good relations that can be subsequently leveraged to promote future developments and expand licensing activities.

The scope of post-agreement activities depends greatly on the license terms. If a paid-up patent license is effected, post-agreement activities will be minimal. For example, if two parties negotiate a license to settle patent infringement litigation calling for a single payment on signing the agreement, with no technology transfer or further administrative requirements for either the licensor or the licensee, both parties can then go on about their business with no further interaction.

On the other hand, a long-term agreement that includes trademark licensing will require considerable post-agreement activity by both the licensor and the licensee. Dolby Laboratories' licensing model, discussed in Appendix A1.1, is a good example of a long-term strategy involving extensive post-agreement activity on the part of both the licensor and the licensees.

BY LICENSOR

Deliverables

The first post-agreement responsibility of the licensor is often to supply technical information, prototype units, tooling, and other deliverables specified in the agreement to the licensee. These technical deliverables can range from nothing (in the case of a paid-up license to an infringed patent) to entire manufacturing facilities.

When a standardized technology is licensed, the technical information is often non-confidential and can be provided prior to the signing of the agreement. A standard licensing manual, containing all information necessary to properly design, manufacture, and (if trademarks are used) mark licensed products, can be prepared by the licensor and distributed as needed. Such a manual can include the following:

- Background information on the licensor
- Theoretical description of the technology being licensed
- Applications information, including block diagrams, sample schematic diagrams, and other engineering details needed to properly design licensed products
- Performance specifications
- Test procedures for confirming that licensed products meet the required specifications and for manufacturing licensed products
- Instructions on how to properly use licensed trademarks and how to mark licensed products
- Descriptions and applications information—if the technology is realized using one or more commercially available building blocks (e.g., integrated circuits)

If the technical deliverables include confidential information, the allowed use and protection of the information should be clearly defined in the license agreement. Confidential information is often partially disclosed prior to the signing of the agreement under an NDA to allow the prospective licensee to evaluate the technology and determine its value. The use of NDAs in technology marketing is discussed further in Chapter 6.

Technology transfer also often includes training, where licensor's technical personnel assist the licensee in rapidly and effectively utilizing the licensed technology. All personnel involved in such training from both the licensor and licensee should not only have a clear understanding of what information is to be transferred but also what information should not be disclosed.

If copyrighted works are licensed (e.g., computer software), the licensed machine and/or source code is usually supplied (on disks, tape, CD-ROM, or via the Internet) when the agreement is signed, and, if escrow is used (as discussed in Chapter 7), the software is placed in the escrow account.

Camera-ready artwork for licensed trademarks should be supplied at the time of signing, along with instructions for its use (artwork can be included in the licensing manual already mentioned). Finally, complete instructions and all necessary forms required for reporting and paying royalties should be supplied to licensee's administrative personnel.

Agreement Maintenance

The scope of maintenance required will depend on the agreement terms. However, many agreements will require some or all of the activities outlined below:

- *Royalties.* The licensor must confirm that all required statements and payments have been made. This is not a trivial undertaking when quarterly statements and payments are required from dozens of licensees. In addition, the licensor may audit its licensees periodically, as discussed later in this chapter.
- *Technology development.* In some cases the licensor agrees to develop the licensed technology further for the licensee (e.g., to design a custom integrated circuit incorporating the technology).
- *Improvements.* Some agreements specify that any improvements made in a defined period of time will be included in the agreement. If this is so, the licensor must notify the licensee of any improvements and transfer the technology.
- *Intellectual property.* Apart from the normal IP maintenance activities outlined below, many agreements require the licensor to defend the licensee against infringement suits brought by third parties.
- *Marketing.* Some agreements, especially those including trademarks, specify joint marketing activities.

IP Maintenance

The means used to initially protect intellectual property, be it trademark registrations, patent filings, or any of the other techniques discussed in Chapter 2, may not ensure continued protection over the life of the intellectual property. Rather, certain intellectual property must be maintained by following legally prescribed steps throughout its life, and a licensor must be aware of the requirements and provide the resources necessary to ensure continued protection.

IP maintenance is a complex subject requiring the advice and assistance of an experienced attorney. However, a few specific IP maintenance concerns are listed below:

- *Patents.* Maintenance fees are due on U.S. and international patents at regular intervals during their life. These fees are in addition to the application and prosecution costs, and in addition to any associated attorney's fees.
- *Trademarks.* Trademarks must be renewed periodically in all countries in which they are registered. Often, proof that the trademark has been used in a particular country is required, along with a fee, before a renewal is granted.
- *Copyrighted works and mask works.* Although registration is not required in the U.S. to obtain protection, important advantages are gained by registering works. Renewals of registrations are generally not required.

Trademark Quality Control

When trademarks are licensed, it is required that some form of quality control be exercised over the licensed products (as discussed in Chapter 2). Generally, the quality control activities fall into two areas: proper trademark usage and conformance to technical specifications.

Checking for proper trademark usage includes making sure that the form, size, and placement of the trademark(s) on the licensed products is correct, and confirming that all required notices are posted on the licensed product and in collateral materials.

Generally, trademark usage guidelines are issued by the licensor and provided to all licensees, and licensed products, product manuals, marketing materials, and any other items (e.g., product packing materials) are submitted to the licensor to check for proper usage. In addition to proper trademark usage, instructions given for using the product and explanations of the licensed technology in the licensee's materials should be checked to ensure that the licensed technology and its use are explained correctly.

The second and often much more extensive component of trademark quality control is checking licensed products to ensure that they conform to required technical specifications. Although the amount and scope of product testing varies among licensors, it is safe to say that more extensive testing provides more extensive trademark protection. A conservative quality control testing program might include the following:

- Submission by licensee and testing of samples of all licensed products manufactured. In addition to confirming that the licensed technology is functioning correctly, the overall operation of the product should be checked to ensure that other aspects of its operation do not negatively affect the operation of the licensed technology. Complete engineering reports containing measured data, details of any substandard performance found, and corrective action required should be provided to the licensee, and follow-up action should to be taken to ensure that all problems have been resolved.
- Review of all new product designs to check for potential problems that might affect performance.
- Visits to the licensee's production facilities to check production-line test procedures, quality control procedures, and to confirm that products are being made to specifications.

The operations listed above can involve considerable time, effort, and expense, but trademark licensors who choose to ignore their quality control responsibilities do so at the risk of losing their trademarks.

BY LICENSEE

In addition to the design, manufacture, and marketing of licensed products, the licensee often has responsibilities and obligations with respect to the agreement, including the items outlined below.

Payments

A primary responsibility of the licensee, one of great interest to the licensor, is the payment of royalties. In many cases an initial payment will be due, either when the agreement is signed or in installments over a period of time. In addition, running royalties often must be paid (and statements provided) over the life of the agreement.

There can be a significant accounting burden associated with the calculation of royalties due, especially when the licensed technology is used in a wide variety of products, which can be manufactured in different locations and sold in different markets. A central accounting operation must gather data from all relevant sources, make the necessary calculations, and prepare and send the statement and payment to the licensor. If foreign operations are involved, tax payments must often be made and foreign currency obtained.

Other Obligations

Other obligations include the following:

- *Trademark licensees.* If a trademark is licensed, the licensee will incur several obligations, including proper use of the trademarks and conformance with product quality specifications, as mentioned above. Technical liaison must be established with the licensor, and product designs and samples must be submitted for testing and approval. In addition, foreign trademark registrations and renewals often require proof of local use of the trademark, and the licensee is often obligated to provide marketing materials and sales invoices to prove such local use.
- *Product marking.* Products incorporating licensed patents and/or copyrighted works must be properly marked.
- *Grant-back of improvements.* If the licensee has agreed to license back improvements to the licensor, documentation, samples, technical assistance, and legal and administrative resources must be provided to do so.
- *IP enforcement.* Depending on the terms of the agreement, the licensee may be required to only notify the licensor of any infringement found or to defend some or all of the licensed intellectual property.
- *Joint marketing activities.* The agreement (especially if trademarks are licensed) might specify joint marketing activities that require the allocation of marketing resources on the part of the licensee.

ROYALTY AUDITING

Under any license agreements that include running royalties, the royalty payment process usually starts with the licensee performing a calculation to determine how much it owes the licensor, based on the terms of the license agreement and the sales of licensed products during the period covered. Many agreements require the licensee to prepare and submit royalty statements and make payments each calendar quarter.

This process, where the licensee determines how much it owes the licensor, is unusual, and can lead to errors, both inadvertent and intentional. In some cases, the royalty terms in the license agreement may be unclear, in which case the calculation method used may not be the method intended by one or both of the parties. In other cases, there may be a difference of opinion as to whether a product sold by the licensee is covered by the agreement. In any case, if the licensee is calculating the royalties due, the method used will reflect its interpretation of the agreement.

Licensors should pay close attention to royalty statements submitted by licensees. Each entry should be checked to ensure that the product listed is covered by the agreement, and royalty calculations should be reviewed for accuracy. In addition, licensors should check, through publicly available information or market intelligence, other similar products made by its licensees but not listed on royalty statements, to ensure that they do not incorporate licensed technology. Any actual or suspected errors should be immediately brought to the licensee's attention for resolution.

Why Audit?

Most license agreements include language giving the licensor the right to periodically audit its licensees' books to confirm that the royalty amounts paid accurately reflect the terms of the agreement. Typical clauses can be found in the sample license agreement in Appendix C. Experienced auditors find that royalty calculations are frequently wrong or performed in a way that favors the licensee. Based on its experience, Andersen estimates that two out of every five royalty reviews result in the identification of calculation errors, with almost all of the errors resulting in underpayments to the licensor. Errors identified in actual audits have ranged from $5,000 to $4,000,000 with the average being nearly $600,000.

Royalty audits help to identify ambiguities, interpretation differences, and royalty calculation errors. Regular royalty audits provide licensors with a wealth of information about calculation methods, calculation accuracy, effectiveness of license agreement language, and use of licensed technology.

Audits can also build and strengthen communication channels between a licensor and its licensees. They can also disrupt relationships, and therefore should be done sensitively and by an experienced and professional auditor. The auditor should have experience reviewing license agreements and evaluating royalty calculations against license agreements, and should be familiar with all accounting components of the revenue cycle. Familiarity with order entry, manufacturing, shipping, billing, and general ledger accounting is important, as royalties are usually based on products manufactured and sold by the licensee. Knowledge of the licensee's industry and the licensed technology is also required, and should be supplemented by the licensor or others as necessary. It is not uncommon for license agreements to include a clause that allows the royalty auditor to engage a technical expert to assist in determination of products covered by the agreement.

Benefits from the royalty audit process include the following:

- Demonstrating to licensees and the business community that you have a well-run licensing organization that actively checks the accuracy of royalty calculations and protects your company's intellectual assets
- Maximizing royalty revenue by quickly identifying and correcting payment errors
- Obtaining feedback on ways to improve future license agreements by making the language clearer and more specific in an effort to minimize disputes and misinterpretations
- Improving the licensee's reporting process by incorporating suggestions that come out of the auditor's review
- Obtaining a better understanding of the uses of the licensed technology

Audit Timing and Frequency

There are many factors to consider when determining whether or not an audit should be performed. The most significant factors include the impact to the licensor/licensee relationship and the amount of money at stake. Because royalty calculations are frequently wrong to the detriment of the licensor, a licensor may decide to conduct audits of all licensees every few years. If done professionally, this should not impact the licensor/licensee relationship.

In rare circumstances, a royalty audit might be performed upon signing of the license agreement to determine the accuracy and reliability of the systems to be relied upon by the licensee, the level of experience and training of the licensee's personnel assigned to calculate royalties, and the level of controls around the calculation process. More frequently, audits will be performed during the term of the license agreement and after the agreement expires. Litigation regarding royalties or patent infringement may also require royalty audits.

Even if a regular auditing program is not in effect, indicators that the calculation and payments might be incorrect and therefore that an audit is called for include the following:

- Late royalty reports
- Incomplete royalty reports
- Revisions to previously submitted royalty reports
- Lower than expected payments based on licensee overall revenues or industry trends
- Early or unexpected termination of the license agreement
- Obvious omission of products covered by the agreement
- Change in ownership of licensee or turnover in personnel responsible for computing the royalties

Other selection criteria includes the following:

- Size of royalty payments
- Size of the licensee
- Licensee growth rate

- New product introductions
- Age of the license agreement
- Upcoming expiration of audit rights

Licensors wishing to maximize royalty revenues should develop an overall audit plan. If regular, periodic audits are planned, licensees can be stratified into various risk levels (e.g., high, medium, low) and each level assigned an audit frequency (e.g., one to three years).

The Audit Process

The audit process includes the following:

- Identifying products that are covered by the license agreement
- Gaining an understanding of the licensee's sales collection system
- Making sure that all sales subject to the license agreement are included in the royalty calculation
- Verifying that the royalty rate(s) specified by the license agreement is being used
- Verifying that the calculation is mathematically correct

The first step is to determine if all products subject to the license agreement are included in the royalty calculation. This step often requires advance preparation of the auditor by the licensor. The licensor should educate the auditor on the technology being licensed and the licensor's understanding of the licensee's use of the technology. The auditor should also perform research into the technology and the licensee's products.

Next, the auditor should request a listing of all of the licensee's products and make an independent evaluation as to which products are covered by the license agreement and confirm this assessment with the licensee. In some cases, this will require discussions with the marketing and product development departments.

Once all of the products covered by the license agreement have been identified, the next step is to determine if all sales of the covered products have been included in the royalty calculation. This can be done through reconciliations to the general ledger or the audited financial statements and through detailed testing of sales or shipping transactions. From this point, it is usually simple to determine if the correct royalty rate has been used and if the calculation is mathematically correct.

A typical royalty audit performed by an independent CPA firm requires a four-person team. A partner typically spends 8 to 16 hours managing the project, while the other team members spend 40 to 80 hours each. This time is broken up into planning, fieldwork, and wrap-up. Planning and wrap-up each account for approximately a quarter of the total effort and fieldwork typically accounts for the remainder of the time. The whole process generally takes around two months to complete.

The auditor will usually ask for some or all of the following:

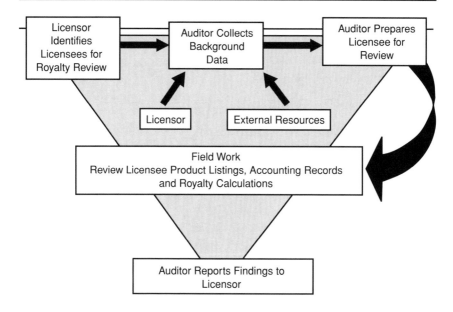

Exhibit 8.1   Royalty Review Methodology

- Master product list by product name/number, highlighting licensed products
- Original royalty reports and supporting calculations
- Historical summary of royalty payments, including any prepayments
- Audited annual and/or interim financial statements for all relevant years
- Reconciliations from the financial statements to the royalty calculations
- Access to shipping logs/documents
- Access to revenue sub-ledgers/sales reports/invoice registers
- Listing of key employees in sales, marketing, manufacturing, engineering, shipping, and royalty reporting processes for interviews
- Listing of evaluation, demonstration, or internal-use units, if applicable
- Names of all sub-licensees or third-party operators

The auditor will prepare a written report describing the work performed and the amount of any over- or underpayments. Due to confidentiality, the content of the auditor's report is typically limited to the cause and amount of any calculation errors. Many license agreements contain language stating that all information provided to the auditor is to be kept confidential by the auditor with the exception of information about the accuracy of the royalty calculation and payments. Additionally, many licensees require auditors to sign a non-disclosure agreement with similar limitations. These limitations protect the licensee's confidential information while allowing for an independent assessment of the accuracy of the royalty calculations and payments on behalf of the licensor.

The auditor may also suggest changing agreement language to reduce ambiguity, to further protect the licensor's intellectual property, or to require additional documentation that will allow the licensor to better judge the accuracy of the royalty statements.

Problems Found in Audits

When miscalculations are identified, the causes often include the following:

- Products that should be included are not. When a licensed product is not or cannot be clearly defined, disputes about what products are covered can arise.
- Subsidiary sales are excluded.
- In agreements where the royalty is based on the net sales price, inappropriate or excessive deductions are made from gross sales amounts. When multiple, sliding, or resetting royalty rates are used, the licensor and licensee can disagree on which rate applies to a given product.
- Excessive exclusions are made of sample, demonstration, training, promotion, or zero dollar sales products.
- Calculation errors are made.

In addition, the wording of the auditing clause of the agreement may be unclear as to what can be reviewed (e.g., "complete and accurate books and records for the purpose of verification of royalties"), which can cause debates or disputes as to the scope of the royalty audit.

Summary of Audit Principles

- Royalty audits can be a powerful tool to maximize revenue and ensure compliance with the terms of a license agreement.
- All licensors should consider using auditing as part of their overall licensing and intellectual property strategies.
- Any audit strategy chosen should reflect the importance of maintaining close and congenial relationships with important licensees.
- Licensors should carefully draft license agreements to minimize the possibility of misunderstanding and confusion in calculating royalties.

LEVERAGING LICENSE AGREEMENTS

Long-term licensing arrangements should be thought of as a partnership. Both the licensor and licensee will gain from the other's success, and should work to promote that success. The licensor should continually strive to improve its technologies and agreement-related services (development and trademark quality control, for example) in order to better serve its licensees. At the same time, the licensee should work to improve its licensed products and marketing efforts to increase sales and provide higher revenues for both itself and the licensor.

The best way to ensure a successful licensing partnership is to maintain regular, open communications between the licensor and licensee. Meetings at the licensee's places of business should be held at least annually, and should be attended by the licensor's technical and marketing liaison personnel (and, if possible, by executive management) and by licensee's designated technical and administrative liaisons, as well as other engineering, marketing, and administrative personnel as needed. A typical agenda for such a meeting would include the following topics:

- If trademarks are licensed, a discussion of all quality control activities that occurred since the last meeting, including sample evaluation results, follow-up activities, and production-line inspections.
- Licensee's plans for new products that will incorporate the licensed technology. New product designs can be reviewed and analyzed at the meeting to help ensure compliance with specifications, and marketing materials can be checked for accuracy and proper trademark usage.
- New technologies can be introduced and demonstrated by the licensor, and proposed terms for their license can be discussed.
- General market trends can be discussed and future needs for technologies and products determined. Licensees are often very knowledgeable about their markets, and information obtained from them can greatly assist a licensor in product planning and market-strategy development.

In addition to regular meetings, information can be provided to licensees by regular mail or e-mail. Mailings can be sent just prior to scheduled meetings so that mailed information can be discussed and questions answered at the meeting.

The personal aspects of licensing should not be overlooked or underestimated. Direct, personal contact between representatives of the licensor and licensee, continuing over a long period of time, will greatly facilitate the promotion of the partnership and the resolution of any problems that may occur. When international licensing is pursued, the use of personnel with experience in the countries of interest and sensitivity to the culture and business practices of those countries is recommended. If a substantial effort is planned in a particular country, local personnel can be retained and a local liaison office established to facilitate communications.

THE LICENSING ORGANIZATION

If significant licensing activity is anticipated, it may be advantageous to set up a formal licensing organization. The responsibilities of the licensing department would include many of the tasks outlined so far in this chapter (agreement maintenance, intellectual property maintenance, and trademark quality control), as well as several other important functions.

Licensing organizations usually evolve over time as the need for licensing-related services grows. Initially there may be no formal organization at all, with licensing functions performed by other departments. The first dedicated licensing person is often hired to coordinate the activities of all the other departments involved. Next, an administrator may be needed to organize the licensing effort and provide continuity while the director is pursuing new business. Then, licensing-related technical responsibilities might be transferred from the engineering department to an independent licensing engineering section. Specialists may at some point assume marketing responsibilities. New technical, marketing, and administrative personnel are added as needed. Over a period of years, the licensing organization might grow into a structure similar to that shown in Exhibit 8.2.

The licensing organization outlined in Exhibit 8.2 would be utilized by a company pursuing international licensing of one or more technologies protected by patents, trademarks, copyright registrations, and as trade secrets. A comprehensive set of technical and administrative services is provided; some of these would not be required for different licensing strategies. For example, if trademarks were not licensed, the product evaluation section would not be needed to conduct trademark quality control. Likewise, foreign liaison offices would not be needed if licensing were restricted to domestic markets.

The licensing operation can be structured as a separate corporation (to obtain certain tax advantages and to shield the main corporation from liability associated with licensing activities), an independent department, or as part of an existing operation (for example, the business development or legal departments). The next six sections describe a licensing organization structured as a department within an existing corporation.

Management

In the organization outlined in Exhibit 8.2, the licensing department is headed by the vice president of licensing, who reports to the president. The responsibilities of the vice president include the following:

- *Long-range strategic planning.* With other management personnel, the vice president of licensing assists in planning the long-term company business strategy and the role of the licensing department in implementing that strategy. This includes primary responsibility for developing both the licensing and IP strategies.
- *Licensing and IP-strategy implementation.* The vice president of licensing is responsible for organizing and staffing the licensing department to effectively implement the licensing and IP strategies.

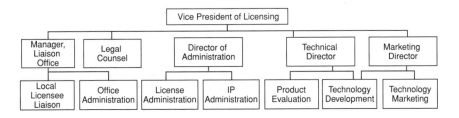

Exhibit 8.2   Typical Licensing Organization

- *Supervising the day-to-day activities of the department.* Working with department managers, the vice president sets short- and long-term goals for each section and develops plans for implementing the goals. If the scope of day-to-day activities is large, a general manager may be needed to assist with this function.
- *Directing the efforts of legal counsel.* This would include ensuring that new technologies are adequately protected, providing for the maintenance of existing intellectual property, directing and assisting in any litigation related to intellectual property or the licensing program, and preparing license agreements to implement existing and planned licensing strategies.
- *Interfacing with other departments.* The vice president of licensing interfaces with other departments at a high level and directs section managers in their interactions. On the administrative side, the licensing department must work closely with the finance department to track and, if necessary, correct royalty statements and payments. This often requires the implementation of computer database systems, which are used by both licensing and finance personnel. Interactions with the engineering department include identifying and developing technologies for license and developing protection strategies for new inventions. Marketing department personnel often assist in conducting market research and developing and implementing technology marketing strategies. In more mature licensing organizations, marketing personnel may be hired directly by the licensing department.
- *Directing the activities of foreign liaison offices.* If international licensing activities are pursued to the extent that the maintenance or establishment of foreign liaison offices is warranted, the vice president of licensing will determine the scope of their responsibilities and direct their overall operation.

Administration

The licensing administration section is headed by a director reporting to the vice president of licensing and is responsible for license and IP administration. In addition to the director, several administrative staff members may be needed to perform the required functions of a typical administration department. License administration includes the following:

- *New licensee support.* Administrative support of the licensing process includes the preparation and mailing of pre-license materials (discussed in Chapter 6) and the maintenance of all related files and databases. When standard agreements are used, agreement copies can be prepared by the administrator for signature. If the agreement is unique, agreements will generally be prepared together by the vice president of licensing and legal counsel.
- *Existing licensee support.* Administrative personnel work together with the finance department to confirm that royalty statements and payments have been submitted when required, and they check them for accuracy. In addition, they assist licensing department management and the engineering section in preparing and sending all communications to licensees. When a large number

of licenses are in place, maintaining the licensee files and databases can require the commitment of substantial administrative resources.

IP administration includes the following:

- *Intellectual property protection.* Administrators assist the vice president and legal counsel in preparing patent filings and trademark and copyright registrations and supply guidelines, training, and documents related to internal IP protection (e.g., employment contracts and NDAs). This might include searching for prior art or registrations, interfacing with inventors, designers, and other employees, preparing related graphical materials, coordinating and scheduling efforts, and creating and maintaining the necessary filing systems.
- *IP maintenance.* For administrative personnel, IP maintenance usually involves liaison between legal counsel (who is responsible for submitting the documents to the appropriate governmental offices) and the licensees (who may be required to submit documentation proving that the patents have been worked or the trademarks used in a particular country). In addition, administrators must ensure that all necessary maintenance is performed as needed.
- *Trademark policing.* As explained in Chapter 2, trademark usage must be policed and any unauthorized or improper use stopped. Administrators check newspapers, magazines, and other publications for proper use of the licensed trademarks and contact licensees and infringers to correct improper usage. In addition, they prepare and provide trademark usage guidelines and artwork to licensees.

Technical Services

The technical services section is responsible for technical quality control of licensed products and for developing and adapting technologies for licensing. It is staffed by engineers and technicians and managed by a technical director, who is also often an engineer or scientist. In an organization in which several different technologies are licensed or widely different markets are exploited, the technical services section may be subdivided by technology, market, or both.

Technical quality control is the process by which licensed products are tested to ensure that they conform to the licensor's performance requirements, and includes the following:

- Developing performance specifications and test procedures that are used in the testing process.
- Receiving, cataloging, and evaluating the performance of samples of licensed products submitted by licensees for testing.
- Preparing an evaluation report for each sample that shows the results and lists any changes that need to be made to meet the specifications.
- Communicating the results to the licensee and ensuring that any needed changes are made.

- Examining relevant production methods and quality control procedures to ensure that the process is adequate to produce conforming licensed products when manufacturing processes affect the performance of licensed products. In many cases, this will require licensing engineers to visit production facilities to examine the manufacturing process.

Technology-development activities vary greatly, but they basically include conducting research to develop new technologies or adapt existing technologies for use in the markets in which they will be licensed, and prototyping, testing, and preparing demonstration units for evaluation by prospective licensees and other marketing functions.

In addition to product evaluation and technology development, licensing engineers often meet with licensees, both at home and at the licensees' facilities, and represent the department at trade shows and other industry events, as discussed in Chapter 6.

Marketing

In the early years of the licensing operation, marketing responsibilities may be handled by the technical staff with assistance from the marketing department. In later years, if the scope of marketing activities expands, and if markets are being exploited that are different from those in which the marketing department is active, it may be advantageous to hire marketing personnel with experience in the markets of interest.

Technology marketing is discussed in detail in Chapter 6. In addition to marketing licensable technologies to prospective licensees and directing public relations activities as described in Chapter 6, marketing personnel are responsible for the following:

- Working together with engineers to identify and develop new technologies for future licensing. Successful new technology introductions are usually market-driven, so marketing personnel should be involved in deciding what new technologies should be developed.
- Maintaining relationships with existing licensees. This may include preparing collateral materials for, and participating in meetings with, existing licensees, introducing new technologies to licensees, supporting licensees' marketing of licensed products, and developing and implementing co-marketing activities with licensees.
- Assisting the vice president and legal counsel in developing strategies to establish and protect IP. In particular, marketing personnel can contribute positively to trademark strategy development.

Legal Counsel

Legal counsel can be provided by in-house attorneys or by retaining one or more independent attorneys. They need expertise in IP law and tax law, and in licensing.

In some cases, separate counsel is retained for obtaining patents, registering trademarks, developing tax strategies, and assisting in licensing. Licensing strategies should be driven by business considerations, and legal counsel should assist in developing IP and other legal strategies that complement the overall business strategy. Some of the contributions made by legal counsel include the following:

- Assisting the vice president of licensing in developing suitable IP and licensing strategies.
- Preparing, filing, and prosecuting patent applications and maintaining issued patents.
- Registering and maintaining trademarks and copyrighted works.
- Advising licensing personnel on matters related to know-how and trade secrets, including preparing employment contracts, guidelines, and NDAs as necessary.
- Drafting and reviewing license agreements and providing counsel on antitrust, tax, and other related concerns.
- Providing liaison with foreign associates used for IP protection overseas.
- Assisting in any litigation related to intellectual property or licensing activities.

Local Liaison Offices

When a large portion of the licensing business is conducted overseas, it is often advantageous to establish a local liaison office in countries with a substantial amount of licensing business. Usually a general manager is responsible for day-to-day management, with administrators and local liaison personnel as needed. The administrators handle local communications, translate and forward licensee communications to the home office, and make travel arrangements for home office personnel visiting the country. Liaison personnel assist in meetings with local licensees (and translate into the local language when necessary), provide technology marketing and research services, and generally assist in communications between the home office and the local licensees and prospective licensees.

It is often possible to utilize a single liaison office for a fairly broad geographical area (e.g., Europe or the Far East), but local sensitivities and cultural differences should be taken into account when considering such an arrangement.

Advantages of Forming a Licensing Organization

The licensing organization described in this section would be appropriate for a mature business in which licensing plays a significant strategic role. As mentioned earlier in this chapter, the sophistication of a licensing organization will grow as the scope of a business' licensing activities grow, and firms in the early stages of implementing a licensing strategy will not need to devote all the resources described immediately. However, there are important advantages to setting up a separate, independent licensing organization.

First and most importantly, a separate organization devoted to licensing demonstrates the licensor's full- and long-term commitment to licensing and to supporting its licensees. By instituting well-defined lines of communication between the organization and its licensees and between the organization and its parent, the responsibilities of both the licensor and the licensees will be carried out more efficiently, and problems will be resolved more quickly. Relying on other departments to provide support to the licensing effort in addition to fulfilling their normal responsibilities can often cause delays and discontinuities in the licensing process that damage the very relationships that are so important to develop and nurture.

Second, an independent organization can have its own profit-and-loss responsibilities within the company, making it easier to measure the performance of the licensing operation. Dedicated licensing personnel who are being judged on the basis of the success of the licensing operation will generally perform better than personnel to whom licensing is of secondary performance.

Third, long-term continuity will be maintained in the licensing operations. Rather than thinking only about one element of the overall strategy, whether it is developing a technology for licensing, licensing the technology to a particular market, or accounting for royalty income, the licensing organization accepts responsibility for all the elements and for merging them into a single coherent strategy. From initial contact to expiration of the agreement, a licensee deals with the same organization, personnel, and procedures.

New developments and changes in the markets can be quickly factored into the overall licensing strategy, and new technologies can be more easily introduced and marketed to licensees. Licensees will interact with the same technical and administrative contacts, and the personal relationships so important to an effective licensing program will be maintained. Such a unified approach is almost guaranteed to be more effective than diverting resources from various other company activities as needed.

For all the reasons just mentioned, it is recommended that any established company seriously considering licensing as a business strategy set up a separate licensing organization. Start-up companies can begin their operations more modestly, but, as licensing activities increase, they, too, should move toward the organizational model discussed in this section.

Appendix A

Case Studies

CONSUMER ELECTRONICS INDUSTRY CASE STUDIES

Licensing Case Study—Dolby Laboratories

Background

Ray Dolby developed A-type noise reduction, intended for use in professional recording, in 1965. Dolby Laboratories continues to manufacture A-type NR, as well as other professional products, to this day. Until recently, none of the professional technologies were licensed, but as new technologies increasingly share both professional and consumer applications (e.g., multi-channel digital audio technology used in both ATSC broadcasting to consumers and in professional film and video mastering), this distinction has lessened.

In 1967, at the request of KLH, Dolby developed a simplified noise reduction (NR) system, intended for consumer applications, which was named B-type NR. Both the technology and two trademarks ("Dolby" and "S/N Stretcher") were licensed for a middle five-figures initial payment and a royalty of 4% of the exfactory price of each tape recorder sold. The license was exclusive to April 1968 and included a technical consultancy agreement.

In 1969 Dolby demonstrated a cassette recorder with external B-type NR at the Audio Engineering Society (AES) convention in New York and to several U.S. and Japanese manufacturers. The first Japanese licensee was Nakamichi, who was already manufacturing for others advanced cassette recorders and the KLH Model 41 R/R recorder with B-type NR.

Evolution of the Current Licensing Model

Around this time, the second-generation license agreement was developed, in which the initial payment was reduced to $5,000 (but separate agreements were required for each type of licensed product) and the royalty rate was 2% for tape recorders, amplifiers, and receivers and 4% for add-on NR units. The agreement included the right to use the "Dolby" and "Double-D" trademarks and consulting services. Four new licensees signed the new agreement in 1970, and that year Dolby opened a Japanese liaison office in Tokyo (still active). European licensee liaison was (and still is) handled through Dolby's European office (where the company was originally established). In light of increased business and a growing customer base in China, a representative office was established in Shanghai in 1998. In 1971, Dolby Laboratories and Signetics announced the development of the first B-type integrated circuit (IC), which further directed attention to the mass market potential of B-type NR. In addition, Dolby announced simplified licensing arrangements and a new, lower-cost royalty structure (a sliding scale starting at 50 cents per circuit for the first 10,000 circuits sold in a calendar quarter, tied to the U.S. consumer cost of living index). A formal quality control program was instituted to maintain compliance with license specifications and ensure quality associated with products bearing the trademark. In 1971, nine companies signed agreements; in 1972, 12 companies signed them, and in 1973, 13 companies. By this time, the 10 largest producers of cassette products had all become licensees.

Symbiosis of Software and Hardware
Dolby Laboratories recognized the importance of software (B-type encoded pre-recorded cassettes) in stimulating sales of hardware and introduced a royalty-free software trademark licensing program to encourage the record companies to produce trademark-bearing B-type encoded cassettes. The program was (and continues to be) very successful. In addition, trademark usage on Dolby Stereo films (*Star Wars, Indiana Jones*, and so on) resulted in widespread public recognition of the trademarks and later served to form the foundation for licensing of home theater decoding products.

Summary of Current Program
1. Consumer technologies are licensed, while certain professional product applications (e.g., cinema processors and multi-channel encoders and decoders) are manufactured by Dolby. This allows Dolby to avoid competing with its licensees. The licensing program is truly international, with well over 100 active licensees in over 40 countries. Current licensing revenues are around $70 to $80 million per year, with around 100 million licensed products made each year.
2. In most cases, patents, trademarks, and know-how are licensed together in a hybrid agreement. All licensees are offered equal terms, which are generally non-negotiable. As the patents age and decrease in value, the trademarks increase in value, justifying maintaining the royalty rate. When the patents expire, the royalty rates are reduced to half (for the trademarks and know-how) on a country-by-country basis. New technologies typically are added to existing agreements by means of side letters.
3. Implementation licenses are issued to companies developing the devices or software implementations needed to integrate the technologies in certain products and product applications. There is a materials fee charged to

cover the deliverables (test kits, test files, reference code, and documentation) and support is provided. Dolby does not charge royalties on the sale of these licensed implementations. It does, however, require quarterly reports of the implementations, quantities, and customers in order to ensure compliance with the terms of the agreement. Implementation licensees are restricted in that they can only provide their products to qualified recipients (typically system licensees of Dolby). An implementation licensing group certifies devices and software prior to their integration in consumer products. Typically, more rigorous tests aimed at the core technology are applied during certification.

4. Active hardware and software quality control programs are maintained. This ensures compliance with trademark licensing law. Equally important, these programs provide a valuable service to the licensees and facilitate open and continuing communication. There are a variety of different licensing groups within Dolby charged with the certification of products in the PC, consumer electronics, test and measurement, and digital television areas. A growing number of engineers, product specialists, and test technicians are charged with handling quality control and technical liaison with licensees. Business meetings and visits with technology partners and key system licensees take place on a regular basis with semi-annual visits to the majority of Far Eastern customers. A licensee information package is prepared and mailed before each visit to provide information on the market and new Dolby technologies.

5. New technologies are introduced to reinforce Dolby Laboratories' image as a long-term provider of technology and to ensure new sources of revenue as older technologies fade and licensed product royalties are reduced when they cover use of the trademarks only. Backward compatibility usually is maintained (e.g., products with Dolby C-type NR can play back Dolby B-type NR encoded cassettes, and Dolby Digital decoders are capable of producing a Dolby Surround compatible stereo signal for Pro Logic decoding). Many new technologies are derived from research originally performed to develop new professional products (e.g., Dolby Pro Logic was derived from Dolby Stereo and Dolby S-type NR was derived from SR).

6. In addition to licensing its own technologies, Dolby Laboratories participates in the licensing of essential patents and know-how associated with the Advanced Audio Codec (AAC) as part of the FADS (Fraunhofer Institute, AT&T, Dolby Laboratories, Sony) group. In recent years, a number of technologies have been licensed in from third parties (e.g., Pro Logic II was licensed from Rockford-Fosgate, Dolby Headphone was licensed from Lake Technology Ltd., and MLP Lossless compression was licensed from Meridian Ltd.).

7. Generally, advertising on the part of its licensees is relied upon to promote the technologies and trademarks. However, the company routinely organizes press visits from trade publications in order to introduce and demonstrate new technologies. This succeeds in favorable and cost-effective press coverage.

Future Trends

Dolby Laboratories has transformed itself from a manufacturer and licensor of analog technologies derived from Ray Dolby's original inventions in analog noise reduction to a digital technology company manufacturing products and licensing technology increasingly sourced from third parties. This transformation has been caused largely by market evolution due to increased use of digital audio/video formats, such as the HDTV and DVD formats, and the increasing rise of PC-based products. Consumer products that incorporate Dolby technologies (e.g., cassette decks) are gradually being replaced by new products that use digital technologies (e.g., DVD players). On the professional side, the transformation involves a move away from studio audio recording products to cinema and professional broadcast products.

Dolby's business strategy has changed from providing somewhat related (NR) technologies to a variety of markets to exploiting the relationship between those markets by providing the enabling links that make it possible for entertainment audio to travel from the creative source through various stages and processes to the consumer's home. For example, Dolby AC-3 multi-channel digital audio technology was originally developed for use in film production and presentation, but it has quickly been positioned in several consumer markets as well, including high-definition television (HDTV), DVD, and home-theater products. The company now offers products, services, and licensed technologies in an interrelated way, all tied together through the common element of its well-known trademarks.

Licensing Case Study—Home THX

Background

The Home THX program is an outgrowth of the THX program for theaters, which in turn was developed to address quality issues in the distribution and exhibition of films produced by Lucasfilm, starting with the *Star Wars* releases. Briefly, the THX theater program provides specifications, test procedures, and certification for release prints and various aspects of theaters, including screens, projection equipment, audio signal processing and reproduction, and room acoustics. The goal of the THX theater program is to provide the same environment in the theater as was available to the producer on the film studio dubbing stage.

Likewise, the goal of the Home THX licensing program is to allow the consumer to assemble a home theater system that will accurately reproduce the sound heard on the film studio dubbing stage. Components (DVD players, signal processors, amplifiers, and speaker systems) are designed and manufactured by licensees to a strict set of standards intended to ensure a consistent and correct presentation. Some components also incorporate patented technologies from Lucasfilm THX. Home THX specifications apply to both audio and video components. A program introduced in 1994 licenses VHS cassettes, DVD's, and Laser Discs to improve the quality of both video and audio transfers and to improve the integration of the sound tracks with home theater equipment. In 1999, THX introduced a two-tier license program for its home theater components. The THX Select trademark applies to a new generation of components suited for smaller home theater environments, while the THX Ultra brand is aimed at high-performance, large-scale systems. A new program licenses desktop PC sound systems, providing engineering design services and applying performance quality standards to the components.

Licensing Model

Prospective licensees are required to sign an NDA before Lucasfilm will send technical or royalty information. This has resulted in widespread speculation among the public and especially the audio press as to the requirements and royalties due for licensed products. Although exact figures are not available, in general the process and payments are as follows:

1. After signing the NDA, the prospective licensee is supplied with trademark usage information, technical specifications, reference circuit designs, and test procedures for the type of product they intend to manufacture. License agreement drafts are available at the same time. A hybrid agreement is used, licensing the intellectual property needed for the particular licensed product (which can include patents and copyrighted works and generally includes trademarks and know-how).

2. The prospective licensee signs the license agreement and returns it with the initial payment to Lucasfilm. Initial payments range from $5,000 to $10,000, depending on the type of product. A sample of each licensed product must be sent for approval prior to sale. To facilitate approval and provide additional service, Lucasfilm engineers are usually involved in licensed-product design from the early conceptual stages. A testing fee is charged for each product evaluation ($1,000 for a loudspeaker, for example).

3. Per-product royalties are charged on a sliding scale, averaging around 1% of the retail price.

Discussion

Home THX is intended to be a profit center. There are currently around 56 licensees. Nearly all licensed products are high-end (and high-cost), so although the average per-unit royalty is high, the total number of licensed products in the market is relatively small, resulting in modest revenues. Expenses associated with the Home THX licensing program include salaries (there are currently four full-time employees and six others who devote part of their time to licensing), travel, advertising, promotional, and other expenses. Although it is reasonable to assume that the program operated at a loss for the first few years, the division is now profitable, with fiscal year 2000 income reportedly exceeding $3 million.

Lucasfilm has obtained other benefits through the Home THX program. First, the THX and Lucasfilm trademarks have attained much wider recognition and value, and their use by licensees has presumably resulted in increased protection in foreign countries. Improved recognition by customers has resulted in more demand for THX-licensed theaters, increasing revenues in this related professional business. Licensed hardware in the market has made it possible for Lucasfilm to institute their software licensing program, another source of revenue. Finally, educational and consulting services provided to designers and installers (e.g., media room design services) provide additional revenues.

Around half the sales of licensed products occur in foreign markets, with Asia and Europe the major contributors. This came as somewhat of a surprise to Lucasfilm, who expected the majority of sales to be domestic.

Audio purists have attacked Home THX for destroying the market for high-end audio equipment by stealing customers, who buy home theater systems, with components not suitable for high-quality music reproduction, instead of high-end audio gear. At the same time, Home THX was criticized for relaxing its standards in the THX Select franchise, so that less expensive Home THX products could be marketed (in larger quantities). This placed Home THX in the unenviable position of defending their claim of being the best while trying to expand their market by relaxing requirements. As already noted, they responded by diversifying their program and creating a range of requirements. In addition, THX has started to leverage the power of its trademark recognition to enter into broader markets and appear on a wider variety of consumer goods.

Lessons to be learned from Home THX

- Expect an initial period of losses while establishing the program, as much as four to five years for a complex technology.
- Take spin-off benefits into account when determining the overall benefit of the program.
- Think internationally.
- Make sure that the size of the opportunity is taken into account when planning investment in the program.
- Plan an orderly and sensible migration down-market when initial products are high-end.
- Develop a trademark strategy that will pave the way for new opportunities.
- Do not alienate potentially valuable allies. Establish and maintain links with high-end reviewers and publications. Keeping technical and licensing details secret can result in speculation, bad feelings, and negative publicity and should be done only to the extent absolutely necessary.

UNIVERSITY LICENSING CASE STUDIES

Licensing Case Study—Stanford University

Introduction
Stanford began one of the first university licensing programs over 30 years ago. The goals of the program are to maximize the public use of and benefit from research through efficient commercialization and to generate revenues for the university and the inventor. Conducted through the Office of Technology Licensing

(OTL), Stanford's program remains one of the most successful of its type, generating total income of $37 million with an operating budget of $2.4 million in fiscal year 1999–2000.

Stanford's royalty-distribution policy is to give one-third of the revenues (after expenses) to the school in which the invention was discovered, one-third to the department, and one-third to the inventor.

OTL received 252 invention disclosures in fiscal year 1999–2000 and a cumulative total of 4,359 since the office opened in 1970. In that 30-year period, a total of 1,050 patents have been issued to Stanford and cumulative income has totaled $454,796,000. On average, over 50% of the patents filed are eventually licensed. Two major royalty-earning inventions have been the Cohen-Boyer Recombinent DNA invention (earning almost $300 million) and the frequency modulation (FM) sound synthesis invention (earning $25 million). Both of these licensing programs will be explored in detail in this case study.

In 1996, Stanford announced the Sondius trademark licensing program, initially to be used with sound-synthesis technologies developed by Stanford's Center for Computer Research in Music and Acoustics (CCRMA). The strategy, execution, and implications of this new (for universities) technique will be explored in the final section.

Cohen-Boyer Recombinant DNA

Background
In 1973 Stanley Cohen of Stanford and Herbert Boyer of the University of California at San Francisco succeeded in developing a process that allowed DNA to be cloned. The potential of their discovery (which eventually allowed the development of the entire bio-technology industry) was immediately obvious to Cohen, Boyer, and their colleagues.

The first published details of their discovery appeared in November 1973 and provoked widespread and wide-ranging discussions of the ethics and safety of creating new life forms. An informal moratorium on recombinant DNA research was agreed to by the academic community, and it was not lifted until after an international conference on the subject was held in December 1974, and only then under strict laboratory-safety guidelines.

Intellectual Property
Niels Reimers, Director of the Stanford OTL, learned of the discovery in May 1974 and contacted Dr. Cohen, who was initially not in favor of obtaining a patent. After discussing the benefits, Dr. Cohen agreed to an investigation of the possibility of patenting the process, to which Dr. Boyer agreed. Reimers then contacted the University of California patent office, and an agreement was reached that OTL would manage the patenting and licensing of the technology, with Stanford and the University of California sharing the royalty income equally after deducting patenting and licensing costs and 15% of the gross royalties for administration.

Three different organizations had sponsored the research: the American Cancer Society, the National Science Foundation (NSF), and the National Institutes of

Health (NIH). Eventually, all agreed that the invention could be administered by Stanford under their institutional patent agreement with the NIH.

A U.S. patent application was filed in November 1974, just before the end of the one-year grace period. Foreign filings were precluded by the November 1973 publication. The application covered both the process and the composition of functional organisms made using the process. The patent office agreed to allow the process claims but not the composition claims, so the application was split into a process application and a product application. The process patent was issued in December 1980. At that time Stanford filed a terminal disclaimer with the patent office, meaning any divisional applications would expire when the process patent expired. The product patent was subsequently divided again into two applications, one covering prokaryotic hosts (without nuclei) and the other covering eukaryotic hosts (with nuclei). The prokaryotic product patent issued in August 1984, and the eukaryotic product patent issued in April 1988.

Licensing Strategy
Stanford decided, because of the fundamental nature of the patents, to pursue a nonexclusive licensing strategy. Because of the wide-ranging applications for the process, it seemed likely that companies both small and large in a number of industries would become licensees. Because of the limited life of the patents and the long product development and approval cycle, the licensing program needed to be initiated quickly.

Because foreign patent protection was not possible, royalty payments needed to be low enough to avoid encouraging offshore production. In order to further encourage licensing, Stanford obtained and publicized a legal opinion stating that unlicensed products manufactured abroad could not be imported into the U.S. under Section 337 of the Tariff Act of 1930.

In addition, Stanford had opened the patent file history to encourage anyone interested in challenging the patent to do so prior to its issuance, thereby effectively discouraging patent challenges later. Prospective licensees were consulted regarding certain critical license terms to avoid problems later in the licensing process.

In August 1981, Stanford announced, with wide media coverage, the availability of licenses. A $10,000 initial payment was required, with $10,000 minimum annual royalty payments. For the first five years of the agreement or until $1 million in licensed product sales occurred in a year, five times the initial and minimum payments was creditable against royalties due, meaning that $60,000 in payments could be credited against up to $300,000 in royalties due. Most licensees took full advantage of this credit.

Royalties ranged from 10% for basic genetic products (chimeric DNA, DNA composed of sequences derived from two or more different sources, and vectors, the agents used to carry the DNA into a cell) to .5% for end products, such as a vaccine or pharmaceutical. Bulk products (intermediate products that will be processed further before sale to the end customer) carried royalty rates of 1% to 3%, and process improvement products (e.g., enzymes) paid 10% of the cost savings or economic benefit.

Results

Stanford announced that the above terms would be valid only for companies executing license agreements before December 15, 1981. No details were given as to what changes would be made after that date (in fact, the five-times credit was reduced to a one-time credit, with other terms remaining unchanged). Representatives visited prospective licensees, prepared collateral materials, and, in general, vigorously promoted licensing. Seventy-three licensees had signed agreements by the cutoff date. Since then, over 300 licenses have been signed.

Licensed products include human insulin (developed by Genentech and marketed by Lilly), human growth hormone (by Genentech), the hepatitis B vaccine (developed by Chiron and marketed by Merck), and tissue plasminogen activator.

Almost $300 million in royalties were generated by the Cohen-Boyer patents, including close to $40 million from licensed products manufactured prior to the December 1997 expiration date but then sold in 1998 and 1999. It has been estimated that over $30 billion in sales of licensed products occurred over the life of the patents.

FM Synthesis

Background

Professor John Chowning developed a technique for generating musical sounds using frequency modulation (FM) in 1971 while working in Stanford's Artificial Intelligence Lab.

After learning of the invention, Reimers of the OTL discussed FM synthesis with several U.S. companies, none of whom were interested. He finally contacted Yamaha, who immediately understood the technology's potential and executed a letter option agreement in July 1974.

Intellectual Property

Stanford was awarded one patent for FM synthesis in April 1977. Yamaha, as a result of their extensive development efforts, assembled a portfolio of FM synthesis-related patents, many of which have not yet expired.

The Exclusive License

After a careful evaluation, Stanford and Yamaha entered into an exclusive license agreement in March of 1975. To ensure timely commercialization, the agreement specified that Yamaha must introduce its first FM synthesis product by 1981. Subsequently, several amendments were added to reflect changes in the marketplace. The amendments addressed such issues as mandatory sublicensing, termination for lack of diligence, rights to future technologies, adjusting royalty rates to reflect the changed market, and royalties and second sourcing for integrated-circuit implementations.

Results

After a lengthy and difficult period of development, in 1981 Yamaha introduced their first FM synthesizer, which cost tens of thousands of dollars. The DX-7 series of synthesizers, introduced in 1983, was a huge success, generating the first significant royalties.

In the early 1990s, Yamaha began selling integrated circuits with limited FM synthesis capability to manufacturers of computer sound cards, which proved to be a large and profitable market. Royalties to Stanford doubled each year from 1991 to 1994, largely from sales of integrated circuits. Because sound cards were largely developed and marketed by U.S. companies, some dissatisfaction with Stanford's exclusive license to Yamaha surfaced, and infringement of the patent became fairly widespread, both by U.S. and foreign companies. Starting in 1994, Yamaha began asserting their patent rights over companies that had introduced competing FM synthesis products.

FM synthesis generated over $25 million in licensing revenues over the life of the patent, which expired in April 1994. These revenues helped to establish and support CCRMA, resulting in further discoveries and inventions, and further established the Stanford OTL as a premier university technology licensing operation.

The Sondius Trademark Licensing Program

University licensing activity has typically centered around patents covering the inventions of researchers. Because most of the technologies licensed are relatively unproven and require substantial additional development before commercialization is possible, the royalties earned are often less than would be justifiable from technologies at a more advanced stage of development. In addition, patents have a limited life span. For some time, Stanford OTL management had been considering ways to add value to their patent portfolio to generate more revenues and extend the life of their license agreements.

Starting in the mid-1980s, researchers at CCRMA, including Professor Julius Smith, developed a new sound synthesis technology known as Waveguide. Based on a physical model of the instrument being synthesized, waveguide sounds have the potential to be more natural than other synthesized sounds, and can be controlled in ways which are similar to those used with real musical instruments. Waveguide sounds can be realized relatively economically using digital signal processors (DSPs).

In 1989 Yamaha was granted an exclusive license (except for North American companies) to the waveguide patents in existence at that time, based on their right of first refusal granted in the FM synthesis license. Stanford's strategy was to allow Yamaha to benefit from their early participation and substantial investment but still allow licensing to domestic companies. Additional patent applications were filed after Yamaha's license was executed.

In 1992 OTL decided to investigate the possibility of developing a trademark which could be licensed together with other intellectual property. The trademark was intended to be used with a variety of technologies. The first technology targeted for inclusion in the trademark program was waveguide.

The first step taken was to develop a business plan. The plan addressed issues associated with developing and protecting the trademark, further technical development needed, the licensing strategy, staffing, markets, and projected expenses and revenues. Elements of the Dolby licensing model were emulated. After a presentation to Stanford management in May 1993, funding was allocated and the project began.

Next, outside firms were contracted to develop a trademark name and logo, and consultants were retained to perform further technical development with the assistance of CCRMA personnel, including the inventors. Hybrid license agreements were drafted, with the waveguide patents, the trademarks, copyrighted works (development tools and the waveguide voices), and know-how included.

In 1994 and 1995, Stanford University funded almost $1 million dollars in development work on the waveguide technology and in obtaining worldwide trademark protection for the Sondius mark. In 1996, licenses were granted to six North American companies to the patents, software, and trademarks bundled in the Sondius licensing program IP portfolio.

Also in 1996, a start-up company was formed by Joe Koepnick, who left OTL to become president of the start-up, and some of the consultants who had worked on the development of the waveguide technology. In exchange for a license granted in early 1997, the new company (named Staccato Systems) gave Stanford a significant amount of equity.

In early 1997, Stanford and Yamaha entered into discussions to combine their respective intellectual property in waveguide technology (Yamaha had by this time over 100 issued patents) into a joint licensing effort, with Stanford to issue the licenses for the combined intellectual property portfolios. Agreements between Stanford and Yamaha were signed in June 1997 and press releases were issued in Japan and the U.S. in July 1997 announcing this new licensing program.

Yamaha introduced waveguide-based licensed products in 1998, and products from other licensees have subsequently found their way to market. As with the introduction of FM, future improvements in price performance of computer memory and processing power will likely lead to new markets for and broader use of waveguide technology in the price-sensitive consumer electronics area.

In 2000, Staccato Systems was acquired by a large electronics company, and Stanford then sold its equity position, providing sufficient return to repay its original investment in the development of the waveguide technology.

PATENT CASE STUDIES

Patent Case Study—Compton's NewMedia

Compton's NewMedia Inc., a subsidiary of the Tribune Company of Chicago, is a small software publishing company located in Carlsbad, CA. Their best-known product is the "Compton's Multimedia Encyclopedia" CD-ROM, first released in 1989. They have since released a number of other CD-ROMs and developed a distribution business that reportedly handled 40% of all CD-ROMs in 1993.

While authoring the Multimedia Encyclopedia, Compton's developed a method for accessing several types of information, such as text, sound, and pictures, simultaneously. In October 1989 they applied for a U.S. patent. Patent 5,241,671, entitled "Multimedia Search Systems Using a Plurality of Entry Path Means Which Indicate Interrelatedness of Information," was granted on August 31, 1993.

Compton's considered itself a pioneer in the CD-ROM business, and had in the past been responsible for expanding channels of distribution and overcoming problems associated with renting software. They believed that supplying content used in future interactive television systems would represent a huge market, and intended to position themselves as the controlling central agency for content distribution. The '671 patent would be used to establish relationships with many developers and achieve sufficient size and clout to be able to negotiate successfully with the other players in the interactive TV market.

Rather than seeing the patent as an immediate source of revenue, they intended to leverage it to establish themselves as the preeminent supplier of content to the interactive television market.

In November 1993, Compton's announced their patent licensing program at Comdex, a large computer industry trade show. Four different licensing arrangements were offered:

1. The patent could be licensed for 1% of the net selling price of the licensed product (a CD-ROM at first) until June 30, 1994, after which the royalty would rise to 3%.
2. In addition to the patent rights, a developer could license Compton's multimedia development kit for a combined royalty of 2.5% of net cash receipts, rising to 4% after June 30, 1994.
3. A developer could become an "Affiliated Label" by giving Compton's the exclusive right to distribute the licensed product and to purchase the product for a 65% discount (standard in the industry) until June 30, 1994, after which the discount would rise to 67%. No other payment would be required.
4. A more intimate "Strategic Partnership" could be established. Terms were not published, and presumably subject to negotiation.

The announcement caused an uproar, with developers and industry analysts accusing Compton's of using the patent to hinder software development at a crucial point in the growth of the market. Several developers and attorneys also indicated that they expected the patent to be challenged on the basis of prior art.

The intensity of the reaction resulted in the commissioner of patents and trademarks requesting that the patent be reviewed by a special examiner, who subsequently rescinded it in March of 1994.

In June of 1994, Compton's reapplied for the patent, slightly narrowing some of the claims, adding new claims, and rebutting the findings of the special examiner. The reapplication was also denied.

Patent Licensing Case Study—SGS-Thomson

Background

SGS-Thomson Microelectronics (SGS) is a $1.5 billion manufacturer of semi-conductors, partly owned by Thomson CSF of France. They have developed an effective system for licensing patent infringers.

Method

The first step in the SGS process is to identify which patents are to be licensed. Technical experts conduct ongoing reviews of the SGS patent portfolio and of products in the marketplace that may utilize proprietary inventions. Patents are usually reviewed by a team consisting of company personnel, outside experts, and team members (often including consultants). The first steps are to understand the patent, estimate if there is high volume use, and then evaluate the use by determining in which companies, what devices, and at what volume use can be detected. After the initial screening a few patents are selected to pursue.

Selected patents then undergo a more detailed evaluation of their particular use over a two- to six-month time frame. A literature search is conducted of catalogs, conference digests, other patents, and so forth. If the selected patent is a circuit patent, samples of products that are suspected of infringement are obtained and their top layers are checked. If a process patent is suspected to be infringed, samples of suspect products are again obtained and a cross-section is checked. If infringement is still believed, more detailed analysis (using high magnification pictures) against the patent claims is conducted.

Legal experts then decide whether to assert or not to assert the infringed patents, and identify key issues that may arise in litigation. If problems are found in a patent, reissue, reexamination, or claim scope changes are considered. SGS has found that only strong patents prevail.

Potential licensees are identified using Dataquest or other market research firms, and SGS usually pursues the largest companies first (>$200MM) to establish credibility. SGS then prepares an "infringement report" in an attempt to avoid long negotiations over whether infringement exists and to show that they are trial ready. Multi-color engineering reports with color coding show which parts of the device infringe which claims, using data sheets, photos, circuits, reverse-engineered circuits, and so forth to locate and label each infringing element. In addition, prior art reports are prepared. If the prior art is significant, SGS applies for reexamination. If not, the report is shown to the potential licensee.

SGS also believes that it is important to understand any vulnerabilities that may exist. In addition to locating and evaluating any prior art, SGS examines the potential licensee's patents in an attempt to determine what may be presented for possible cross-licensing. A position paper is prepared which addresses any vulnerabilities found.

When all of the above elements are in place, a solicitous letter is sent to the targeted potential licensee requesting a meeting.

Negotiations

The purpose of the ensuing negotiation is to convince the other side that they cannot win. Negotiations can be both offensive (licensing out) or defensive (licensing in).

Two main rules are followed to help ensure a favorable outcome. The first is to make sure that the SGS team is well prepared, including developing a negotiating strategy, having well-researched infringement reports and position papers, and knowing about the targeted company. Databases are used to find out the size, sales, affiliates, details of previous patent litigation, and other relevant facts about the company.

Second, SGS feels that it is important to maintain a position of strength by showing respect for the opponents and avoiding threats and loss of temper. Only with extreme caution should deadlines be set.

Litigation Strategy

Litigation should be avoided, but if negotiations fail, the first step is to create a litigation team consisting of a specialist, a team coordinator, and leaders for the various team functions. Team leaders must develop a winning strategy; if no winning strategy can be developed, the effort should be abandoned. Once the strategy has been developed, personnel are assigned to the team and trained (in particular, lawyers must understand the technology), and a quality monitoring procedure is established for the team.

SGS feels that the winner is the one who has a winning strategy, the best talent, is well prepared, and executes the strategy flawlessly.

All information is given to other side at the beginning. A dual-path legal strategy is followed, consisting of an International Trade Commission (ITC) filing under Section 337 and, at same time, an infringement action in district court. For an ITC filing the manufacturer must practice the invention in the U.S. SGS can get an exclusion order to prohibit entry at any U.S. port, and a general exclusion order, which stops all imports, even by other companies. There is a time limitation (quick trial) associated with an ITC filing. Infringement actions in district court provide for damages, and SGS can pick a favorable forum (if a district court action is not filed, the opponent will file in an unfavorable forum). Only the district court can determine the validity of a patent. The disadvantage of the dual-path approach is its cost because two actions must be pursued.

Settlement

The successful settlement of litigation will result in a license to the infringer. Two types are offered, the guillotine license, featuring a fixed term followed by renegotiation, and the peace treaty, with a long term (10 years or the life of patent). By licensee choice, all agreements negotiated so far have been paid up. Royalty rates are based on what other companies are charging in the industry, what courts have awarded, and what is fair (what SGS would be willing to pay).

Follow-through

Yearly correspondence is maintained with all licensees. Included is a booklet with a list of all new patents. SGS tries to ensure the ongoing value of the licensing arrangement.

Patent Case Study—The Auction of the Wang Laboratories[1] Patent Portfolio

In late 1995, we[2] were contacted by Albert A. Notini, then General Counsel for Wang Laboratories. Wang had just emerged from a Chapter XI reorganization and changed from a computer research, development, manufacturing, and marketing company to primarily a service company[3], repairing and installing computers and computer systems. Wang had a portfolio of about 250 issued U.S. utility patents, some pending U.S. applications, and about 500 counterpart foreign patents and patent applications. Most of the patents and applications had filing dates in the 1980s, when Wang was one of the most creative and dynamic computer companies in the world. The portfolio covered a wide range of computer-related technologies, such as computer architecture, telecommunications, and computer operating systems, to name just a few.

Wang was interested in extracting value from its patent portfolio. My partner, Robert A. Pressman, and I had recently completed a three-year stint as CEO and General Counsel, respectively, of a digital cellular patent licensing company[4], and had generated about $125 million in licensing revenue. We had previously been at Unisys Corporation[5], where we initiated the very successful Lempel-Zev-Welch data compression algorithm patent licensing program, and sold some valuable semiconductor patents, so we had a good knowledge of the computer and telecommunications industries. Bert Notini felt that our backgrounds suited us to the task of extracting maximum value from the patent portfolio for the benefit of the Wang shareholders.

The first thing we had to do was get familiar with the patent portfolio and develop a sense of which patents were valuable. For this purpose, we had to review all of the patents and, because some of the technologies were beyond our expertise, we engaged consultants to help us, when needed, in this assessment[6]. We also consulted with former Wang patent attorneys, who often had very good insights about the patents and were familiar with file histories. This helped us get up to speed more rapidly than would otherwise have been the case. None of this is cheap and, although we never calculated how much Wang spent for supporting consultants and patent attorneys (they did approve all major expenses in advance), it was a significant sum, but proved to have been well spent.

While this preliminary evaluation was being done, Wang was in litigation

---

[1]Now known as GetronicsWang.
[2]Bramson & Pressman.
[3]It had an imaging software division, which it later sold, as noted below.
[4]InterDigital Patents Corporation.
[5]Where I had been General Patent and Technology Counsel and Rob Pressman had been Senior IP Counsel.
[6]When we identified exciting patents that we thought were infringed or were likely to be infringed, we created claim charts for discussion with interested prospects. Out of 215 utility patents in the auction, I would estimate that about 10% were truly interesting (in a very good portfolio based on very creative engineering), and that's what drove the auction.

with some imaging patents it owned, and we used that opportunity to initiate a licensing program for some of those patents. That was where we started, because, as a result of the litigation, there was more knowledge about which patents were valuable and why, applicable prior art, prospective infringers, and so on.

It took almost a year to complete our analysis of the portfolio and understand which patents were valuable. We could have done this more quickly, but at first we were focusing on the imaging patents. Also, the Internet was not as well developed in 1995–1996 as it is now, so the kind of detailed product information that is now so readily available on company Web sites was harder to come by then.

In late 1996, Wang sold its imaging business, together with all of the related imaging patents, and Bert Notini asked us to focus on generating revenue from the rest of the portfolio, which constituted about 215 U.S. utility patents, 400 foreign counterparts, and 30 design patents[7].

The first thing we did was to categorize the remaining Wang patents into 27 technology groups (e.g., computer architecture, data compression, database, graphics systems, Internet, pen-based computing, and telecommunications). Each group had about five to ten patents, although the number varied considerably. We felt that it would be easier for prospective buyers to focus on the patents of interest to them if the patents were organized this way, and this organization also made it easier for us to understand better what was in Wang's portfolio.

We talked about how best to generate value from the portfolio. We had identified some patents that were infringed, but Wang decided that it wasn't interested in getting involved in expensive, time-consuming lawsuits, and would rather generate shorter-term revenues by outright patent sales. We knew, due to the activities of companies such as Texas Instruments, IBM, and Lucent, that there was a great deal of cross-licensing activity in the computer and telecommunications industries, and that this created a market for the sale of patents to less patent-rich companies in these industries, to be used for cross-licensing or other purposes.[8] We knew many of the potentially interested companies from our prior experiences, and whom to contact within those companies. One of the important qualities to look for in engaging a representative is how good is their contact file?[9]

We all decided that an auction was the best vehicle for selling the remaining Wang patents because we felt that it would help focus the prospects on meeting our proposed auction deadlines. It was also a convenient vehicle for

---

[7]There was no interest in the design patents, and we anticipated that, so our focus was on the utility patents.

[8]We had experience at Unisys in selling the semiconductor patents in its portfolio, which became extraneous when Unisys shut down its semiconductor design and manufacturing facilities, and decided to buy its components from established component suppliers.

[9]When we prepare mailings, whether for an auction or a patent sale, we prepare the letters and mailing labels ourselves because we don't want to release our valuable contact information.

presenting to the interested companies all of the different groups of patents, without having to focus on selling particular patents to particular companies, which would have been more expensive and inefficient. Also, it would allow us to sell the less exciting patents in each group in conjunction with the more exciting patents, and not leave us with a bunch of less interesting patents on which Wang would have to pay maintenance fees, and then figure out what to do with them.

Fortunately, Bert Notini was familiar and comfortable with the auction process. Before Wang, he had been a partner in the bankruptcy group at Hale & Dorr, the well-known Boston law firm, and we had no trouble getting him to agree on the idea of an auction. Based on his bankruptcy experience with auctions, he recommended that we structure the auction as a two-step process, and we followed his suggestion. We were concerned about the "bird in the hand" aspect of selling some patents to an interested buyer who wanted to circumvent the auction process, and we dealt with that prospect too.

We decided to put a set of non-confidential materials in an Auction[10] Book, which we would mail to priority prospects and make available to other prospects that expressed an interest. The contents of the Auction Book[11] were:

- The history of Wang's patent portfolio
- A brief auction overview
- The auction procedure (rules)
- The list of the 27 patent groups for sale and the minimum price for each group[12]
- The proposed Patent Assignment Agreement, which Wang would sign to transfer the patents to the highest bidder for each patent group
- A list (organized by patent group) of the patents available for sale and the foreign counterparts to each U.S. patent and the status of each (issued or pending)
- The cover page of each U.S. patent, again organized by patent group (with an index tab naming each group)
- A cross-index of patent numbers and groups, organized sequentially by patent number (so someone looking for a particular patent would know where it was)
- An auction registration form, registering a company in the auction, to be sent to Arthur Andersen, the firm we engaged to process the bids

---

[10]Bert Notini was concerned that investors might identify the word "auction" with financial difficulties (which Wang did not have by then) and that this could have an adverse effect on Wang's stock price. So we called the auction a "limited offering" and, to my knowledge, it had no adverse effect on Wang's stock price. In our meetings and conversations with prospective buyers, we (and they) referred to the process as an auction.

[11]The Auction Books were expensive to print and bind. Wang paid about $15 for each book plus a couple of dollars for each CD-ROM containing its patents.

[12]Called the "reserve" in auction parlance.

- A Confidentiality Agreement, for execution by companies desiring to see confidential information, such as claim charts and existing license agreements[13]
- An Offer Form, for prospective buyers to use in submitting bids
- A file history order form[14]
- A CD-ROM containing copies of all of the Wang U.S. patents[15] in the auction was supplied to companies that registered for the auction

We then needed to create a mailing list for the auction materials. We did that from our own contacts file. We supplemented that as we felt necessary, but because of our experience, our contacts file had most of the names and addresses we needed. The principal focus of our mailing was the person responsible for patents or licensing in corporations in the relevant industries (electronics and telecommunications). Each of these persons got a copy of the Auction Book.

We also sent letters to a large number of the patent and IP attorneys in our contact files who we knew dealt in the applicable technology space or were in firms that dealt in the space. The letter gave a brief description of the auction and included a copy of the index for the Auction Book and a request form to ask for a copy of the Auction Book. We got many requests. We eventually mailed out about 200 Auction Books.

We engaged Arthur Andersen[16] to receive and manage the bids because we felt that some companies would want to keep their identities and bids confidential. It was not a major task, and therefore was not expensive and seemed to have been a worthwhile expenditure.

Companies that were interested in any of the Wang patents registered for the auction by returning the registration forms and the Confidentiality Agreements, both of which were in the Auction Books. Upon receiving these, we sent them the CD-ROM containing all of the U.S. patents (based on receipt of the registration form), and copies of the claim charts and licenses (based on receipt of the Confidentiality Agreement).

The timetable for the auction was:

- Auction Books and letters (to those not receiving books) were sent out in early September 1997

---

[13]Wang had about eight outstanding royalty-free, non-exclusive licenses, which did not materially affect the value of the patents, but were required to be disclosed and were identified in the Patent Assignment Agreement form.

[14]We made arrangements with a large patent service company to retain a master of each file history, so that they could be readily available for interested parties. Today, we get all of the U.S. patents, the important file histories, and most applicable prior art and have them copied onto a non-confidential CD-ROM, which we make available as part of the Auction Book.

[15]See footnote 16.

[16]Now called Andersen.

- Wang reserved the right to sell or license any patent groups outside the auction process on or before October 31, 1997,[17] and would then notify all registered parties of the patent groups sold or licensed prior to that date.
- A First Offer as to each patent group was due by January 31, 1998. All offers had to be presented on the Offer Form included in the Auction Book, which incorporated by reference the Patent Assignment Agreement.
- By February 20, 1998, the three highest bidders for each patent group were notified by Andersen of the amount of the highest bid for that group.
- Those three bidders had until March 20, 1998, to make a Second and Final Offer as to that group. The patent group was then sold to the bidder that made the highest Second and Final Offer. If no Second and Final Offer was received for that patent group which exceeded the highest First Offer, the patent group was sold to the highest First Offer bidder.
- Wang then completed and signed the Patent Assignment Agreement and sent it to the highest bidder for each group, which signed and returned it.
- Closings and payment were due by May 1, 1998.
- After the closing, Wang sent the applicable patent files to the successful buyer.

After we got the auction registration forms and confidentiality agreements, and began to send out the confidential materials, we began scheduling meetings with interested prospects. Since some of the interested companies were in Japan, Korea, and Taiwan, we had to arrange a travel schedule so that we could use the time efficiently.

We engaged local representatives in Japan, Korea, and Taiwan, to assist us in the scheduling and selling process because of the need to have representatives who understood the local language and culture and whose contacts supplemented ours. In Taiwan we gave several seminars about the portfolio to interested companies, many of which were not on our mailing list. The seminars proved to be very helpful. In total, we made about six trips to Asia in this selling process. Asian companies purchased some of the patent groups. This readily justified the considerable expense of travel in Asia.

Some bidders wanted to meet with us and discuss the patents in detail. Other bidders were content to do the evaluations on their own, and called us from time to time if they had questions.

On the cut-off date, Andersen received a flurry of First Offers. They then sent responses to the three highest bidders for each patent group, identifying to them the amount of the highest First Offer for that group.

In most instances, Andersen received Second and Final Offers that exceeded the First Offers, and the highest Second and Final Offer won the auction for the applicable patent group. In those few instances in which there was no higher Second and Final Offer, the highest First Offer bought that patent group.

---

[17]We had gotten a head start on selling a few of the patent groups, so that it was realistic to contemplate completing some sales between September and October, and indeed we did sell some patent groups before that date and notified the prospective buyers accordingly.

In those few instances in which the highest First Offer did not exceed the reserve, we talked to the interested companies and then worked out deals outside of the auction process.

Wang signed the applicable Patent Assignment Agreements,[18] inserting in the forms the name of the buyer, the amount of the purchase price, and the identity of the patent group being sold, and returned the appropriate agreements to the winning bidders for execution and delivery. All closings were conducted by express delivery service (for document transfer), telephone, and wire transfer of funds. Everything went very smoothly, without a hitch.

The final result was net revenues (gross revenues minus all consultant fees and expenses) that made Wang very happy. The number is confidential, but the happy result is not.

---

[18]We were gratified to find that our Patent Assignment Agreement forms were acceptable to all bidders.

Appendix B

Sources of
Additional Information

ORGANIZATIONS

There are literally thousands of organizations in existence, both domestic and international, devoted to a wide range of subjects related to licensing and intellectual property. Many publish journals or proceedings with articles of interest to the membership and organize conventions and conferences.

Several reference works listing organizations can be purchased or found in libraries, including the *Encyclopedia of Associations, Research Centers Directory*, and *International Organizations*, all published by Gale Research, Inc., Detroit, MI, at (800) 877-GALE.

A few well-known associations related to licensing and technologies commonly licensed are listed below. It is recommended that the reader refer to the references listed below for further information.

Licensing and Intellectual Property Associations

Licensing Executives Society International, Inc. (LESI)
The Licensing Executives Society International (LESI) is an association of 27 national and regional societies, each composed of men and women who have an interest in the transfer of technology, or licensing of intellectual property rights—from technical know-how and patented inventions to software, copyright, and trademarks. There are more than 10,000 members worldwide, representing more than 60 different countries. Interested individuals may apply for membership with their country's national society.

Web Site: http://www.les.org/
Publication: les Nouvelles®, Journal of the Licensing Executives Society

Licensing Executives Society (LES)—U.S. and Canada

The Licensing Executives Society (U.S. & Canada), Inc. is a professional society comprised of nearly 5,000 members who are involved in the transfer, use, development, manufacture, and marketing of intellectual property. LES members include professionals in the field of law, academics, science, government, and the private sector. LES (U.S & Canada), Inc. is a member society of the Licensing Executives Society International (LESI).

Address:
Licensing Executives Society
1800 Diagonal Rd.,
Suite 280
Alexandria, VA 22314-2840
Phone: (703) 836-3106
Web Site: http://www.usa-canada.les.org/

Association of University Technology Managers (AUTM)

The AUTM® is a not-for-profit association with a membership of more than 2,300 technology managers and business executives who manage intellectual property—one of the most active growth sectors of the U.S. economy. The AUTM's members represent over 300 universities, research institutions, teaching hospitals, and a similar number of companies and government organizations. AUTM publishes the *Journal of the Association of University Technology Managers.* AUTM also publishes a quarterly newsletter, an annual journal, and a three-volume *Technology Transfer Practice Manual.*

Address:
AUTM
60 Revere Dr., Suite 500
Northbrook, IL 60062
Phone: (847) 559-0846
Fax: (847) 480-9282
E-mail: autm@autm.net
Web Site: http://www.autm.net
Publication: Journal of the Association of University Technology Managers

American Intellectual Property Law Association (AIPLA)

The American Intellectual Property Law Association (AIPLA) is a 12,000 member national bar association constituted primarily of lawyers in private and corporate practice, in government service, and in the academic community. The AIPLA represents a wide and diverse spectrum of individuals, companies, and institutions involved directly or indirectly in the practice of patent, trademark, copyright, and unfair competition law, as well as other fields of law affecting intellectual property. Members represent both owners and users of intellectual property.

Address:
American Intellectual Property Law Association
2001 Jefferson Davis Highway, Suite 203
Arlington, VA 22202-3694
Phone: (703) 415-0780
Fax: (703) 415-0786
Web Site: http://www.aipla.org
Publication: American Intellectual Property Law Association Quarterly Journal

American Bar Association Section of Intellectual Property Law

Formerly the Section of Patent, Trademark, and Copyright Law, this Section was the second Section created by the ABA and the first Section organized to deal with a special branch of the law. Since 1894 it has contributed significantly to the development of our system for the protection of intellectual property rights. With 20,035 total members as of 8/31/00 (17,295 lawyer members, 753 associate members, and 1,987 law student members), the Section is the largest intellectual property organization in the world.

Address:
Membership Department
American Bar Association
541 N. Fairbanks Ct.
Chicago, IL 60611
Phone: (800) 285-2221
Fax: (312) 988-5528
Web Site: http://www.abanet.org/intelprop/
Publication: Intellectual Property Law Newsletter

Association of Patent Law Firms

The Association of Patent Law Firms (APLF) is a national association of law firms that devote a majority of their practice to patent law. Practicing attorneys of member firms are skilled and experienced in the areas of patent application work, litigation, and counseling services. They seek to fill a void that has been left by other organizations that have broadened their base to the general field of "intellectual property law." As an alliance strictly of patent law firms, a major objective is to jointly promote the advantages realized by clients when they select a patent law firm for patent application work, litigation, and counseling services.

E-mail: info@aplf.org
Web Site: http://www.aplf.org/

Intellectual Property Management Institute

The Intellectual Property Management Institute (IPMi) is a not-for-profit organization dedicated to professional development in the field of intellectual property management. Intellectual property has become vitally important in international commerce and its effective management has become an essential skill in business. The mission of IPMi is therefore to encourage the development of intellectual property management theory and practice, and to provide recognition for those who, through educational and professional development, have attained professional status.

Address:
AUS Consultants
155 Gaither Dr., P.O. Box 1050
Moorestown, NJ 08057-1050
Attention: IPMi Membership Administrator
Web Site: http://ipinstitute.org/

International Trademark Association
The International Trademark Association (INTA) is a not-for-profit worldwide membership organization of trademark owners and advisors. INTA represents trademark owners to protect and advance the importance of trademarks as essential elements of international commerce. INTA shapes public policy, advances practitioner's knowledge, and educates business, the media, and the public on the significance of trademarks.

Address:
International Trademark Association
1133 Avenue of the Americas
New York, NY 10036
Phone: (212) 768-9887
Fax: (212) 768-7796
Web Site: http://www.inta.org/
Publication: THE TRADEMARK REPORTER®

World Intellectual Property Organization
The World Intellectual Property Organization (WIPO) is an international organization dedicated to promoting the use and protection of works of the human spirit. These works—intellectual property—are expanding the bounds of science and technology and enriching the world of the arts. Through its work, WIPO plays an important role in enhancing the quality and enjoyment of life, as well as creating real wealth for nations. With headquarters in Geneva, Switzerland, WIPO is one of the 16 specialized agencies of the United Nations system of organizations. It administers 21 international treaties dealing with different aspects of intellectual property protection. The organization counts 177 nations as member states.

Address:
Headquarters of WIPO
WIPO, 34, chemin des Colombettes, Geneva
Mailing address: P.O. Box 18, CH-1211 Geneva 20

Telegraphic address: OMPI Geneva
Phone: +41-22 338 9111
Fax: +41-22 733 54 28
Telex: 412912 ompi ch

WIPO Coordination Office at the United Nations in New York, United States of
America:
Direct Phone Numbers with Personal Voice Mail
Address: 2 United Nations Plaza, New York, NY 10017, Suite 2525
Phone: +1-212 963 6813
Fax: +1-212 963 4801
Telex: 420544 UNH UI
Web Site: http://www.wipo.org/

Federal Laboratory Consortium for Technology Transfer (FLC)

The Federal Laboratory Consortium for Technology Transfer (FLC) was organized in 1974 and formally chartered by the Federal Technology Transfer Act of
1986 to promote and to strengthen technology transfer nationwide. Today, more
than 700 major federal laboratories and centers and their parent departments and
agencies are FLC members.

Address:
Federal Laboratory Consortium for Technology Transfer
317 Madison Ave., Suite 921
New York, NY 10017-5391
Phone: (212) 490-3999
Web Site: http://flc2.federallabs.org/
Publication: NewsLink

Technical/Trade Organizations

Software & Information Industry Association (SIIA)

The Software & Information Industry Association (SIIA) is the only trade association with a global reach that provides a credible, unifying voice for all businesses that provide the software and information that underpin the digital
economy. It has 1,200 member companies from around the world. SIIA provides
a neutral business forum for its members to understand business models, technological advancements, industry trends, and "best practices."

Address:
The Software & Information Industry Association
1730 M St. NW, Suite 700
Washington, D.C. 20036-4510
Phone: (202) 452-1600
Web Site: http://www.siia.net/

Biotechnology Industry Organization

Biotechnology is one of the most significant industries of this century. Thousands of people and organizations are conducting breakthrough research, and companies are delivering biotechnology products to consumers worldwide. As the industry has grown, so has the Biotechnology Industry Organization (BIO). Its roster includes more than 950 members, almost a 50% increase since the industry organization was established in 1993.

Address:
1625 K St., NW, Suite 1100
Washington, D.C. 20006
Phone: (202) 857- 0244
Fax: (202) 857- 0237
Web Site: http://www.bio.org/
Publication: Your World, Our World

Electronic Industries Association (EIA)

A trade association representing the U.S. high technology community, EIA began in 1924 as the Radio Manufacturers Association. The EIA sponsors a number of activities on behalf of its members, including conferences and trade shows. In addition, it has been responsible for developing some important standards such as the RS-232, RS-422, and RS-423 standards for connecting serial devices.

Address:
2001 Pennsylvania Ave. NW
Washington, D.C. 20006-1813
Phone: (202) 457-4900
Web Site: www.eia.org

Institute of Electrical and Electronic Engineers (IEEE)

The IEEE helps advance global prosperity by promoting the engineering process of creating, developing, integrating, sharing, and applying knowledge about electrical and information technologies and sciences for the benefit of humanity and the profession. IEEE provides the latest information and the best technical resources to members worldwide. Today, IEEE connects more than 350,000 professionals and students to the solutions to tomorrow's technology needs.

Address:
IEEE-USA
1828 L Street, NW, Suite 1202
Washington, D.C. 20036-5104
Phone: (202) 785-0017
Web Site: http://www.ieee.org/
Publications: IEEE Xplore, IEEE Spectrum

American Institute of Chemical Engineers (AIChE)
The American Institute of Chemical Engineers, AIChE, was founded in 1908. AIChE is a professional association of more than 50,000 members that provides leadership in advancing the chemical engineering profession. Its members are creative problem-solvers who use their scientific and technical knowledge to develop processes and design and operate plants to make useful products at a reasonable cost. Chemical engineers are also at the forefront of research to assure the safe and environmentally sound manufacture, use, and disposal of chemical products. AIChE fosters and disseminates chemical engineering knowledge, supports the professional and personal growth of its members, and applies the expertise of its members to address societal needs throughout the world.

Address:
3 Park Ave.
New York, NY 10016-5991
Phone: 1-800-AIChemE
Web Site: http://www.aiche.org/
Publications: AIChE Journal, Chemical Engineering Progress

Telecommunications Industry Association (TIA)
The Telecommunications Industry Association (TIA) is the leading trade association in the communications and information technology industry with proven strengths in market development, trade promotion, trade shows, domestic and international advocacy, standards development, and enabling e-business. Through its worldwide activities, the association facilitates business development opportunities and a competitive market environment. TIA provides a market-focused forum for its more than 1,100 member companies that manufacture or supply the products and services used in global communications.

Address:
Telecommunications Industry Association
2500 Wilson Blvd., Suite 300
Arlington, VA 22201
Phone: (703) 907-7700
Fax: (703) 907-7727
Web Site: http://www.tiaonline.org/
Publication: Industry Beat (weekly bulletin)

Society of Manufacturing Engineers (SME)
SME, headquartered in Dearborn, Michigan, is the world's leading professional society serving the manufacturing industries. Through its publications, expositions, professional development resources, and member programs, SME influences more than 500,000 manufacturing executives, managers, and engineers. Founded in 1932, SME has some 60,000 members in 70 countries and supports a network of hundreds of chapters worldwide.

Address:
International Headquarters
One SME Dr.
Dearborn, MI 48121
Phone: (800) 733-4763
Outside the U.S.: (313) 271-1500
Fax: (313) 271-2861
Web Site: www.sme.org
Publications: Forming & Fabricating, Manufacturing Engineering

Audio Engineering Society (AES)
The Audio Engineering Society (AES), now in its fifth decade, is the only professional society devoted exclusively to audio technology. Its membership of leading engineers, scientists, and other authorities has increased dramatically throughout the world, greatly boosting the society's stature and that of its members in a truly symbiotic relationship. The AES serves its members, the industry, and the public by stimulating and facilitating advances in the constantly changing field of audio. It encourages and disseminates new developments through annual technical meetings and exhibitions of professional equipment, and through the *Journal of the Audio Engineering Society*, the professional archival publication in the audio industry.

Address:
International Headquarters
60 East 42nd St., Room 2520
New York, NY 10165-2520
Phone: (212) 661-8528
Fax: (212) 682-0477
E-mail: *HQ@aes.org*
Web Site: http://www.aes.org/

BioWorld
http://www.bioworld.com/

BioWorld Online
3525 Piedmont Rd.
Building 6, Suite 400
Atlanta, GA 30305

Customer Service:
In the U.S. and Canada:
1-800-688-2421
Outside the U.S.:
1-404-262-5476
E-mail: customerservice@bioworld.com

PUBLISHING RESOURCES

Name	Location	Resource	Subject
BNA Books http://www.bna.com/bnabooks/	Washington, DC	Books	Licensing/IP
Computer Literacy Bookshops http://www.fatbrain.com/	San Jose, CA	Reports	Computing
Datapro Information Services http://www.gartnerweb.com/ public/static/datapro/main.html	Delran, NJ	Reports	Computing
Forward Concepts http://www.fwdconcepts.com/	Tempe, AZ	Books, Newsletters	DSP
Information Gatekeepers http://www.igigroup.com/	Boston, MA	Newsletters	Telecom
Knowledge Industry Publications http://www.pbimedia.com/ refresh.html	White Plains, NY	Books	Video/other
Mass High Tech http://www.masshightech.com/	Woburn, MA	Database	Software
Matthew Bender http://www.bender.com/	Albany, NY	Books	Licensing/IP
Meckler Corporation http://www.internet.com/	Westport, CT	Shows, Reports, other	Various
Phillips Business Information http://www.pbimedia.com/	Potomac, MD	Newsletters	Various
Prentice Hall Law & Business http://vig.prenhall.com/	Upper Saddle River, NJ	Books	Licensing/IP
Publications Resource Group PRGGuide.com	North Adams, MA	Several	Communications
Seybold Publications http://www.seyboldreport.com/	Media, PA	Reports, Newsletters	Multimedia, other
Technologic Partners http://www.technologicpartners. com	New York, NY	Reports, Newsletters	Various
TMA Associates http://www.tmaa.com/	Encino, CA	Reports, Newsletters	Speech Recognition
Van Nostrand Reinhold http://www.wiley.com	New York NY	Books	Communications
West Group http://www.westgroup.com/	Eagan MN	Books	Licensing/IP
John Wiley & Sons http://www.wiley.com	New York, NY	Books	Licensing/IP

BioVenture View
http://www.pjbpubs.com/bvv/

Company Locations:
Worldwide
BioVenture View
18/20 Hill Rise, Richmond
Surrey TW10 6UA, UK

U.S.
PharmaBooks Ltd
1775 Broadway, Suite 511
New York, NY 10019

Genesis Report
Adis' Business Intelligence division offers three newsletters addressing the broad spectrum of emerging technology, market development, and business development issues in the health care industry today. Each of these is thoroughly researched.

Web Site: http://www.adisinsight.com/default.asp
United States/Canada
Adis International Inc.
860 Town Center Dr.
Langhorne, PA 19047
Phone: (215) 741-5200
Fax: (215) 741-5202
E-mail: adisinsight@adis.com

Genetic Engineering News
Genetic Engineering News (GEN) is the source for news on biotechnology, bioregulation, bioprocess, bioresearch, and technology transfer. In addition to news and feature articles, each issue of GEN includes BioProcess Tutorials, New Products, Wall $treet Biobeat, Clinical Trials Update, Collaborations and Agreements, University Gene Beat, People, Calendar, and Biotechnology on the World Wide Web. GEN fuses industry, academia, and government, and fosters collaborations and agreements in the biotechnology industry. It is the industry standard.

Web Site: http://www.genengnews.com/

COMPANY INFORMATION

BioIndex
A continuously updated, fully searchable database. Tracks almost 4,000 products as they move through the medical industry's development pipeline.

Web Site: http://bioindex.com/

BioScan
Product information is divided into three areas —PET/Nuclear Medicine Equipment and Services, General Instrumentation for Biochemistry and Molecular Biology, and Service and Technical Support.

Web Site: http://BioScan.com/

Corporate Technology Directory
A comprehensive source of information on America's 50,000 technology manufacturers. Over 80% of the companies are privately held or operating units of larger companies. Company profiles are quite extensive, including details of ownership, executives, products, address, phone/fax/e-mail/sales, employee count, and past and future employment growth.

Address:
OneSource Information Services, Inc.
300 Baker Ave.
Concord, MA 01742
Phone: (978) 318-4300
Fax: (978) 318-4690

Web Site: http://www.corptech.com

Dun & Bradstreet
D&B Million Dollar Database provides the professional, marketer, and sales executive with information on approximately 1,600,000 U.S. and Canadian leading public and private businesses. Company information includes industry information with up to 24 individual 8-digit SICs, size criteria (employees and annual sales), type of ownership, principal executives, and biographies.

Web Site: http://www.dnb.com/

Pharmaprojects
Pharmaprojects is the leading source of global business intelligence on drugs in R&D and provides users with a comprehensive view of product development. Pharmaprojects monitors every significant new drug currently under development, tracking all new drug candidates under active international R&D—approximately 6,000 at any one time. Overall, Pharmaprojects contains details on over 26,000 new drug candidates that have been investigated since 1980, including those currently in research and those whose development has been discontinued.

Web Site: http://www.pjbpubs.com/pharma/

Recombinant Capital
The purpose of the ReCap Web site is to provide a resource to biotechnology executives who are involved with financing, business development, licensing, and

other strategic planning essential to the development and commercialization of biotechnology, pharmaceuticals, diagnostics, and medical devices. Although not specifically aimed at investors, sophisticated investors may appreciate good information and analysis of these factors as well.

Address:
Recombinant Capital, Inc.
2121 N. California Blvd., Suite 250
Walnut Creek, CA 94596
Phone: (925) 952-3870
Fax: (925) 952-3871
E-mail: *info@recap.com*
Web Site: http://www.recap.com/

Standard & Poor's
Standard & Poor's is the pre-eminent provider of independent financial information and analytical services. Real-time market data gives the world financial community high-caliber tools and information for financial decision making.

Web Site: http://www.standardpoor.com/

Thomas Register of American Manufacturers
A listing of over 168,000 companies (U.S. and Canada). Use of the online searchable database is free.

Web Site: http://www.thomasregister.com/

Value Line Publishing Inc.
Value Line publishes more than a dozen print and electronic products utilized by more than half a million investors for timely information on stocks, mutual funds, special situations, options, and convertibles. The company is best known for The Value Line Investment Survey, the most widely used independent investment service in the world.

Web Site: http://www.valueline.com/index.html

Venture Economics
Institutional investors, venture capital firms, investment banks, consulting firms, and notable media circles have identified Venture Economics as the indispensable source for accurate, complete, and timely coverage of investment, exit, and performance activity in the private equity industry. Its coverage of firms, funds, and companies is frequently sourced to support today's headlines in *The Wall Street Journal*, *The Red Herring*, *Forbes*, *The Industry Standard*, and other media outlets.

Web Site: http://www.ventureeconomics.com/

TYPICAL TRADE PUBLICATIONS

Name	Subject	Publisher	Location
Advanced Imaging	Imaging	Cygnus Business Media	Melville, NY
Communications News	Communications	Nelson Publishing	Nokomis, FL
Computerworld	Computing	CW Publishing	Framingham, MA
Electronic Musician	Audio	Intertec Publishing	Overland Park, KS
EQ	Audio	PSN Publications	Fort Washington, PA
InfoWorld	Computing	InfoWorld Publishing	New York, NY
Laser Focus World	Optics & Lasers	Penwell Publishing	Tulsa, OK
Macworld	Computing	Macworld Communications	San Mateo, CA
Medialine	Replication	Miller Freeman PSN	New York, NY
Nature	Science	Nature Publishing Group	New York, NY
New Media	Multimedia	HyperMedia Communications	London, England
PC World	Computing	PC World Communications	Manhasset, NY
Photonics Spectra	Optics & Lasers	Lauren Publishing	Pittsfield, MA
Pro Sound News	Audio	Miller Freeman PSN	New York, NY
Science	Science	American Association for the Advancement of Science	New York, NY
Sound & Communications	Duplication	Sound & Communications Pubs.	Washington DC
Streaming Media	Internet	Penton Media	San Francisco, CA
Surround Professional	Audio	Miller Freeman PSN	New York, NY
Systems Contractor News	Sound & Video Systems	United Entertainment Media	New York, NY
Upside	Hi-tech Business	Upside Media	San Francisco, CA
Windows	Computing	CMP Publications	Manhasset, NY
Wired	Multimedia	Wired Ventures	San Francisco, CA

TRADE SHOWS

The largest shows of interest include Comdex (computers), Semicon (semiconductors), and the Consumer Electronics Show (CES). A host of other shows specialize in the Internet, wireless technologies, professional audio, lasers, biotechnology, and many other subjects. The use of search engines and the Internet is a great way to find out more information about trade shows.

Appendix C

Annotated Sample License Agreements

The purpose of this appendix is to introduce the reader to the structure, subject matter, and typical wording of license agreements. The reader is cautioned not to use the sample agreements as templates for his or her license agreement; rather, they should be used as educational tools to illustrate some of the important concepts and techniques that could be used in an actual agreement. All license agreements should be reviewed by an IP attorney.

Two sample license agreements are reproduced with comments, observations, and possible variations for certain sections. The first is a hybrid agreement that would typically be used to license technology for use in hardware products. The technology licensed in the sample agreement is for digital signal processing (DSP); however, most of the wording would apply equally well to other technologies. The second is a computer software distribution agreement.

HYBRID TECHNOLOGY LICENSE AGREEMENT

A hybrid agreement licenses several types of intellectual property (in this case patents, trademarks, copyrights, and know-how) together. Although it is possible to license each individually, determining reasonable royalty rates is made more difficult by the decreasing life of the patents (lowering their value), the (hopefully) increasing value of the trademarks, possible eventual publication of the know-how, and so forth. By lumping all in one agreement, it is easier to defend the royalty rates by arguing that even though some of the licensed technology may have fallen in value, the value of other technology or of the trademarks has increased, making the rates reasonable. In addition, the licensee will have less incentive to challenge the licensed patents, as their obligation to pay royalties will not totally cease. See Chapter 7 for more information on license structure and further discussion of the benefits of hybrid and separate licenses.

Four broad classes of intellectual property are used in the agreement: patents (including applications), copyrights, know-how (everything technical not included in the previous two classifications), and trademarks. The reader is referred to Chapter 2 for further discussion of intellectual property. General provisions are included for providing transfer of technical information, training, joint development, and follow-up support. Marketing and sales rights are included in "Licenses Granted."

The wording of the sample agreement is adapted from several existing license agreements and from legal reference books (see bibliography).

The sample agreement is quite long; however, in some cases large sections of the text are not needed (e.g., if trademarks are not licensed), and there is some duplication of text to cover different situations. Actual agreements are usually shorter.

Each article of the sample agreement (and sometimes an individual section) is preceded by a discussion of the purpose of and the philosophy behind the proposed text. The explanations, which occur throughout the agreement, are set in italics.

A. Cover Page—Essential information and signatures can be included on the front page as shown below:

DIGITAL SIGNAL PROCESSOR SYSTEM LICENSE AGREEMENT

AN AGREEMENT BY AND BETWEEN

_____ (hereinafter called "LICENSOR")

of _____

and

_____ (hereinafter called "LICENSEE")

of _____

Facsimile telephone number of LICENSOR for transmission of quarterly royalty reports (Section 4.05):

LICENSOR's bank and account number for wire transfer of royalty payments (Section 4.05):

Bank:
Address:
Account Name:
Account Number:
ABA Number:

Identification of bank with respect to whose prime rate interest is calculated on overdue royalties (Section 4.06):

Address of LICENSEE for communications not otherwise specified (Section 8.04):

SIGNATURES:

On behalf of LICENSOR   On behalf of LICENSEE

By: ....   By:................................

Title: ....   Title: ....

Witnessed by: ....   Witnessed by: ....

....

Date: ....   Date: ....

Initial Payment: $

B. Index:

DIGITAL SIGNAL PROCESSING SYSTEM LICENSE AGREEMENT

INDEX

Preamble

Section 8.12—Company Representation and Warranty
Section 8.13—Execution

Appendix A—Scheduled Patents
Appendix B—Digital Signal Processing System
Appendix C—Preliminary Specifications for Digital Signal Processing System
Appendix D—Licensee Information Manual
Appendix E—Schedule for Development of Licensed Device
Appendix F—Schedule for Development of Licensed Product
Appendix G—Rates for Expenses Associated with Development of Licensed Product

C. Preamble—The preamble consists of "recitals" (whereas clauses) and should provide basic information on the licensor, the licensee, and the nature of the agreement. The example below could be used for a company that wants to use the DSP processor in their consumer products.

DIGITAL SIGNAL PROCESSING SYSTEM LICENSE AGREEMENT

WHEREAS, LICENSOR is engaged in the development, manufacture, and sale of integrated circuits (hereinafter referred to as "ICs") used in digital signal processing (hereinafter referred to as DSP) systems and has developed DSP systems useful for communications and for other applications;

WHEREAS, LICENSOR's DSP systems have acquired a reputation for excellence and LICENSOR's trademarks have acquired valuable goodwill;

WHEREAS, LICENSOR has licensed other companies to make, use, and sell consumer hardware and ICs incorporating LICENSOR's DSP systems and marked with LICENSOR's trademarks; and

WHEREAS, LICENSOR has developed a DSP system which uses new techniques for processing of signals in digital form with improved processing speed and reduced processor complexity;

WHEREAS, LICENSOR's DSP system and its manufacture are the subject of substantial know-how owned by LICENSOR;

WHEREAS, LICENSOR's DSP system and its manufacture embody inventive subject matter which is the subject of international patents and patent applications owned or licensable by LICENSOR,

WHEREAS, the manufacture and sale of LICENSOR's DSP system requires the reproduction of copyrighted works owned or licensable by LICENSOR;

WHEREAS, LICENSOR represents and warrants that it has rights to grant licenses under such know-how, patents, patent applications, and copyrighted works and under its trademarks;

WHEREAS, LICENSEE is engaged in the manufacture of consumer hardware products which utilize DSP technology;

WHEREAS, LICENSEE believes it can develop a substantial demand for products using LICENSOR's DSP system technology;

WHEREAS, LICENSEE desires a license to manufacture and sell products using LICENSOR's DSP system under LICENSOR's trademarks, know-how, copyrighted works, patents, and patent applications; and

WHEREAS, LICENSOR is willing to grant such a license under the terms and conditions set forth in this Agreement.

NOW, THEREFORE, it is agreed by and between LICENSOR and LICENSEE as follows:

A more modern way to open an agreement not utilizing "whereas" clauses follows:

AGREEMENT

Effective . . . . , ... , a California corporation, ..., a . . . . , agree as follows:

Article I - Background

(The information in the whereas clauses goes here)

D. Definitions—Accurate and complete definitions are very important, especially those for the product or technology being licensed, the price to be used to calculate royalties, and the licensed intellectual property. Some definitions can be more or less standard, but in many cases definitions must be drafted for each situation.

ARTICLE I

DEFINITIONS

Section 1.01—"LICENSOR" means . . . ., a corporation of the State of California, having a place of business as indicated on the title page of this Agreement, and its successors and assigns.

Section 1.02—"LICENSEE" means the corporation identified on the title page of this Agreement and any subsidiary thereof of whose ordinary voting shares more than 50% are controlled directly or indirectly by such corporation, but only so long as such control exists.

Note: By defining LICENSEE this way, extra wording is not required in the body of the agreement to cover subsidiaries. In some cases considering wholly owned subsidiaries to be covered by the agreement should present no problems, and in fact excluding them can result in extra administrative work when separate agreements are required for each subsidiary. In other cases, multiple agreements (and initial payments, calculation of quantity discounts, and so forth) with a licensee and its subsidiaries might be desirable.

Section 1.03—"Application" means an application for the protection of an invention or an industrial design; references to an "Application" shall be construed as references to applications for patents for inventions, inventors' certificates, utility certificates, utility models, patents or certificates of addition, inventors' certificates of addition, utility certificates of addition, design patents, and industrial design registrations.

Section 1.04—"Patent" means patents for inventions, inventors' certificates, utility certificates, utility models, patents or certificates of addition, inventors' certificates of addition, utility certificates of addition, design patents, and industrial design registrations.

Section 1.05—"Related Application" means an Application, whether international or in the same or another country or region, which

(1) is substantially the same as (e.g., it does not include any new matter in the sense of the United States Patent Law) an Application or Patent listed in Appendix A, entitled "Scheduled Patents and Applications," which is attached hereto and forms an integral part of this Agreement (e.g., without limiting the foregoing, a continuation

Application, a corresponding Application, an Application to reissue, or a refiled Application), or

(2) is substantially only a portion of (e.g., it contains less than an Application or Patent listed in Appendix A and, it does not include any new matter in the sense of the United States Patent Law) an Application or Patent listed in Appendix A (e.g., a divisional Application, or a corresponding or refiled Application in the nature of a divisional Application).

Section 1.06—"Related Patent" means:
(1) a Patent granted on an Application listed in Appendix A,
(2) a Patent granted on a Related Application,
(3) a reissue of a Patent of Sections 1.06(1) or 1.06(2), and
(4) a reexamination certificate of a Patent of Sections 1.06(1), 1.06(2), or 1.06(3).

Section 1.07—"Scheduled Patents" means the Applications and Patents listed in Appendix A together with Related Applications and Related Patents.

Applications and Patents which contain not only common subject matter but also additional subject matter going beyond the disclosure of Applications and Patents of this Section (e.g., without limiting the foregoing, a continuation-in-part Application, or a corresponding or refiled Application in the nature of a continuation-in-part Application) shall be deemed to be Scheduled Patents only with respect to that portion of their subject matter common to the Applications and Patents of this Section.

Note: These sections (and Appendix A) define what patents are included in the agreement very precisely.

Section 1.08—"DSP System Specifications" means the specifications for the DSP System, comprising the claims and teachings of the Scheduled Patents, the DSP System operating parameters as specified in Appendix B entitled "DSP System," the "Preliminary Specifications for DSP System" as specified in Appendix C, the Licensed Copyrighted Works and the Know-How. Appendices B and C are attached hereto and form an integral part of this Agreement.

Note: Additional sections (and Appendices) may be required if more than one technology is being licensed.

Section 1.09—"Licensed Trademark" means one or more of the following: (a) the word mark "[trademark]", and
(b) the device mark "[trademark]".

Section 1.10—"Licensed Device" means a DSP System circuit having DSP System Specifications, whether made in discrete component, integrated circuit, or other forms, for processing digital signals and performing related control and interface functions.

Section 1.11—"Licensed Product" means a complete ready-to-use electronic product which:
(1) contains one or more Licensed Devices, and
(2) is intended or designed for use in transmitting, receiving, or processing a digital signal in communications or other related systems.

A Licensed Product is not a semiconductor chip, a partially assembled product, a product in kit form, or a knocked-down or semi-knocked-down product.

Note: Delineating between licensed devices and licensed products can be useful because a) higher royalties are paid for products containing more licensed devices (royalties are based on the number of licensed devices in a product) and b) it is easy to distinguish between the final product (which bears the trademarks and therefore is subject to quality control) and the processor. This concept is useful in some cases (especially when trademarks are licensed), but it will be inappropriate in others.

Section 1.12—"Patent Rights" means:

(1) the Scheduled Patents; and

(2) such Patents and Applications directed to Licensed Products that LICENSOR may own or gain rights to license during the term of this Agreement and which LICENSOR may agree to include in the Patent Rights without payment of additional compensation by LICENSEE.

The Patent Rights do not include such other Applications and Patents as LICENSOR does not agree to include in the Patent Rights without payment of additional compensation by LICENSEE.

Note: Again, this narrowly defines what patents are included in the agreement and allows the inclusion of future patents as licensor sees fit. In some cases this definition could be modified to include certain future patents in the patent rights.

Section 1.13—"Know-How" means all proprietary information, trade secrets, skills, experience, recorded or unrecorded, accumulated by LICENSOR, from time to time prior to and during the term of this Agreement, or licensable by LICENSOR, relating to the Licensed Devices and the Licensed Products and all designs, drawings, reports, memoranda, blue-prints, specifications, and the like, prepared by LICENSOR or by others and licensable by LICENSOR, insofar as LICENSOR deems the same to relate to and be useful for the development, design, manufacture, sale, or use of Licensed Products. Know-How does not include Licensed Copyrighted Works, whether or not published.

Note: Know-how does not include licensed copyrighted works because of the different (three year) treatment of know-how.

Section 1.14—"Confidential Information" means non-technical proprietary information of LICENSOR or LICENSEE, including, without limiting the foregoing, marketing information, product plans, business plans, royalty, and sales information.

Note: Know-how and confidential information have been separated into technical and non-technical parts. Technical information is subject to export control requirements, whereas non-technical information is not.

Section 1.15—"Non-Patent Country" means a country in which there do not exist, with respect to a Licensed Product, any Scheduled Patents including any pending Application or unexpired Patent, which, but for the licenses herein granted, is (or in the case of an Application, would be if it were an issued Patent) infringed by the manufacture, and/or use, lease, or sale of such Licensed Product.

Note: In order to allow licensing in countries where patents have not been filed or where patents have expired, a separate (lower) royalty structure is introduced. In this case, the license covers trademarks, know-how, and copyrights.

Section 1.16—"LICENSEE's Trade Name and Trademarks" means any trade name or trademark used and owned by LICENSEE.

Section 1.17—"Other-Trademark Purchaser" means any customer of LICENSEE who, with LICENSEE's knowledge, intends to resell, use, or lease the Licensed Products under a trademark other than LICENSEE's Trade Name and Trademarks.

Note: Original Equipment Manufacturing (OEM) business, where a licensee manufactures products under another company's trademark, is allowed.

Section 1.18—"Licensed Copyrighted Works" means all copyrighted works owned by LICENSOR or owned by others and which LICENSOR has the right to sublicense, relating to the DSP System and the reproduction of which are required in order for LICENSEE to make or have made for it Licensed Products, and to use, lease, and sell the same. Licensed Copyrighted Works exclude Mask Works fixed in a semiconductor chip product.

Note: Mask Works are protected under the Semiconductor Chip Protection Act, and can also be licensed if necessary (as Licensed Mask Works).

Section 1.19—The "Consumer Price Index" means the U.S. City Average Index (base of 1984-1986=100) of the Consumer Price Index for All Urban Consumers as published by the Department of Labor, Bureau of Labor Statistics of the United States Government. In the event that said Index ceases to be published under its present name or form or ceases to be published by the same government entity, reference shall be made to the most similar index then available.

Note: If a long-term agreement is envisioned, royalties can be adjusted by a cost-of-living factor so that inflation-adjusted royalty rates remain constant. This strategy is appropriate when royalty rates are fixed, but usually not necessary when the royalty is a percentage of the net sales price, in which case the product price (and thus the royalty) will increase with inflation.

Section 1.20   The "Effective Date" of this Agreement is the date of execution hereof by the last party to execute the Agreement, or, if this Agreement requires validation by any governmental or quasi-governmental body, the "Effective Date" is the date of validation of this Agreement.

Note: In many agreements the royalty paid is a percentage of the sales price of the Licensed Product. In this case a precise definition of the sales price is needed. Usually rebates, sales commissions, returns, and other expenses associated with product sales are allowed to be deducted for purposes of calculating the sales price. In addition, licensed products are often transferred between subsidiaries at a price which may be either lower or higher than the market price; the method for determining the sales price in such cases should be outlined in the definition.

E. Licenses Granted: Two examples are given, the first covering patents, trademarks, copyrights, and know-how and allowing for reduced royalties in non-patent countries and the second covering patents, copyrights, and know-how. The first wording basically charges royalties for use of the patents and allows use of the other IP as long as those royalties are paid, while the second lumps everything together and includes limited exclusivity.

Although not shown in these examples, it is often beneficial to separate the patent license (and, therefore, royalty payments) from the license for other intellectual property. When this is done, the license will remain (partially) in effect even if the patents expire or are invalidated.

Example 1) ARTICLE II

LICENSES GRANTED

Section 2.01—Licenses Granted to LICENSEE

LICENSOR hereby grants to LICENSEE:

(1) a personal, non-transferable, indivisible, and non-exclusive license throughout the world under the Patent Rights, subject to the conditions set forth and LICENSEE's performance of its obligations, including paying royalties due, to make or have made for it Licensed Products, and to use, lease, and sell the same;

Note: A license to make includes a license to have made, so subcontracting cannot be forbidden. Handling of confidential information when subcontracting should be addressed.

(2) a personal, non-transferable, indivisible, and non-exclusive license throughout the world to use the Know-How and to reproduce the Licensed Copyrighted Works in connection with the design, manufacture, and sale of the Licensed Products and to use the Licensed Trademarks on the Licensed Products and in connection with the advertising and offering for sale of Licensed Products bearing one or more of the Licensed Trademarks subject to the conditions set forth in this Agreement and LICENSEE's performance of its obligations:

(i) without any further payment of royalties with respect to use of the Know-How, Licensed Trademarks, or reproduction of the Licensed Copyrighted Works in countries in which there is an Application or Patent included in the Scheduled Patents, so long as the license under the Patent Rights in sub-part (1) of this Section remains in force and royalties are payable thereunder;

(ii) but, as provided in Section 4.06, with the payment of royalties for the use of the Know-How, Licensed Trademarks, or Licensed Copyrighted Works in each other country unless LICENSEE exercises its option, set forth in Section 6.03, to terminate its license under this Agreement with respect to a Non-Patent Country, and

(3) a personal, non-transferable, indivisible, non-exclusive, and royalty-free license throughout the world under the Patent Rights to use the Know-How and to reproduce the Licensed Copyrighted Works in connection with the manufacture, use, lease, and sale of spare parts solely for the repair of Licensed Products manufactured by LICENSEE under this Agreement.

Example 2) ARTICLE II

LICENSES GRANTED

Section 2.01—Licenses Granted to LICENSEE

LICENSOR hereby grants to LICENSEE:

(1) a personal, non-transferable, indivisible, and non-exclusive license throughout the world under the Patent Rights to make Licensed Devices and to use, lease, and sell the same, and to use the Know-How and to reproduce the Licensed Copyrighted Works in connection with the design, manufacture, and sale of the Licensed Devices subject to the conditions set forth and LICENSEE's performance of its obligations, including paying royalties due;

(2) a personal, non-transferable, and indivisible license throughout the world under the Patent Rights to make Licensed Products and to use, lease, and sell the same, and to use the Know-How and to reproduce the Licensed Copyrighted Works in connection with the design, manufacture, and sale of the Licensed Products, subject to the conditions set forth and LICENSEE's performance of its obligations, including paying royalties due:

(i) which is exclusive in _____, and;

(ii) which is non-exclusive in the rest of the world except for _____, where no license is granted; and

(3) the right to sublicense the Patent Rights in _____.

Note:The next section deals with what is not licensed. The first example is intended for a licensing situation in which a manufacturer is making consumer products incorporating licensed technology and bearing licensed trademarks, while the second is for an integrated-circuit-development license.

Example 1) Section 2.02—Limitation of Licenses Granted

Notwithstanding the licenses granted under Section 2.01:

(1) no license is granted to lease, sell, transfer, or otherwise dispose of any part of a Licensed Product, including, without limiting the foregoing, a semiconductor chip specially adapted for use in a Licensed Product, which part (a) is a material part of an invention which is the subject of a Scheduled Patent and which part is not a staple article or commodity of commerce suitable for substantial non-infringing use or (b) is not a spare part solely for the repair of a Licensed Product manufactured by Licensee under this Agreement;

(2) no license is granted under this Agreement to lease, sell, transfer, or otherwise dispose of any partially assembled products, products in kit form, and knocked-down or semi-knocked-down products;

(3) no license is granted under this Agreement with respect to LICENSOR's other proprietary technologies;

(4) no license is granted under this Agreement to use any Licensed Trademark in connection with offering for sale or in advertising and/or informational material relating to any Licensed Product which is not marked with the mark specified in Section 3.01(1) of this Agreement;

(5) no license is granted under this Agreement with respect to the use of any Licensed Trademark on or in connection with products other than Licensed Products;

Note: the trademarks can only be used on Licensed Products and, if they are used, must be used as specified.

(6) no right is granted with respect to LICENSOR's trade name "[licensor]" except with respect to the use of said tradename on and in connection with Licensed Products in the trademark acknowledgment and license notice required by Sections 3.01(6) and 3.09, respectively;

(7) no license is granted to prepare, make, or have made derivative works based on the Licensed Copyrighted Works; and

(8) no right to grant sublicenses is granted under this Agreement.

Example 2) Section 2.02—Limitation of Licenses Granted

Notwithstanding the licenses granted under Section 2.01:

(1) no license is granted under this agreement with respect to LICENSOR's other proprietary technologies;

(2) no right is granted with respect to LICENSOR's trade name "[licensor]" except with respect to the use of said trade name on and in connection with Licensed Products in the license notice required by Section 3.09;

(3) no right to grant sublicenses except as specifically laid down in Section 2.01(2) is granted under this agreement; and

(4) notwithstanding the provisions hereunder, LICENSOR shall have no obligation to LICENSEE to grant a license to use nor to disclose know-how developed based on a third party's proprietary information, to the extent prohibited by the secrecy agreement and/or custom development agreement between LICENSOR and said third party.

F. Other obligations: This section contains provisions regarding trademark usage and protection, required markings on licensed products, and handling of know-how and confidential information. Sections 3.01, 2, and 3 are not required and Section 3.05 can be greatly simplified if trademarks are not licensed.

Licensee obligations that cannot be required include:

1. Exclusive or assignment grant-back of improvements. Nonexclusive grant-backs are allowed.

2. Licensee's agreement not to contest the licensed patents. They have the right to contest and to not pay royalties during the time that the lawsuit is pending.

ARTICLE III

OTHER OBLIGATIONS OF THE LICENSOR AND LICENSEE

Section 3.01—Use of Licensed Trademarks

The Licensed Trademarks have acquired a reputation for high quality among professionals and consumers around the world. The performance capability of the DSP System is such that LICENSOR is willing to allow the use of the Licensed Trademarks on Licensed Products and in connection with their advertising and marketing to indicate that the quality of such products conforms with the general reputation for high quality associated with the Licensed Trademarks. LICENSEE's use of the Licensed Trademarks is optional, however, if LICENSEE opts to use one or more Licensed Trademarks, such use shall be subject to the obligations of this Agreement as well as detailed regulations issued from time to time by LICENSOR. Detailed regulations current at the time of execution of this Agreement and additional to those set forth in this Agreement are set forth in the section entitled "Trademark Usage" in the Licensee Information Manual of Appendix D which is attached hereto and forms an integral part of this Agreement. LICENSEE shall comply with the requirements of the body of this Agreement and those of the Licensee Information Manual of Appendix D and such additional regulations as LICENSOR may issue and shall ensure that its subsidiaries, agents, distributors, and dealers throughout the world comply with such requirements (in the case of any inconsistencies among the body of this Agreement, the Licensee Information Manual of Appendix D and any additional regulations, the body of this Agreement shall govern):

(1) LICENSEE shall prominently mark the Licensed Product on the fascia thereof in the following way:

[Logo]

(2) The mark specified in subsection (1) of this Section 3.01, shall also be used at least once in a prominent manner in all advertising and promotions for such Licensed Product; such usages shall be no less prominent and in the same relative size as the most prominent other trademark(s) appearing on such Licensed Product or in the advertising and promotion thereof.

(3) LICENSEE may not use the Licensed Trademarks in advertising and promotion of a product not marked in accordance with subsection (1) of this Section 3.01, even if such product is a Licensed Product.

(4) In every use of a Licensed Trademark, except on the main control surface of a Licensed Product, LICENSEE shall give notice to the public that such Licensed Trademark is a trademark by using the superscript letters "TM" after the respective trademark, or by use of the trademark registration symbol "®" (the capital letter R enclosed in a circle) as a

superscript after the respective trademark. LICENSOR shall inform LICENSEE as to which notice form is to be used.

(5) LICENSOR's ownership of Licensed Trademarks shall be indicated whenever used by LICENSEE, whether use is on a product or on descriptive, instructional, advertising, or promotional material, by the most relevant of the following acknowledgment: "'[trademark]' is a trademark of [licensor]" On Licensed Products such words shall be used on an exposed surface, such as the back or the bottom. LICENSEE shall use its best efforts to ensure that such an acknowledgement appears in advertising at the retail level.

(6) Licensed Trademarks shall always be used in accordance with established United States practices for the protection of trademark and service mark rights, unless the requirements in the country or jurisdiction in which the product will be sold are more stringent, in which case the practice of such country or jurisdiction shall be followed. In no event shall any Licensed Trademark be used in any way that suggests or connotes that it is a common, descriptive, or generic designation. Whenever the word "[trademark]" is used, the first letter shall be upper-case. The word "[trademark]" shall be used only as an adjective referring to a digital signal processing product, never as a noun or in any other usage which may contribute to a generic meaning thereof. In descriptive, instructional, advertising, or promotional material or media relating to Licensed Products, LICENSEE must use the Licensed Trademarks and expressions which include the Licensed Trademark "[trademark]" with an appropriate generic or descriptive term (e.g., "[trademark] digital signal processor," etc.), with reference to Licensed Products and their use.

(7) All uses of the Licensed Trademarks are subject to approval by LICENSOR. LICENSOR reserves the right to require LICENSEE to submit proposed uses to LICENSOR for written approval prior to actual use. Upon request of LICENSOR, LICENSEE shall submit to LICENSOR samples of its own usage of the Licensed Trademarks and usage of the Licensed Trademarks by its subsidiaries, agents, distributors, and dealers.

(8) Licensed Trademarks shall be used in a manner that distinguishes them from other trademarks, service marks, symbols, or trade names, including LICENSEE's Trade Name and Trademarks.

(9) LICENSEE may not use the Licensed Trademarks on and in connection with products that do not meet LICENSOR's quality standards.

(10) LICENSEE may not use the Licensed Trademarks on and in connection with products other than Licensed Products.

Section 3.02—Ownership of the Licensed Trademarks

LICENSEE acknowledges the validity and exclusive ownership by LICENSOR of the Licensed Trademarks.

LICENSEE further acknowledges that it owns no rights in the Licensed Trademarks nor in the trade name "[trademark]."

LICENSEE acknowledges and agrees that all rights that it may accrue in the Licensed Trademarks and in the trade name "[trademark]" will inure to the benefit of LICENSOR.

LICENSEE further agrees that it will not file any application for registration of the Licensed Trademarks or "[trademark]" in any country, region, or under any arrangement or treaty. LICENSEE also agrees that it will not use nor will it file any application to register in any country, region, or under any arrangement or treaty any mark, symbol or phrase, in any language, which is confusingly similar to the Licensed Trademarks or "[licensor]."

Section 3.03—Maintenance of Trademark Rights

The expense of obtaining and maintaining Licensed Trademark registrations shall be borne by LICENSOR. LICENSOR, as it deems necessary, will advise LICENSEE of the grant of registration of such trademarks. As LICENSOR deems necessary, LICENSEE and LICENSOR will comply with applicable laws and practices of the country of registration, including, without limiting the foregoing, the marking with notice of registration and the recording of LICENSEE as a registered or licensed user of such trademarks. The expense of registering or recording LICENSEE as a registered user or otherwise complying with the laws of any country pertaining to such registration or the recording of trademark agreements shall be borne by LICENSEE. LICENSEE shall advise LICENSOR of all countries where Licensed Products are sold, leased, or used.

Note: The next section outlines what actions should be taken when notified of infringement. The first wording requires the licensee to inform the licensor and assist when asked, but requires the licensor to do nothing. Adding the second wording requires the licensor to settle all infringement that affects licensee's use of the licensed technology or refund royalties paid. In general, the licensor should not allow the licensee to force litigation due to third party infringement, as this can damage the licensed patents (the infringement should be substantial before litigation is initiated).

Example 1) Section 3.04—Patent, Trademark, and Copyright Enforcement

LICENSEE shall immediately inform LICENSOR of all infringements, potential or actual, which may come to its attention, of the Patent Rights, Licensed Trademarks, or Licensed Copyrighted Works. It shall be the exclusive responsibility of LICENSOR, at its own expense, to terminate, compromise, or otherwise act at its discretion with respect to such infringements. LICENSEE agrees to cooperate with LICENSOR by furnishing, without charge, except out-of-pocket expenses, such evidence, documents, and testimony as may be required therein.

Additional Wording for Section 3.04:

3.04(2)—In the event of the institution of any suit against LICENSEE alleging that LICENSEE's manufacture, use, or sale of Licensed Devices or Licensed Products violates any intellectual property right of any third party (hereinafter "Third Party Rights"), or shall become the subject of claim for violation of Third Party rights, LICENSEE shall promptly notify LICENSOR of such alleged violation.

3.04(3)—Following such notice, LICENSOR agrees, at its own expense and option, to defend or to settle any such claim, suit, or proceeding brought against LICENSEE to the extent that the alleged violation is due to infringement of the Patent Rights, Licensed Copyrighted Works, or Know-How. LICENSOR shall have sole control of any such action or settlement negotiations, and LICENSOR agrees to pay, subject to the limitations hereinafter set forth, any final judgment entered against LICENSEE on the issue of such violation of Third Party Rights, and any settlement payment as a result of such negotiation conducted by LICENSOR, in any such suit or proceeding defended by LICENSOR. LICENSEE agrees that LICENSOR, at its sole option, shall be relieved of the foregoing obligation unless LICENSEE notifies LICENSOR promptly in writing of such claim, suit, or proceeding and gives LICENSOR authority to proceed as contemplated herein, and at LICENSOR's expense, gives its best efforts assistance to settle and/or defend any such claim, suit, or proceeding.

3.04(4)—In the event of any adjudication that the Patent Rights, the Licensed Copyrighted Works, the Know-How, or any part thereof violates any such Third Party Rights, and if the manufacture, use, and sale of such Licensed Device or Licensed Product is enjoined, LICENSOR shall, at its option and expense:

(i) Procure for LICENSEE the right under such Third Party Rights to manufacture, use, and sell Licensed Devices and Licensed Products, or

(ii) Modify the Patent Rights, Licensed Copyrighted Works, or Know-How to eliminate the infringement of such Third Party Rights; or

(iii) Refund an equitable portion of the license fee paid by LICENSEE to LICENSOR hereunder based upon the relative value of the enjoined Patent Rights, Licensed Copyrighted Works, or Know-How with respect to the Patent Rights, Licensed Copyrighted Works, or Know-How licensed hereunder and the remaining commercial life of such enjoined Patent Rights, Licensed Copyrighted Works, or Know-How.

3.04(5)—LICENSOR's obligation pursuant to this Section 3.04 shall not exceed the total amounts paid by LICENSEE under Article 4 to the time in question, provided, however, that LICENSOR shall from time to time advise LICENSEE with respect to the handling of such action or settlement negotiation and that if the settlement would impose on LICENSEE any payment of consideration to LICENSOR or such third party exceeding the down payment provided for in Article 4, it shall be subject to LICENSEE's prior consent.

Section 3.05—Other-Trademark Purchasers

To the extent only that technical standardization, equipment or signal source interchangeability, product identification and usage of the Licensed Trademarks are affected, the following conditions shall apply if LICENSEE sells or leases Licensed Products on a mass basis to an Other-Trademark Purchaser who does not hold a license with terms and conditions substantially similar to this Agreement. LICENSEE shall inform LICENSOR of the name, place of business, trademarks, and trade names of the Other-Trademark Purchaser before such Other-Trademark Purchaser sells, leases, or uses Licensed Products. LICENSEE shall obtain agreement from such Other-Trademark Purchaser not to modify, install, use, lease, sell, provide written material for or about, advertise, or promote Licensed Products in any way which is in conflict with any provision of this Agreement. It shall be the responsibility of LICENSEE to inform the Other-Trademark Purchaser of the provisions of this Agreement, to notify such Other-Trademark Purchaser that the provisions of this Agreement shall be applicable, through LICENSEE, in the same way as if the Licensed Products were sold by LICENSEE under LICENSEE's Trade Names and Trademarks, to ensure by all reasonable means that such provisions are adhered to and, if requested by LICENSOR, to provide to LICENSOR samples on a loan basis of the Other-Trademark Purchaser's embodiment of the Licensed Products, as well as copies of such Other-Trademark Purchaser's advertising, public announcements, literature, instruction manuals, and the like.

Section 3.06—Patent Marking

LICENSEE shall mark each Licensed Product in the form, manner, and location specified by LICENSOR, with one or more patent numbers of Patents in such countries under which a license is granted under this Agreement.

Note: In some licensing situations the types of copies of the copyrighted works made by the licensee can be restricted (as in section 3.08, example 1). See Example 1 below. When developing and manufacturing integrated circuits, the licensee may very well have to make various types of copies; if given the right to do so, the licensee must be required to place the correct notice on all copies. Example 2 covers this situation. The right to copy should only be granted when necessary.

Example 1) Section 3.07   Copyright Notice

3.07(1)—Where Applied—LICENSEE shall apply the copyright notice specified in subsection 3.07(2) of this Section 3.07:

(a) to all Licensed Products in such a manner that the first use of the Licensed Product by a purchaser thereof requires the breaking of a wrapping or seal prominently displaying the copyright notice; and

(b) to all media in which the program is distributed as permitted by this Agreement, whether as an integral part of a Licensed Product or as a spare part solely for the repair of a Licensed Product.

3.07(2)—Form of Notice—LICENSEE shall apply the following copyright notice as required in subsection 3.07(1) of this Section 3.07:

This product contains one or more programs protected under international and U.S. copyright laws as unpublished works. They are confidential and proprietary to [licensor]. Their reproduction or disclosure, in whole or in part, or the production of derivative works therefrom without the express permission of [licensor] is prohibited. Copyright [year] by [licensor]. All rights reserved.

Example 2) Section 3.07—Copyright Notice

3.07(1)—Where Applied—LICENSEE shall apply the copyright notice specified in subsection 3.07(2) of this Section 3.07:

(a) to all Licensed Devices; and

(b) as a structure (metal polygons) to the layout of the Licensed Devices; and

(c) to all printed copies made of the Licensed Copyrighted Works; and

(d) to all technical information relating to the Licensed Devices.

3.07(2)—Form of Notice—LICENSEE shall apply the following copyright notice:

(i) as required in subsections 3.07(1)(a) and (b) of this Section 3.07:

The letter "c" enclosed in a circle (the "copyright sign") followed by the word "[licensor]".

(ii) as required in subsections 3.07(1)(c) and (d) of this Section 3.07:

Notice: contains one or more programs protected under international and U.S. copyright laws as unpublished works, which are confidential and proprietary to [licensor]. Their reproduction or disclosure, in whole or in part, or the production of derivative works therefrom without the express permission of [licensor] is prohibited. Copyright [year] by [licensor]. All rights reserved.

Note: The first wording of Section 3.08, along with Section 3.10, is intended for product licensing. The second wording (with Section 3.10 deleted) would be appropriate for an integrated-circuit-development agreement.

Example 1) Section 3.08—Furnishing of Copyrighted Works; Use of Copyrighted Works

Subject to any restrictions under the export control regulations of the United States or any other applicable restrictions, LICENSOR will promptly after the Effective Date, furnish to LICENSEE copies of all programs constituting the Copyrighted Works in the form of object code (machine readable code). LICENSEE agrees to use such programs only for the purpose of programming read only memories (ROMs) forming an integral part of Licensed Products and constituting spare parts solely for the repair of Licensed Products. LICENSEE agrees (1) it will not otherwise reproduce Copyrighted Works, in whole or in part, (2) it will not prepare derivative works from Copyrighted Works, and (3) it will not disclose the Copyrighted Works, in whole or in part. LICENSEE further agrees that it will not decompile or otherwise reverse engineer the object code constituting the Licensed Copyrighted Works, or any portion thereof.

Upon termination of this Agreement, LICENSEE shall promptly return to LICEN-

SOR, at LICENSEE's expense, all documents and things supplied to LICENSEE as Licensed Copyrighted Works, as well as all copies and reproductions thereof.

Example 2) Section 3.08—Furnishing and Use of Copyrighted Works and Know-How

3.08(1)—By LICENSOR

Subject to any restrictions under the export control regulations of the United States or any other applicable restrictions, LICENSOR will promptly after the Effective Date, furnish to LICENSEE:

(1) copies of all programs constituting the Copyrighted Works in the form of object code (machine readable code); and

(2) copies of all documents and things comprising the Know-How; and

(3) when requested by LICENSEE, provide, as LICENSOR deems reasonable, consulting services regarding design considerations and general advice relating to the Licensed Devices and Licensed Products and the sale and use thereof, for all of which LICENSEE will reimburse LICENSOR for travel and reasonable per diem expenses.

3.08(2)—By LICENSEE

LICENSEE shall have the right to make copies of the Licensed Copyrighted Works for use in developing and manufacturing Licensed Devices subject to the marking requirements of Section 3.07.

During the term of this Agreement, LICENSEE agrees to furnish LICENSOR in writing all updates, improvements, or modifications made by LICENSEE to the Copyrighted Works and Know-How delivered to LICENSEE under Section 3.08(1). LICENSOR shall bear the actual expenses incurred by LICENSEE in connection with preparation and transfer of the documentation on such updates, improvements or modifications.

LICENSEE shall have the right to apply for patents and/or utility model rights and to register mask work rights in any country of the world relating to any products which LICENSEE may develop using the Copyrighted Works and Know-How during the life of this Agreement. When LICENSEE files application or makes registration, LICENSEE shall submit to LICENSOR within ninety (90) days thereafter a copy of such application or registration. This right of LICENSEE shall not limit LICENSOR's patent, utility model, copyright, or mask work rights in the Patent Rights, Copyrighted Works, or the Know-How.

LICENSEE further agrees to grant to LICENSOR a royalty-free license to use and incorporate such updates, improvements, or modification for the development, manufacture, use, and sale of LICENSOR's products.

Note: When an improvement is made that affects a technology that has become a standard, it is important that the rights to the improvement be made available to all companies licensing the core technology. If not, the improvement is of limited worth, as all licensees cannot use it. Additionally, improvements of this type can be used by the licensee, for all intents and purposes, to make a nonexclusive license exclusive. Therefore, the licensor should not only have the right to use the improvements in its products but should also have the right to sublicense the improvements to other licensees. In this case the licensor can give the licensee a share of the royalties obtained from sublicensing. See the "Improvements Pool" section at the end for another approach to this problem.

Section 3.09—License Notice

On all Licensed Products, LICENSEE shall acknowledge that the Licensed Products are manufactured under license from LICENSOR. The following notice shall be used by

LICENSEE on an exposed surface, such as the back or the bottom, of all Licensed Products: "DSP System manufactured under license from [licensor]." Such notice shall also be used in all instruction and servicing manuals unless such acknowledgment is clearly and unambiguously given in the course of any textual descriptions or explanations.

Section 3.10—Furnishing of Know-How

Subject to any restrictions under the export control regulations of the United States or any other applicable restrictions, LICENSOR will promptly after the Effective Date, furnish to LICENSEE:

(1) copies of all documents and things comprising the Know-How; and

(2) when requested by LICENSEE, provide, as LICENSOR deems reasonable, consulting services regarding design considerations and general advice relating to the Licensed Products and the sale and use thereof, for all of which LICENSEE will reimburse LICENSOR for travel and reasonable per diem expenses.

Section 3.11—Use of Know-How and Confidential Information

3.11(1)   By LICENSEE

LICENSEE shall use all Know-How and Confidential Information obtained heretofore or hereafter from LICENSOR solely for the purpose of manufacturing and selling Licensed Products under this Agreement, shall not use such Know-How or Confidential Information in an unauthorized way, and shall not divulge such Know-How or Confidential Information or any portion thereof to third parties, unless such Know-How or Confidential Information (a) was known to LICENSEE prior to its obtaining the same from LICENSOR; (b) becomes known to LICENSEE from sources other than either directly or indirectly from LICENSOR; or (c) becomes public knowledge other than by breach of this Agreement by LICENSEE or by another licensee of LICENSOR. The obligations of this subsection 3.11(1) shall cease three (3) years from the date on which such Know-How or Confidential Information are acquired by LICENSEE from LICENSOR under this Agreement.

Upon termination of this Agreement, with respect to Know-How or Confidential Information subject to the obligations of this subsection 3.11(1), LICENSEE shall promptly return to LICENSOR, at LICENSEE's expense, all documents and things supplied to LICENSEE as Know-How, as well as all copies and reproductions thereof.

Example 1) 3.11(2)—By LICENSOR

Except as provided by Article IV of this Agreement, LICENSEE is not obligated to disclose to LICENSOR any information that it deems proprietary or confidential. Except as provided by Article IV of this Agreement, LICENSOR has no obligation to treat in confidence, nor to restrict, in any way, the use, reproduction, or publication of information obtained from LICENSEE, including, without limiting the foregoing, information obtained by LICENSOR in the course of providing consulting services under Section 3.10(2) of this Agreement and information obtained by LICENSOR in the course of exercising its right to maintain quality control over LICENSEE's Licensed Products under Sections 5.01 and 5.02 of this Agreement.

Example 2) 3.11(2)—By LICENSOR

Except as provided in Section 3.08(2) of this Agreement, LICENSEE is not obligated to disclose to LICENSOR any information that it deems proprietary or confidential. Except for information provided under Section 3.08(2) of this Agreement, LICENSOR has no obligation to treat in confidence, nor to restrict, in any way, the use, reproduction, or publication of information obtained from LICENSEE, including, without limiting the foregoing, information obtained by LICENSOR in the course of providing consulting services under Section 3.08(1) of this Agreement.

LICENSOR shall use all Know-How and Confidential Information obtained from LICENSEE under the provisions of Section 3.08(2) of this Agreement heretofore or hereafter solely for the purpose of manufacturing and selling ICs, shall not use such Know-How or Confidential Information in an unauthorized way, and shall not divulge such Know-How or Confidential Information or any portion thereof to third parties, unless such Know-How or Confidential Information (a) was known to LICENSOR prior to its obtaining the same from LICENSEE; (b) becomes known to LICENSOR from sources other than either directly or indirectly from LICENSEE; or (c) becomes public knowledge other than by breach of this Agreement by LICENSOR. The obligations of this subsection 3.11(2) shall cease three (3) years from the date on which such Know-How or Confidential Information are acquired by LICENSOR from LICENSEE under this Agreement.

Note: In Example 1 there is no obligation for the licensee to provide any know-how or confidential information, and licensor has no obligation to treat any information received as confidential. This approach, which provides licensor with the best protection, is good for situations where information will flow only from the licensor to the licensee, but will not work when joint development is envisioned, in which case Example 2 can be used. See Chapter 2 for more details on handling confidential information.

3.12—Explanation and Training

LICENSOR shall provide to LICENSEE's technical personnel, at no additional charge, full disclosure including explanations and training concerning the Know-How and Copyrighted Works delivered to LICENSEE under Sections 3.10 and 3.08. Such explanation and training shall be furnished at LICENSOR's main office and/or other appropriate location in the most appropriate manner so that LICENSEE's technical personnel may be able to understand and utilize said information fully and in reasonable detail. LICENSEE, however, shall not interfere with LICENSOR's normal business operations. The number of days and LICENSEE's technical personnel sent to LICENSOR shall be limited to ten (10) days at LICENSOR's facility for a group of up to six (6) qualified personnel initially and thereafter to five (5) days for each updated product released hereunder pursuant to Paragraph 3.13. Any expense, including travel, lodging, and other out-of-pocket expenses incurred by LICENSEE's technical personnel shall be borne by LICENSEE.

3.13—Updating of Know-How and Copyrighted Works

During the term of this Agreement, LICENSOR agrees to furnish to LICENSEE in writing all updates, improvements or modifications made by LICENSOR to the Know-How and Copyrighted Works delivered to LICENSEE under Sections 3.10 and 3.08. Such updates, improvements, or modifications shall include changes to fix bugs or to improve speed or yield, but exclude Know-How and Copyrighted Works not related to Licensed Devices. LICENSEE shall bear the actual expenses incurred by LICENSOR in connection with preparation and transfer of the documentation on such updates, improvements, or modifications.

LICENSOR further agrees to grant to LICENSEE the same license as provided under Paragraph 2.1 to use and incorporate such updates, improvements, or modification.

3.14—Development of Licensed Device

LICENSOR shall develop the Licensed Device according to the schedule set forth in Appendix E. Should LICENSOR become unable to continue the development of the

Licensed Device due to any reasons beyond its reasonable control or should the prototype samples of the Licensed Device not become available to LICENSEE due to any
reasons attributable to LICENSOR within ninety (90) days of the date established
as the target therefor in Appendix E or within such other time period as may be from
time to time agreed upon between the parties, LICENSEE shall not be required to
pay the second installment of the license fee provided for in Section 4.01. Further, LI-
CENSOR shall make a full and complete disclosure to LICENSEE of such portion of
the Know-How and Copyrighted Works which LICENSOR then owns or controls in
reasonable detail for LICENSEE to continue the development of the Licensed Device
by itself.

3.15—Development of Licensed Product
   (1) LICENSOR shall develop the Licensed Product according to the division of work
and the schedule set forth in Appendix F. LICENSEE may dispatch to LICENSOR one
(1) engineer, at LICENSEE's cost, in order to participate in the development.
   (2) LICENSEE shall bear its own expenses and costs incurred for the performance of
its part of the development. In addition, LICENSEE shall bear half of the actual expenses
and costs incurred by LICENSOR within the maximum amount to be agreed upon between the parties when the final specifications and the development schedule are finalized. The actual expenses as herein provided shall consist of the engineering labor costs
including computer charges at the rates provided for in Appendix G, and traveling expenses and engineering material cost directly expended for the design of the Licensed
Product and shall be paid by LICENSEE on a monthly basis at the end of each month
against LICENSOR's invoice for such expenses received by LICENSEE by the end of the
previous month.
   (3) Should LICENSOR become unable to continue the development of the Licensed
Product due to any reasons beyond its reasonable control or should the prototype samples
of the Licensed Product not become available to LICENSEE due to any reasons attributable to LICENSOR within ninety (90) days of the date established as the target therefor in
Appendix F or within such other time period as may be from time to time agreed upon between the parties, LICENSEE shall not be required to pay the second installment of the license fee provided for in Section 4.02 or bear thereafter the expenses provided for in the
preceding Subsection 3.15.2. Further, LICENSOR shall make the full and complete disclosure to LICENSEE of such portion of the Know-How and Copyrighted Works which
LICENSOR then owns or controls in reasonable detail for LICENSEE to continue the development of the Licensed Product by itself.

*G. Payments: There are many different possible payment schemes. Two are shown below;
the first is used by a well-known licensor for the majority of their consumer product licensing. Note the sliding scale, cost-of-living and half-rate provisions, and reporting requirements. More information on royalty structures and rates can be found in Chapter 5.
   The tax treatment of royalty payments should be carefully considered when developing
the royalty scheme, especially with respect to foreign licensees. The examples below allow the deduction of foreign withholding tax from royalty payments to the extent the withholding can be deducted from licensor's own tax payments (due to the provisions of the
various tax treaties). This method works well when the licensor has substantial tax liabilities that can be offset; if the majority of the licensor's income comes from royalties, it is
likely that much of the benefit of such offsets will be lost.*

Example 1) ARTICLE IV

PAYMENTS

Section 4.01—Initial Payment
LICENSEE shall promptly upon the Effective Date of this Agreement pay LICEN-SOR the sum specified on the title page and shall pay all local fees, taxes, duties, or charges of any kind and shall not deduct them from the royalties due unless such deductions may be offset against LICENSOR's own tax liabilities.

Section 4.02—Royalties
Subject to the provisions of Section 4.05, LICENSEE shall pay to LICENSOR royalties on Licensed Devices manufactured by or for LICENSEE and incorporated in Licensed Products which are used, sold, leased, or otherwise disposed of by LICENSEE, except for Licensed Devices incorporated in Licensed Products returned to LICENSEE by customers of LICENSEE, other than in exchange for an upgraded product, on which a credit has been allowed by LICENSEE to said customers. The royalty payable shall be based on the number of Licensed Devices, hereinbefore defined, contained in Licensed Products, which are used, sold, leased, or otherwise disposed of by LICENSEE in successive calendar quarters from the effective date hereof, according to the amount of royalty specified below:

Number of Licensed Devices Disposed of in Quarter	Royalty Payable
Up to 10,000	50 cents per device
On those from 10,001 to 50,000	25 cents per device
On those from 50,001 to 250,000	10 cents per device
On those from 250,001 to 1,000,000	8.5 cents per device
On those above 1,000,000	7.5 cents per device

On the Effective Date of this Agreement, and annually thereafter on first day of each calendar year, the rate at which the royalties are calculated shall be adjusted in accordance with the Consumer Price Index. The adjustment shall be made by multiplying the royalties calculated as specified above by the ratio between the Consumer Price Index for the last month of the year preceding the year in which the adjustment takes place and the Consumer Price Index for the month of January 2001. LICENSOR will, during the first quarter of each calendar year, or as soon as such information is known, if later, inform LICENSEE of the adjustment ratio to be applied to royalties due in that year. The first adjustment to royalty rates shall be made in the quarter commencing January 1, 2002.

Section 4.03—Manufacture of Licensed Products by Another Licensee
If LICENSEE purchases Licensed Products from or has Licensed Products made for it by another party holding a Licensed Product license then LICENSEE shall have no royalty obligation under this Agreement, but all other rights and obligations of LICENSEE under this Agreement shall be fully effective.

Section 4.04—Royalty Applicability
A Licensed Product shall be considered sold under Section 4.02 when invoiced, or if not invoiced, delivered to another by LICENSEE or otherwise disposed of or put into use by LICENSEE, except for consignment shipments, which will be considered sold when the payment for such shipments is agreed upon between LICENSEE and customer.

Section 4.05—Royalty Payments and Statements

Unless Licensed Products are manufactured for LICENSEE under the provisions of Section 4.03 of this Agreement, LICENSEE shall render statements and royalty payments as follows:

(1) LICENSEE shall deliver to the address shown on the cover sheet of this Agreement or such place as LICENSOR may from time to time designate, quarterly reports certified by LICENSEE's chief financial officer or the officer's designate within 30 days after each calendar quarter ending with the last day of March, June, September, and December. Alternatively, such reports may be delivered by facsimile by transmitting them to LICENSOR's facsimile telephone number shown on the cover sheet of this Agreement or such other number as LICENSOR may from time to time designate. Royalty payments are due for each quarter at the same time as each quarterly report and shall be made by wire transfer in United States funds to LICENSOR's bank as identified on the cover sheet of this Agreement or such other bank as LICENSOR may from time to time designate. LICENSEE shall pay all local fees, taxes, duties, or charges of any kind and shall not deduct them from the royalties due unless such deductions may be offset against LICENSOR's own tax liabilities.

Each quarterly report shall:

(a) state the number of each model type of Licensed Products leased, sold, or otherwise disposed of by LICENSEE during the calendar quarter with respect to which the report is due;

(b) state the number of Licensed Devices in each model type of Licensed Product; and

(c) contain such other information and be in such form as LICENSOR or its outside auditors may prescribe. If LICENSEE claims less than full product royalty (under Section 4.06) or no royalty due (under Section 6.03), LICENSEE shall specify the country in which such Licensed Products were made, the country in which such Licensed Products were sold, and the identity of the purchasers of such Licensed Products.

(2) Any remittance in excess of royalties due with respect to the calendar quarter for which the report is due shall be applied by LICENSOR to the next payment due.

(3) LICENSEE's first report shall be for the calendar quarter in which LICENSEE sells its first Licensed Product.

(4) LICENSEE shall deliver a final report and payment of royalties to LICENSOR certified by LICENSEE's chief financial officer or the officer's designate within 30 days after termination of this Agreement throughout the world. Such a final report shall include a report of all royalties due with respect to Licensed Products not previously reported to LICENSOR. Such final report shall be supplemented at the end of the next and subsequent quarters, in the same manner as provided for during the Life of the Agreement, in the event that LICENSEE learns of any additional royalties due.

(5) LICENSEE shall pay interest to LICENSOR from the due date to the date payment is made of any overdue royalties or fees, including the Initial Payment, at the rate of 2% above the prime rate as is in effect from time to time at the bank identified on the cover page of this Agreement, or another major bank agreed to by the LICENSOR and LICENSEE in the event that the identified bank should cease to exist, provided however, that if the interest rate thus determined is in excess of rates allowable by any applicable law, the maximum interest rate allowable by such law shall apply.

Note: Section 4.06 provides for lower royalties when products are made and sold in countries where patents were never obtained or where the scheduled patents have expired. This is a strategy for extending the life of the agreement beyond expiration of the patents.

Section 4.06—Royalties in Non-Patent Country

If a Licensed Product is manufactured in a Non-Patent Country and used, sold, leased or otherwise disposed of in a Non-Patent Country, be it the same or a different Non-Patent Country, royalties for the manufacture, use, sale, lease, or other disposal of the Licensed Products in such Non-Patent Country or Countries under the Know-How, Licensed Copyrighted Works, and the Licensed Trademarks license shall be payable at the rates specified in Section 4.02; however, each Licensed Device of such Licensed Products shall count as fifty one-hundredths (0.50) of a Licensed Device. This provision shall not apply and full royalties shall be payable under Section 4.02:

(1) when Licensed Products are manufactured in any country which is not a Non-Patent Country or are used, sold, leased, or otherwise disposed of in any country which is not a Non-Patent Country, be it the same country as the country of manufacture or a different country; or

(2) when LICENSEE knows or has reason to know that the Licensed Products manufactured in a Non-Patent Country and used, sold, leased, or otherwise disposed of in a Non-Patent Country are destined for use by consumers or for sale, lease, or other disposal to consumers in a country which is not a Non-Patent Country and LICENSOR deems such sale to be for the purpose of defeating the royalty provisions of this agreement.

Section 4.07—Books and Records

LICENSEE shall keep complete books and records of all sales, leases, uses, returns, or other disposals by LICENSEE of Licensed Products.

Note: The licensor has the right to audit the licensee's books to ensure that royalties are being calculated and paid correctly.

Section 4.08—Rights of Inspecting Books and Records

LICENSOR shall have the right, through a professionally registered accountant at LICENSOR's expense, to inspect, examine, and make abstracts of the said books and records insofar as may be necessary to verify the accuracy of the same and of the statements provided for herein but such inspection and examination shall be made during business hours upon reasonable notice and not more often than once per calendar year. LICENSOR agrees not to divulge to third parties any Confidential Information obtained from the books and records of LICENSEE as a result of such inspection unless such information (a) was known to LICENSOR prior to its acquisition by LICENSOR as a result of such inspection; (b) becomes known to LICENSOR from sources other than directly or indirectly from LICENSEE; or (c) becomes a matter of public knowledge other than by breach of this Agreement by LICENSOR.

Example 2) ARTICLE IV

PAYMENTS

Section 4.01—Payment for the Licensed Device

In consideration for the licenses and rights granted for the Licensed Device LICENSEE shall pay to LICENSOR one million dollars (U.S. $1,000,000) according to the following schedule:

(1) $500,000 within thirty (30) days after the Effective Date.

(2) $500,000 within thirty (30) days after the date on which the prototype sample of the Licensed Device is available to LICENSEE.

Section 4.02—Payment for the Licensed Products

In consideration for all the licenses and rights granted and for the Licensed Product LICENSEE shall pay to LICENSOR two million dollars (U.S. $2,000,000) according to the following schedule:

(1) $1,000,000 within thirty (30) days after the Effective Date.

(2) $1,000,000 within thirty (30) days after the date on which the prototype sample of the Licensed Product is available to LICENSEE.

Section 4.03—Payment Manner

All the payments due to LICENSOR under this Agreement shall be made in United States funds by wire transfer to LICENSOR's bank as identified on the cover sheet of this Agreement or such other bank as LICENSOR may from time to time designate. LICENSEE shall pay all local fees, taxes, duties, or charges of any kind and shall not deduct them from the royalties due unless such deductions may be offset against LICENSOR's own tax liabilities.

H. Trademark Quality Control: When trademarks are licensed, the licensor must institute a quality-assurance program to protect the reputation of the trademarks (see Chapter 8).

ARTICLE V

STANDARDS OF MANUFACTURE AND QUALITY

Section 5.01—Standardization and Quality

LICENSEE shall abide by the DSP Processor Specifications, hereto appended in Appendix C and as modified from time to time by mutual agreement between LICENSOR and LICENSEE. LICENSEE shall abide by reasonable standards of quality and workmanship. Such quality standards shall apply to Licensed Devices and to aspects of Licensed Products not directly relating to the Licensed Devices but which nevertheless influence or reflect upon the quality or performance of the Licensed Devices as perceived by the end user. LICENSEE shall with respect to all Licensed Equipment conform to any reasonable quality standards requirements as specified by LICENSOR within a period of ninety (90) days of such specification in writing.

Licensed Products shall not be designed, presented or advertised in any way which contributes to confusion of the DSP System with any of LICENSOR's other proprietary technologies.

Section 5.02—Right to Inspect Quality

LICENSEE shall provide LICENSOR with such non-confidential information concerning Licensed Products as it may reasonably require in performing its right to enforce quality standards under this Agreement. LICENSEE will, upon request, provide on a loan basis to LICENSOR a reasonable number of samples of Licensed Products for testing, together with instruction and service manuals. In the event that LICENSOR shall complain that any Licensed Product does not comply with LICENSOR's quality standards, excepting newly specified standards falling within the ninety (90) day time limit of Section 5.01, it shall promptly so notify LICENSEE by written communication whereupon LICENSEE shall within ninety (90) days suspend the lease, sale, or other disposal of the same.

I. Termination: Two examples follow. The first can be used when a long term is desired, and reflects the philosophy from Section II that the royalties are paid for the use of the patents. Note, however, that the expiration date is that of the last-to-expire patent in the world, not the licensee's country. Newly issued patents can be added to the scheduled patents to extend the life of the agreement almost indefinitely.

It is often better to license a dead-beat company and keep them licensed, even if problems develop, because many of the provisions in the agreement protect the licensor. If there is no agreement or the agreement is canceled, the licensor is no longer as well protected. The second example is for a simple, fixed-term agreement.

Example 1) ARTICLE VI

TERMINATION AND EFFECT OF TERMINATION

Section 6.01—Expiration of Agreement

Unless this Agreement already has been terminated in accordance with the provisions of Section 6.02, this Agreement shall terminate in all countries of the world upon the expiration of the last-to-expire Patent under the Scheduled Patents. The Agreement is not extended by Patents in the Patent Rights that are not Scheduled Patents.

Section 6.02—Termination for Cause

At the option of LICENSOR, in the event that LICENSEE breaches any of its material obligations under this Agreement, subject to the conditions of Section 6.04, this Agreement shall terminate upon LICENSOR's giving sixty (60) days advance notice in writing, effective on dispatch of such notice, of such termination, giving reasons therefor to LICENSEE, provided however, that, if LICENSEE, within the sixty (60) day period, remedies the failure or default upon which such notice is based, then such notice shall not become effective and this Agreement shall continue in full force and effect. Notwithstanding the sixty (60) day cure period provided under the provisions of this Section 6.02, interest due under Section 4.05 shall remain payable and shall not waive, diminish, or otherwise affect any of LICENSOR's rights pursuant to this Section 6.02.

Note: According to this section, only the licensor has the right to terminate for cause.

Section 6.03—Option to Terminate in a Non-Patent Country

Subject to the provisions of Section 6.04, unless this Agreement already has been terminated in accordance with the provisions of Section 6.01 or Section 6.02, LICENSEE shall have the option to terminate its license under this Agreement with respect to a Non-Patent Country at any time after three years from the Effective Date of this Agreement. Said option to terminate with respect to such country shall be effective when LICENSOR receives LICENSEE's written notice of its exercise of such option and shall be prospective only and not retroactive.

Note: The licensee has the right to opt out of the half-rate royalty provision for non-patent countries (Section 4.06), but (of course) cannot use the trademarks in this case.

Section 6.04—Effect of Termination

Upon termination of the Agreement, as provided in Sections 6.01 or 6.02, or upon termination of the license under this Agreement with respect to a Non-Patent Country in accordance with the option set forth in Section 6.03, with respect to such country only, all licenses granted by LICENSOR to LICENSEE under this Agreement shall terminate, all rights LICENSOR granted to LICENSEE shall revest in LICENSOR, and all other rights and obligations of LICENSOR and LICENSEE under this agreement shall terminate except that the following rights and obligations of LICENSOR and LICENSEE shall survive to the extent necessary to permit their complete fulfillment and discharge, with the exception that subsection (9) shall not apply in case of termination under Section 6.01:

(1) LICENSEE's obligation to deliver a final royalty report and supplements thereto as required by Section 4.05;

(2) LICENSOR's right to receive and LICENSEE's obligation to pay royalties, under Article IV, including interest on overdue royalties, accrued or accruable for payment at the time of termination and interest on overdue royalties accruing subsequent to termination;

(3) LICENSEE's obligation to maintain books and records and LICENSOR's right to examine, audit, and copy as provided in Sections 4.07 and 4.08;

(4) any cause of action or claim of LICENSOR accrued or to accrue because of any breach or default by LICENSEE;

(5) LICENSEE's obligations with respect to Know-How and Confidential Information under Section 3.11(1) and LICENSOR's obligations with respect to Confidential Information under Section 4.08;

(6) LICENSEE's obligations to cooperate with LICENSOR with respect to Patent, Trademark, and Copyright enforcement under Section 3.04, with respect to matters arising before termination;

(7) LICENSEE's obligation to return to LICENSOR all documents and things furnished to LICENSEE, and copies thereof, under the provisions of Sections 3.08 and 3.11;

(8) LICENSEE's and LICENSOR's obligations regarding public announcements under Section 8.03; and

(9) LICENSEE shall be entitled to fill orders for Licensed Products already received and to make or have made for it and to sell Licensed Products for which commitments to vendors have been made at the time of such termination, subject to payment of applicable royalties thereon and subject to said Licensed Products meeting LICENSOR's quality standards, provided that LICENSEE promptly advises LICENSOR of such commitments upon termination.

The portions of the Agreement specifically identified in the sub-parts of this Section shall be construed and interpreted in connection with such other portions of the Agreement as may be required to make them effective.

Example 2) ARTICLE VI

TERMINATION AND EFFECT OF TERMINATION

Section 6.01—Expiration of Agreement
    This Agreement shall terminate in all countries of the world five years after the Effective Date.

Section 6.02—Termination for Cause
    In the event that LICENSEE or LICENSOR, respectively, breaches any of its material obligations under this Agreement, subject to the conditions of Section 6.04, LICENSOR or LICENSEE, respectively, shall have the option to terminate this Agreement by giving sixty (60) days advance notice in writing, effective on dispatch of such notice, of such termination, giving reasons therefor, provided however, that, if LICENSEE or LICENSOR, respectively, within the sixty (60) day period, remedies the failure or default upon which such notice is based, then such notice shall not become effective and this Agreement shall continue in full force and effect.

    If a validated export license which permits transfer of the Know-How and Copyrighted Works is required and has not been obtained from the U.S. Government within six (6) months after the Effective Date LICENSEE may, upon fifteen (15) days written notice to LICENSOR, cancel this Agreement, and LICENSOR shall refund to LICENSEE the payments made under Sections 4.1 and 4.2 without interest thereon within ten (10) days after the effective date of such cancellation. Upon such cancellation, this agreement shall become null and void and all rights, licenses and privileges granted by each party to the other shall cease.

Note: This simpler wording allows both companies to terminate the agreement for cause.

Section 6.04—Effect of Termination

Upon termination of the Agreement, as provided in Sections 6.01 or 6.02, all licenses granted under this Agreement shall terminate, all rights LICENSOR granted to LICENSEE shall revest in LICENSOR and all rights LICENSEE granted to LICENSOR shall revest in LICENSEE, and all other rights and obligations of LICENSOR and LICENSEE under this agreement shall terminate except that the following rights and obligations of LICENSOR and LICENSEE shall survive to the extent necessary to permit their complete fulfillment and discharge:

(1) any cause of action or claim of LICENSOR accrued or to accrue because of any breach or default by LICENSEE;

(2) LICENSEE's obligations with respect to Know-How and Confidential Information under Section 3.11(1) and LICENSOR's obligations with respect to Confidential Information under Section 4.08;

(3) LICENSEE's obligations to cooperate with LICENSOR with respect to Patent and Copyright enforcement under Section 3.04, with respect to matters arising before termination;

(4) LICENSEE's and LICENSOR's obligation to return all documents and things furnished, and copies thereof, under the provisions of Sections 3.08 and 3.11; and

(5) LICENSEE's and LICENSOR's obligations regarding public announcements under Section 8.03.

The portions of the Agreement specifically identified in the sub-parts of this Section shall be construed and interpreted in connection with such other portions of the Agreement as may be required to make them effective.

J. Limitations: These provisions are designed to protect the licensor's technology and to define the extent of the licensor's liability. If the technology or product being licensed is not proven, additional wording should be added to detail licensor's liability if the technology or product does not perform as expected.

ARTICLE VII

LIMITATIONS OF RIGHTS AND AUTHORITY

Section 7.01—Limitation of Rights

No right or title whatsoever in the Patent Rights, Know-How, Licensed Copyrighted Works, or the Licensed Trademarks is granted by LICENSOR to LICENSEE or shall be taken or assumed by LICENSEE except as is specifically laid down in this Agreement.

Section 7.02—Limitation of Authority

Neither party shall in any respect whatsoever be taken to be the agent or representative of the other party and neither party shall have any authority to assume any obligation for or to commit the other party in any way.

Section 7.03—Disclaimer of Warranties and Liability; Hold Harmless

LICENSOR has provided LICENSEE the rights and privileges contained in this Agreement in good faith. However, nothing contained in this Agreement shall be construed as (1) a warranty or representation by LICENSOR as to the validity or scope of any Patent included in The Patent Rights; (2) a warranty or representation that the DSP System technology, Patent Rights, Know-How, Licensed Copyrighted Works, Licensed Trademarks, or any Licensed Device, Licensed Product, or part thereof embodying any of them will be free from infringement of Patents, copyrights, trademarks, service marks, or other proprietary rights of third parties; or (3) an agreement to defend LICENSEE against actions or suits of any nature brought by any third parties.

LICENSOR disclaims all liability and responsibility for property damage, personal injury, and consequential damages, whether or not foreseeable, that may result from the manufacture, use, lease, or sale of Licensed Devices, Licensed Products, and parts thereof, and LICENSEE agrees to assume all liability and responsibility for all such damage and injury.

LICENSEE agrees to indemnify, defend, and hold LICENSOR harmless from and against all claims (including, without limitation, product liability claims), suits, losses, and damages, including reasonable attorneys' fees and any other expenses incurred in investigation and defense, arising out of LICENSEE's manufacture, use, lease, or sale of Licensed Devices, Licensed Products, or parts thereof, or out of any allegedly unauthorized use of any trademark, service mark, Patent, copyright, process, idea, method, or device (excepting Licensed Trademarks, Patent Rights, Know-How, Confidential Information, and Licensed Copyrighted Works) by LICENSEE or those acting under its apparent or actual authority.

Note: The wording of Section 7.03 will depend on the provisions of Section 3.04 (dealing with infringement of third party rights). In some cases licensees will require assurances as to the validity of the licensed patents, in which case the licensor can: (1) guarantee the validity of its patents (not recommended); (2) obtain and give the licensee opinions of counsel stating that the patents are valid; (3) agree to assume the defense of the patents if an infringement suit is initiated; and/or (4) agree to let the licensee withhold royalty payments during litigation or to use the royalties due for the defense.

Section 7.04—Limitation of Assignment by LICENSEE

The rights, duties and privileges of LICENSEE hereunder shall not be transferred or assigned by it either in part or in whole without prior written consent of LICENSOR. However, LICENSEE shall have the right to transfer its rights, duties and privileges under this Agreement in connection with its merger and consolidation with another firm or the sale of its entire business to another person or firm, provided that such person or firm shall first have agreed with LICENSOR to perform the transferring party's obligations and duties hereunder.

Note: According to this section, if the licensee's business is sold in its entirety the license can be transferred if the new owner agrees to accept all the obligations.

Section 7.05—Compliance with U.S. Export Control Regulations

(1) LICENSEE agrees not to export any technical data acquired from LICENSOR under this Agreement, nor the direct product thereof, either directly or indirectly, to any country in contravention of United States law.

(2) Nothing in this Agreement shall be construed as requiring LICENSOR to export from the United States, directly or indirectly, any technical data or any commodities to any country in contravention of United States law.

K. Miscellaneous

ARTICLE VIII

MISCELLANEOUS PROVISIONS

Section 8.01—Language of Agreement; Language of Notices

The language of this Agreement is English. If translated into another language, this English version of the Agreement shall be controlling. Except as may be agreed by LICENSOR and LICENSEE, all notices, reports, consents, and approvals required or permitted to be given hereunder shall be written in the English language.

Section 8.02—Stability of Agreement

No provision of this Agreement shall be deemed modified by any acts of LICENSOR, its agents, or employees or by failure to object to any acts of LICENSEE which may be inconsistent herewith, or otherwise, except by a subsequent agreement in writing signed by LICENSOR and LICENSEE. No waiver of a breach committed by either party in one instance shall constitute a waiver or a license to commit or continue breaches in other or like instances.

Section 8.03—Public Announcements

Neither party shall at any time heretofore or hereafter publicly state or imply that the terms specified herein or the relationships between LICENSOR and LICENSEE are in any way different from those specifically laid down in this Agreement. LICENSEE shall not at any time publicly state or imply that any unlicensed products use the DSP System Specifications. If requested by one party, the other party shall promptly supply the first party with copies of all public statements and of all publicity and promotional material relating to this Agreement, the DSP System Specifications, Licensed Devices, Licensed Products, Licensed Trademarks, and Know-How.

Section 8.04—Address of LICENSOR and LICENSEE for all Other Communications

Except as otherwise specified in this Agreement, all notices, reports, consents, and approvals required or permitted to be given hereunder shall be in writing, signed by an officer of LICENSEE or LICENSOR, respectively, and sent postage or shipping charges prepaid by certified or registered mail, return receipt requested showing to whom, when and where delivered, or by Express mail, or by a secure overnight or one-day delivery service that provides proof and date of delivery, or by facsimile, properly addressed or transmitted to LICENSEE or LICENSOR, respectively, at the address or facsimile number set forth on the cover page of this Agreement or to such other address or facsimile number as may from time to time be designated by either party to the other in writing. Wire payments from LICENSEE to LICENSOR shall be made to the bank and account of LICENSOR as set forth on the cover page of this agreement or to such other bank and account as LICENSOR may from time to time designate in writing to LICENSEE.

Section 8.05—Applicable Law

This Agreement shall be construed in accordance with the substantive laws, but not the choice of law rules, of the State of California.

Note: The next section deals with disputes. The first wording is quite simple and does not limit resolution to arbitration (some, including many lawyers, do not favor arbitration). The second requires arbitration. Arbitration is private, faster than litigation, can utilize experts who are as qualified as federal judges (in fact, many are federal judges), can be less expensive, and generally leaves both parties feeling better. On the other hand, some (including the Justice Department) do not feel arbitration should be used to resolve patent disputes.

Example 1) Section 8.06—Choice of Forum; Attorneys' Fees

To the full extent permitted by law, LICENSOR and LICENSEE agree that their choice of forum, in the event that any dispute arising under this agreement is not resolved by mutual agreement, shall be the United States Courts in the State of California and the State Courts of the State of California.

In the event that any action is brought for any breach or default of any of the terms of this Agreement, or otherwise in connection with this Agreement, the prevailing party shall be entitled to recover from the other party all costs and expenses incurred in that action or any appeal therefrom, including without limitation, all attorneys' fees and costs actually incurred.

Example 2) Section 8.06—Arbitration; Attorneys' Fees

All disputes, controversies, or differences which may arise between the parties, out of or in relation to or in connection with this Agreement, or the breach thereof, shall be finally settled by arbitration pursuant to the Japan-American Trade Arbitration Agreement of September 16, 1952, by which each party hereto is bound. Such arbitration shall be conducted by three (3) arbitrators with reasonable technical knowledge of and experience in the semiconductor industry, selected by the mutual agreement of the parties, or, failing such agreement, as selected according to the applicable rules specified below. The parties shall bear the costs of such arbitrators equally.

If LICENSOR shall request arbitration under this Agreement, the arbitration shall be conducted in the Japanese language in Tokyo, Japan, under the Commercial Arbitration rules of the Japan Commercial Arbitration Association. If LICENSEE shall request arbitration under this Agreement, the arbitration shall be conducted in the English language in San Francisco, California, under the Commercial Arbitration Rules of the American Arbitration Association and its Supplementary Procedures for International Commercial Arbitration. Any decision of the arbitrators shall be in writing and shall state the reasons for the conclusions reached.

In the event that any action is brought for any breach or default of any of the terms of this Agreement, or otherwise in connection with this Agreement, the prevailing party shall be entitled to recover from the other party all costs and expenses incurred in that action or any appeal therefrom, including without limitation, all attorneys' fees and costs actually incurred.

Section 8.07—Construction of Agreement

This Agreement shall not be construed for or against any party based on any rule of construction concerning who prepared the Agreement or otherwise.

Section 8.08—Captions

Titles and captions in this Agreement are for convenient reference only and shall not be considered in construing the intent, meaning, or scope of the Agreement or any portion thereof.

Section 8.09—Singular and Plural

Throughout this Agreement, words in the singular shall be construed as including the plural and words in the plural shall be construed as including the singular.

Section 8.10—Complete Agreement

This Agreement contains the entire agreement and understanding between LICENSOR and LICENSEE and merges all prior or contemporaneous oral or written communication between them. Neither LICENSOR nor LICENSEE now is, or shall hereafter be, in any way bound by any prior, contemporaneous, or subsequent oral or written communication except insofar as the same is expressly set forth in this Agreement or in a subsequent written agreement duly executed by both LICENSOR and LICENSEE.

Section 8.11—Severability
Should any portion of this Agreement be declared null and void by operation of law, or otherwise, the remainder of this Agreement shall remain in full force and effect.

Section 8.12—Company Representation and Warranty
LICENSEE represents and warrants to LICENSOR that it is not a party to any agreement, and is not subject to any statutory or other obligation or restriction, which might prevent or restrict it from performing all of its obligations and undertakings under this License Agreement, and that the execution and delivery of this Agreement and the performance by LICENSEE of its obligations hereunder have been authorized by all necessary action, corporate or otherwise.

Note: The licensor warrants nothing in this wording. Some licensees will require such a warranty, in which case the following can be used:

LICENSOR represents and warrants to LICENSEE that it is not a party to any agreement, and is not subject to any statutory or other obligation or restriction, which might prevent or restrict it from performing all of its obligations and undertakings under this License Agreement, and that the execution and delivery of this Agreement and the performance by LICENSOR of its obligations hereunder have been authorized by all necessary action, corporate or otherwise.

Section 8.13—Execution
IN WITNESS WHEREOF, the said LICENSOR has caused this Agreement to be executed on the cover page of this Agreement, in the presence of a witness, by an officer duly authorized and the said LICENSEE has caused the same to be executed on the cover page of this Agreement, in the presence of a witness, by an officer duly authorized, in duplicate original copies, as of the date set forth on said cover page.
This concludes the sample agreement. Two other ideas follow that may be useful in some situations:

L. Most-favored nation clause: Some licensees will want the licensor to ensure that the terms of their license are and will remain as favorable as the terms of any other equivalent license. The licensor may want to restrict this promise to agreements executed subsequently and only if the licensee agrees to accept any other restrictions or requirements also included in the subsequent licenses.

Section 3.16—Revision of Terms
If LICENSOR hereafter grants to another party a license to make Licensed Products for sale in the Market at a royalty rate which is lower than that granted to LICENSEE, LICENSOR shall so notify LICENSEE, and LICENSOR, at its own option, either shall grant such lower royalty rate to LICENSEE on a retroactive basis to the date of such other license or shall inform LICENSEE of any special conditions related to such other license which justify said lower royalty rate. In the event LICENSEE believes that such special conditions are insufficient to make the present Agreement equitable to LICENSEE, then LICENSEE may inform LICENSOR of its belief in writing and the reasons for such belief, whereupon the LICENSEE and LICENSOR shall bargain in good faith with the view toward revising this Agreement so as to make its terms reasonably equivalent to those

granted to such other party. In the event LICENSEE and LICENSOR cannot, within ninety (90) days after LICENSOR has received said written notice from LICENSEE, resolve this situation, then the parties hereto shall within thirty (30) days following the end of such ninety (90) day period submit in good faith the problem for resolution to a group of three disinterested persons, one chosen by LICENSEE, one chosen by LICENSOR and the third to be chosen jointly by the first two persons. The majority opinion of this group shall be binding upon the parties hereto. The expense of such submission shall be borne equally by the parties.

M. Improvements pool: If a technology has become a standard and one licensee develops an improvement, the improvement is only useful if all licensees can use it. In this case, it may be useful to have a pool of such improvements, where all licensees contribute their improvements for the benefit of all.

Unfortunately, there are problems with such an approach, including the following:

- *The licensees don't like to give up their improvements, especially to their competitors*
- *If the licensor accepts information from a licensee about an improvement and happens to be working on the same thing, it could affect the licensor's ability to protect the development*
- *There may be unwanted confidentiality obligations associated with accepting the information.*

If standardization is not an issue and there are several licensees, an improvements pool can be offered where licensor's improvements are offered after a certain date only to those licensees who join and contribute their improvements to the pool.

In addition, a licensor can license its improvements to its licensees unilaterally. In actual practice the improvements clause is rarely used. Therefore, there would seem to be few occasions where provisions for an improvements pool are needed; however, if such an occasion arises, the following can be considered:

Section 3.17—Improvements

If the LICENSOR has heretofore brought about or shall hereafter during the term of this Agreement bring about any improvements, including improvements brought about by LICENSOR's vendors or subcontractors to which LICENSOR may become entitled, the LICENSOR shall promptly offer to disclose such improvements to the LICENSEE and if such improvements reasonably appear to be patentable, LICENSOR shall file patent applications thereon in the name and at the expense of the LICENSOR and such applications and any patents issuing thereon shall be included in the Patent Rights.

The LICENSEE agrees not to divulge to any third parties any information concerning such improvements or such patent application which has been disclosed to it by LICENSOR unless such information (a) was known to the LICENSEE prior to its receipt from the LICENSOR; (b) becomes known to the LICENSEE from sources other than directly or indirectly from LICENSOR; or (c) becomes a matter of public knowledge other than by breach of this Agreement by LICENSEE. The above obligations of LICENSEE shall in any event cease three (3) years from the date on which such information has been acquired from LICENSOR.

With the restriction that Improvements shall specifically be defined as only those improvements which already come within the scope of one or more claims of the Patent Rights, and furthermore only those improvements which are directly useful for the making and use of Licensed Devices and Licensed Products which are the subject of this Agreement, if the LICENSEE has heretofore brought about or shall hereafter during the term of this Agreement bring about any Improvements, including Improvements brought about by LICENSEE's vendors or subcontractors to which LICENSEE may become entitled, excepting improvements brought about by another licensee holding a DSP System license, the LICENSEE shall promptly offer to disclose such improvements to the LICENSOR in confidence and if such improvements reasonably appear to be patentable LICENSOR shall file and prosecute patent applications thereon in LICENSEE's name, the expense of which shall be borne by the LICENSOR, for the securing and maintaining of patent protection in such countries of the world as agreed between LICENSOR and LICENSEE and such application and any patents issuing thereon shall be included in the Patent Rights.

If either LICENSOR or LICENSEE, as a first party, shall inform the other party that it has decided not to file such patent application in any country or shall fail, within sixty (60) days after written inquiry by the other party on the patent status of an improvement, to file such patent applications as specified above or to prosecute such pending applications under the above provisions, the other party shall have the right to do so at its own expense and the said first party shall promptly assign to said other party its entire right, title, and interest in and to such patent applications. Said first party, on the other party's request, shall sign or cause to be executed all lawful documents and perform all lawful acts to effectuate fully such assignments to the other party.

Section 3.18—Improvements Pool

Within eighteen months of the disclosure by the LICENSEE to the LICENSOR of any improvement under the terms of 3.17 above or within twelve months of the commencement of production incorporating the improvements, whichever occurs first, LICENSOR shall receive from LICENSEE a non-exclusive, royalty-free license, together with the right to grant sublicenses to other licensees holding DSP System licenses, under each of said patent applications and any patents issuing thereon.

If the LICENSOR receives, from another DSP System licensee, a non-exclusive, royalty-free license, together with the right to grant sublicenses, of the type described above under patent applications and/or patents issuing thereon covering Improvements, LICENSOR shall immediately inform LICENSEE of such Improvements and shall include such patent applications and/or patents issuing thereon in the Patent Rights.

SOFTWARE DISTRIBUTION AGREEMENT

The sample agreement that follows would be used to license the distribution of a computer software application program. Computer software is primarily protected as a copyrighted work. As discussed in Chapter 2, there is a bundle of rights associated with a copyrighted work, including the right to use the work, the right to copy and distribute the work, and the right to prepare derivative works.

In this case, the licensor is granting the licensee the right to use, copy, and distribute the software but is not granting the right to prepare derivative works. This would be appropriate when, for example, an Internet browser application intended for use on personal computers is provided by its owner to a computer magazine to distribute to its readers on a CD-ROM to be included with an upcoming issue. This agreement would not be appropriate if the licensee intended to make changes to the software to adapt it for a particular use, in which case the right to prepare derivative works would be needed.

The boilerplate clauses are included in the first section of the agreement, while Exhibit A is used for any special terms needed for a particular licensee. This format is convenient when the same basic agreement is used, with minor variations, for a number of different licensing applications.

As with the hybrid agreement, comments are in italics.

Software Distribution Agreement

This Software Distribution Agreement (*"Agreement"*) is made as of [date] (the *"Effective Date"*) by and between [licensor name], a [place of incorporation] corporation with a place of business at [address], (*"Licensor"*), and the individual or entity identified below (*"Licensee"*).

In exchange for valuable consideration consisting of cross promotion, Licensor and Licensee agree to enter into the following arrangement:

A. Section 1 includes a basic description of the license grant and restrictions. The grant is further defined in Exhibit A, where terms specific to this particular agreement are included.

1. LICENSE

LICENSE GRANT. Subject to the terms and conditions of this Agreement, Licensor hereby grants to Licensee a non-exclusive license to use the Software (described in Exhibit A) solely in accordance with the license terms set forth in Exhibit A attached hereto, the terms of which are incorporated into this Agreement by reference.

LICENSE RESTRICTIONS. Except as expressly provided in this Agreement, Licensee may not use, copy, modify, or transfer the Software, or any copy thereof, in whole or in part. Any attempt to transfer any of the rights, duties or obligations hereunder is void.

B. Section 2 contains language protecting Licensor's ownership of the software and requiring that certain notices be included on all copies made by the licensee.

2. OWNERSHIP AND PROPRIETARY RIGHTS NOTICES.

OWNERSHIP. All right, title, and interest in the Software will at all times remain the property of Licensor. The Software is licensed, not sold, to Licensee for use only under the terms of this Agreement, and Licensor reserves all rights not expressly granted to Licensee. Licensee owns the media, if any, on which the Software is recorded, but Licensor retains ownership of all copies of the Software itself.

PROPRIETARY RIGHTS NOTICES. All proprietary rights notices or legends in the Software and any related documentation provided by Licensor, including trade names, trademarks, copyright designations, and authorship attributions shall be retained in any and all copies of the Software. Any publication by or on behalf of Licensee that refers to the Software shall state that the Software was created by Licensor.

C. Section 3 defines the responsibilities of the licensee with respect to confidential information supplied by licensor. There are no provisions regarding disclosure of confidential information by the licensee. If the licensee will disclose confidential information, the language should be changed to reflect this.

3. CONFIDENTIALITY.

CONFIDENTIAL INFORMATION AND TRADE SECRETS. Except as specifically permitted herein, Licensee will not disclose to any third party or to Licensee's employees (unless they have a reasonable need to know), nor use any Software or other information disclosed to it by Licensor (*"Confidential Information"*), and will cause its employees to, take all reasonable measures to maintain the confidentiality of all Confidential Information in its possession or control, which will in no event be less than the measures it uses to maintain the confidentiality of its own information of equal importance. Licensee acknowledges that the Software contains valuable trade secrets of Licensor, the disclosure of which would cause substantial harm to Licensor that could not be remedied by the payment of damages alone. Accordingly, Licensor will be entitled to seek preliminary and permanent injunctive and other equitable relief for any breach of this Section 3.

Exceptions. "*Confidential Information*" will not include information that: (a) is in or enters the public domain without breach of this Agreement; (b) Licensee received from a third party without restriction on disclosure and without breach of a nondisclosure obligation; or (c) Licensee develops independently, which it can prove with written evidence.

D. Sections 4 and 5 limit the licensor's liability for any damages that may occur as a result of the licensee's use of the software.

4. DISCLAIMER OF WARRANTY. The Software is provided to Licensee "As Is" with no warranty whatsoever. Licensor expressly disclaims all warranties, including the implied warranties of merchantability, fitness for a particular purpose, and non-infringement. No oral or written information or advice given by Licensor, its employees, or agents shall increase the scope of the above warranties or create any new warranties.

5. LIMITATION OF LIABILITY. Regardless of whether any remedy set forth herein fails of its essential purpose or otherwise, in no event will Licensor be liable to Licensee or to any third party for any lost profits, lost data, interruption of business, or other special, indirect, incidental or consequential damages of any kind, whether in contract, tort (including negligence) or otherwise, arising out of the use or inability to use the Software or any data supplied therewith, even if Licensor has been advised of the possibility of such loss or damage and whether or not such loss or damages are foreseeable.

E. Section 6, together with the term section of Exhibit A, state the term of the agreement and under what circumstances the agreement can be terminated earlier.

6. TERM AND TERMINATION.

TERM. This Agreement will be effective as of the Effective Date, and shall continue for the period set forth in Exhibit A, or until earlier terminated as set forth herein.

TERMINATION FOR BREACH. Licensor may terminate this Agreement immediately at any time upon written notice to Licensee if Licensee breaches any term of this Agreement.

TERMINATION FOR CONVENIENCE. At any time, Licensee may terminate this Agreement for any reason by providing Licensor with ninety (90) days written notice of the date of the intended termination.

EFFECT OF TERMINATION. Termination of this Agreement will not limit either party from pursuing any other remedies available to it, including but not limited to injunctive relief. If this Agreement is terminated, Licensee will: (a) cease using the Software, and (b) certify to Licensor within ten (10) days that Licensee has, at the election of Licensor, either returned or destroyed all copies of the Software in its possession and removed all license keys (if any). Sections 1.2, 2, 3, 4, 5, 6, 7, 9 and 10 will survive any termination of this Agreement.

F. Section 7 is intended to protect the licensor from any legal consequences if the licensee exports the software illegally.

7. EXPORT LAW. The Software and related technology may be subject to export or import regulations in the U. S. and other countries. Licensee agrees to strictly comply with all such laws and regulations and acknowledges that Licensee has the responsibility to obtain

such licenses to export, re-export or import as may be required. Licensee agrees to strictly comply with all of the applicable country laws and regulations when either exporting or re-exporting or importing the Software or any underlying information or technology.

8. FEES. Licensee shall pay the license fees for the Software as set forth in Exhibit A.

G. Section 9, together with Exhibit A, defines the support that the licensor will provide. The scope of support provided by the licensor will vary greatly depending on the situation.

9. NO SUPPORT. Licensor shall have no obligation to provide any support and/or maintenance services to Licensee hereunder except as set forth in Exhibit A. Licensor shall, however, provide updates and/or additions to the Software, including bug fixes, as they are generally released, which shall be included in the definition of "Software" hereunder.

H. Section 10 is a condensed version of the "Miscellaneous Provisions" section (Article 8) of the hybrid agreement.

10. GENERAL. This Agreement will be governed by the internal laws of the State of California, without regard to choice of law principles. Each party agrees to comply with all applicable laws, rules, and regulations in connection with its activities under this Agreement. If Licensor takes legal action to enforce the provisions of this Agreement and prevails in such action, Licensee will pay all costs incurred by Licensor in connection with the legal action, including reasonable attorneys' fees. Except for actions relating to Section 3, any dispute arising out of or in connection with this Agreement will be finally settled in arbitration under the rules of the American Arbitration Association by one or more arbitrators appointed in accordance with such rules, to be conducted in Santa Clara County, California. The relationship of the parties is solely that of independent contractors, and not partners, joint venturers or agents. All notices required to be sent hereunder will be in writing and will be deemed to have been given when sent by certified mail, overnight express, or confirmed facsimile to the recipient's address listed below. In the event any provision of this Agreement is held to be unenforceable, the remaining provisions will remain in full force and effect. The waiver by either party of any default or breach of this Agreement will not constitute a waiver of any other or subsequent default or breach. Any waiver, amendment, or other modifications of this Agreement will be effective only if in writing and signed by the parties. Neither party will be liable by reason of failure of performance if the failure arises out of causes beyond that party's reasonable control. This Agreement, together with its attachments, is the complete and exclusive statement of the agreement between the parties that supersedes any proposal or prior agreement, written or oral, and any other communications between the parties relating to the subject matter hereof.

In witness whereof, the authorized representatives of each party have signed this Agreement as of the Effective Date:

[Licensor] (Licensor)	[Licensee] (Licensee)
By:	By:
Name:	Name:
Title:	Title:
Date:	Date:
Address:	Address:
Phone:	Phone:
Facsimile:	Facsimile:

Exhibit A

Commercial License

This is Exhibit A (Commercial License) to the Software Distribution Agreement ("Agreement") dated [date] by and between [licensor] ("Licensor") and [licensee] ("Licensee").

I. A complete description of the software being licensed and any accompanying documentation should be included.

SOFTWARE. The Software shall include each of the following software components:

Product   Documentation

_____

_____

_____

FEES. $[amount]

TERM. 1 year

J. License grant terms specific to this agreement are included in the next section.

LICENSE TERMS. The following terms shall be incorporated into and made part of the Agreement.

Definitions. For purposes of this Exhibit A, "Licensed Software" shall mean versions of [software] intended for use by consumers as an application on a Windows-based personal computer.

License Grant. Subject to the terms and conditions of this Agreement, Licensor hereby grants to Licensee a non-exclusive, royalty-free, nontransferable license to copy and distribute the Licensed Software.

K. When licensing the distribution of software, it is important to ensure that all licensed software distributed by the licensee includes an appropriate end-user license agreement. The next section addresses this issue.

End-User Distribution Requirements. All distribution of Licensed Software (whether for fee or otherwise) must be made subject to an end-user license that includes (at least): restrictions against copying, reverse engineering, and sublicensing; and disclaimers (at least on behalf of Licensor) of all warranties including fitness, merchantability, and non-infringement. All copies of Licensed Software distributed to any third parties must include labeling and displays attributing Licensor and including appropriate trademarks, trademark acknowledgments, and copyright notices, as reasonably specified by Licensor. All customer support shall be solely the obligation of Licensee. Licensee will provide monthly reports to Licensor summarizing end-user inquiries and will contact Licensor on an as-needed basis regarding end-user issues. All communications regarding end-user issues will be directed to [licensor's e-mail address] or such other address as Licensor may specify.

Publicity. Licensee may publish promotional materials (Web pages, press releases, etc.) promoting the Licensed Software. Licensor shall be provided copies of all such materials. Licensor may issue press releases and other promotional materials publicizing the Agreement.

L. The last two sections include any other terms agreed to between the parties that don't logically fit in the preceding sections.

Other Responsibilities of Licensee.

Licensee will provide a prominent link and banner on its Web site that promotes Licensor's Web site using Licensor's logo and branding guidelines.

Licensee will provide free of charge distribution for the Licensed Software.

At Licensor's request, Licensee will include, at no cost to Licensor, marketing materials provided by Licensor with the Licensed Software when it is distributed to end-users.

Other Responsibilities of Licensor.

Licensor will provide Licensee with the Licensed Software in a form suitable for distribution to end-users.

Licensor will provide to Licensee in a timely manner updates to the Licensed Software.

Licensor will provide technical support to Licensee as needed for problems arising from its servers and electronic programming guide.

Appendix D

Glossary of
Intellectual Property Terms[*]

Abandonment—Loss of rights in IP[**]. Abandonment can occur by (1) an intentional act of abandonment by the IP owner, (2) failure to file an applicable fee, or (3) in the case of a Patent Application, failure to respond to an Office Action within the allotted time period.

Accused Device—A product that is alleged to infringe a Patent.

Active Inducement—Patent Infringement by virtue of active inducement of (aiding and abetting) Direct Infringement by third parties (e.g., by advertising an infringing use). 35 U.S.C. § 271(b). Requires a Direct Infringement by someone else.

ADR—Alternate dispute resolution. ADR can be mediation (which is non-binding) or arbitration (which is binding).

All Elements Rule—A limitation on the Doctrine of Equivalents, under which *each element* of a Claim must be found in the Accused Device to constitute Direct Infringement. Therefore, the Doctrine of Equivalents *may not* be applied to the Claim as a whole, in disregard of the *Claim elements.*

Anticipation—A single Prior Art Patent or publication which is substantially identical to a Claim and thus invalidates the Claim under 35 U.S.C. §102(b).

Anti-Dilution—Statutory provisions and legal doctrines which protect well-known Trademarks in product areas in which they are not in use. *See*, e.g., 15 U.S.C. §1125(c).

Assignee—Buyer.

Assignment— Sale of an IP right.

---

[*]These definitions are accurate, but were written to be simple and clear, rather than legally perfect, and are based on an understanding of U.S. law. For more legalistic definitions, see *McCarthy's Desk Encyclopedia of Intellectual Property*, 2nd edition (1995), published by the Bureau of National Affairs.

[**]Defined terms are referred to in this Glossary with initial capital letters.

Assignment in Gross—Assignment of a Trademark without Assignment of the associated goodwill. An Assignment in Gross is invalid.

Assignor—Seller.

Assignor Estoppel—A legal principle under which the Assignor of an IP right (e.g., a Patent) is Estopped from denying later the Validity of the assigned right (e.g., the assigned Patent).

Berne Convention—An international Copyright treaty, which most countries, including the United States, have signed. Among its provisions, a Copyrightable work created in one member country is automatically protected (no registration is required) in all member countries. Partial exception: although the United States does not require Copyright registration by a non-U.S. resident to file a Copyright suit, residents must first obtain a Copyright registration. *See* 17 U.S.C. §411(a).

Best Efforts—In American parlance, usually a reasonable level of effort, but courts may vary in their interpretations. (It is better to use "reasonable diligence.")

Best Endeavors—The counterpart in England to Best Efforts, but judicially interpreted in England to mean a very high level of effort.

Blocking Patent—A Patent whose Infringement cannot be avoided in a particular type of product, system, or service. *Example*, the AT&T Shockley transistor patent. *See* Essential Patent.

Bundling—Selling two separate products as one unit. For example, Windows® software sold with a Compaq® computer. *See also* Unbundling.

"But for" License—A Patent License grant and/or Royalty payment provision in which the License grant or Royalty payment obligation is based on products (or processes) "which would, *but for* this Agreement, Infringe one or more Claims of Licensed Patents."

CAFC—*See* Court of Appeals for the Federal Circuit.

CAGR—Compound Annual Growth Rate.

Claim—A numbered paragraph in a Patent which verbally defines the legal rights protected by the Patent. Note: The legal right embodied in a Claim is an Exclusionary Right.

Claim Chart—A two- or three-column chart, comparing all of the words and phrases of a Claim against the features of an allegedly Infringing product or process. One hundred percent correspondence of words and features constitutes Infringement. If there is not 100% correspondence, there may still be Infringement. *See* Doctrine of Equivalents.

Claim Differentiation Doctrine—A doctrine of Claim interpretation, under which each Claim is interpreted to be different from each other Claim in the same Patent, that is, a narrower Claim cannot be used to restrict a broader Claim.

Clayton Act. 15 U.S.C. §§ 12-27—An anti-trust statute prohibiting the acquisition of an asset (e.g., Patent), the tendency of which is to substantially lessen competition.

Click Wrap License—A License of software or a database that is accessed and downloaded online. The License is created online when the potential Licensee is presented with a screen of license terms and agrees to the terms by a click of the cursor.

Common Law—The federal and state laws of the U.S. which are not statutory (made by legislatures) but were made by judges and inherited from British law.

Comprising—An open-ended term used in a Claim, interpreted to mean "including" (but not limited to) or "containing."

Compulsory License—A non-exclusive License under a Patent required by law or judicial decree to be granted by a Patent owner to third parties. Compulsory Licenses are not required by law in the U.S., but are required by the laws of some countries, often to pharmaceutical patents.

Conception—The mental part of making a patentable invention.

Consisting of—A closed term used in a Claim, which closes or limits the Claim to those elements recited in the Claim. *Compare* with Comprising.

Constructive Notice—An act having the same legal effect as *actual* notice. For example, actual notice of Patent Infringement is telling the infringer that it is infringing a particular Patent. The same legal result can be achieved (constructive notice is given) when the Patent owner's Patented product or package is marked with (bears) the Patent number, 35 U.S.C. §287. The concept of Constructive Notice also applies to registered Trademarks and Copyrights. Various legal benefits derive from the giving of actual or Constructive Notice.

Constructive Reduction to Practice—Filing a U.S. Patent Application.

Contributory (Patent) Infringement—The act of selling a *non-staple* article which is an element of an article or is used in a process which Infringes a Patent. *See* 35 U.S.C. § 271(c). A non-staple article is one that has no substantial non-Infringing uses. There are also Copyright and Trademark doctrines of Contributory Infringement. As to Copyright, *see Sony Corp. v. Universal City Studios, Inc.*, 464 417, 441 (1984); as to Trademark, *See Inwood Labs. Inc. v. Ives Labs. Inc.*, 456 844, 854 (1982).

Convoyed Goods—Unlicensed products that are sold together with or as part of a sale of a Patented product. Example, a Patented DNA probe which is sold with or drives the sale of unpatented reagents. The reagents are Convoyed Goods. *See Promega Corp. v. Lifecodes Corp.*, 53 USPQ 2d 1463 (D.Utah 2000).

Copyright—A federal right granted to the creator of an original work that is fixed in a tangible medium of expression. 17 USCA §§ 100 *et seq.*

Court of Appeals for the Federal Circuit—The federal appeals court which is empowered to decide all appeals (from U.S. District Courts around the country) involving Patent rights. Also called the Federal Circuit or CAFC.

Covenant Not to Sue—A personal covenant or promise (express or implied) not to sue a third party for a Tort or contract breach. A non-exclusive License is sometimes considered by the courts to be a Covenant Not to Sue by the Licensor and therefore is deemed not transferable. When a Patent owner grants a Covenant Not to Sue, the grantee cannot pass along its immunity from Infringement of the Patent to its customers (unless expressly permitted by the agreement).

Declaratory Judgment Suit—A lawsuit filed in federal court by an alleged Patent Infringer, seeking a declaration of the court that a Patent is Invalid, not Infringed and/or not enforceable.

Defensive Suspension—A provision of (1) a License agreement or (2) a standards-based undertaking to License an Essential Patent, by which the License or undertaking is suspended if the licensee or prospective licensee sues the Patent owner for Patent Infringement or declaration of Invalidity or non-Infringement.

Dependent Claim—A Claim that is derived from and incorporates by reference all of the terms of another Claim.

Design Around—A way of avoiding Patent Infringement by using a design of a product or process which is competitive to the patented product or process but does not infringe the Patent being considered. Also called "Work Around."

Design Patent—A Patent that protects the aesthetic aspects of a product.

Direct Infringement—Patent Infringement that occurs when an Accused Device or process is (1) Literally Infringed or (2) Infringed under the Doctrine of Equivalents. 35 U.S.C. § 271(a).

Discounted Cash Flow Analysis—An approach used in determining an applicable Royalty, by discounting (to present value) the cash flows that the Licensee would expect to receive from the sale of the Licensed Product.

DJ Action—Same as Declaratory Judgment Suit.

Doctrine of Equivalents—A rule of Claim construction for establishing Patent Infringement, under which a word or phrase in a Claim may be interpreted to include an "equivalent" element, which performs *substantially the same function in substantially the same way to achieve substantially the same result*. For example, the word *rivet* in a Claim may cover other elements such as nuts-and-bolts.

Doctrine of Exhaustion—The first sale of a Patented, Copyrighted, or Trademarked item by the owner or Licensee exhausts the IP right, so that the owner or Licensee cannot control resale of the item. *See also* First Sale Doctrine.

Enhancement—A modification of a computer program to add new or improved features or functionality.

Entire Market Value Rule—A Patent Infringement damages rule that, if a product (e.g., radio) includes a Patented component (e.g., amplifier), and the customer demand for the product is based on the component, the Infringement damages may be based on the market value of the product.

EPO—The European Patent Office. The EPO is located in Munich, Germany.

Essential Patent—*See* Blocking Patent. The term is usually used in Standards Licensing.

Estopped—Barred. *See* Estoppel.

Estoppel—A legal principle under which a person or company is barred, by its actions, from doing something. In the Patent field, it comes up when an action by a Patent owner in obtaining the Patent, limits or estops the owner from interpreting a Claim broadly. *See* File Wrapper Estoppel.

Exclusionary Right—The right of a Patent owner *to exclude* an Infringer of one or more Claims from making, having made, offering for sale, selling, using, or importing any Infringing product or process. That is to say, merely having a Patent on an invention does *not* give the Patent owner the right to make, use, sell, etc. that invention *if* the manufacture, use, or sale of the Patented invention Infringes someone else's Patent.

Exclusive License—A License grant by the owner of an IP right of exclusive (as opposed to non-exclusive) rights under the IP right. Under U.S. law, an Exclusive License is equivalent to an assignment of the IP rights.

Federal Circuit—*See* Court of Appeals for the Federal Circuit.

Field of Use—A particular product area or service market.

Field of Use License—An IP License which is restricted to a Field of Use. For example, a Patent or technology applies to batteries and License A is restricted to portable computers and License B is restricted to wireless telephones. (Of course, there could be a problem when portable computers and wireless telephones integrate, and that problem illustrates the need for careful drafting.)

File Wrapper Estoppel—A legal doctrine under which a Claim is barred (Estopped) from being more broadly interpreted because of a limitation inserted in the Claim by an applicant (or his or her Patent attorney) in response to a Rejection of a predecessor to that Claim as Unpatentable over Prior Art, he is estopped (barred) from recapturing the interpretation of the claim *to include the prior art element as an equivalent*. This rule negates application of the Doctrine of Equivalents. Also called "Prosecution History Estoppel."

First Sale Doctrine—Same as Doctrine of Exhaustion. *See* 17 U.S.C. § 109(a) as to Copyright.

Force Majeure Clause—A contract provision which excuses performance by a party when a specified situation outside the party's control (e.g., an earthquake, fire, or strike) prevents the performance. For example, a Licensor is obligated to deliver to the Licensee a sample of a Licensed composition, but is prevented by a fire at the plant making the composition.

Forward Citation Analysis—The analysis, with respect to a given Patent, of subsequently issued Patents which cite the given Patent.

Foundry Right—The right, under a Patent license, enabling the Licensee to manufacture (act as a foundry for) Licensed products for a non-Licensee which designed the products. This term is usually used in the computer, electronics, and telecommunications industries.

GAAP—Generally accepted accounting principles.

GAAPCA—Generally accepted accounting principles, consistently applied.

Georgia Pacific Factors—A comprehensive list of fifteen evidentiary facts relevant to the determination of a reasonable royalty in the computation of damages in a Patent Infringement lawsuit. Some of the facts are: the established profitability of the product made under the Patent and its commercial success; the extent to which the Infringer made use of the Invention; and the Royalties received by the Patent owner from other Licensees of the Patent. *Georgia-Pacific Corp. v. United States Plywood Corp.*, 318 F.Supp. 1116 (S.D.N.Y. 1970).

Goodwill—An intangible asset, often associated with a Trademark or Service Mark.

Grant-Back—A license of IP improvement rights (usually Patents) from a Patent Licensee (of other IP rights) to the Licensor.

Have Made Right—The right of a Patent Licensee to have a Licensed product manufactured by a third party for sale by the Licensee.

Heads of Agreement—An outline of the proposed terms of a contract, in the form of an outline of essential terms of the contract, and intended *not to be legally binding*. Used in international transactions. Unless the Heads of Agreement has language negating a binding contract, it might create a binding contract or at least questions about whether or not it is a binding contract (itself troublesome). *See* Letter of Intent, Term Sheet, and Memorandum of Understanding.

Human Capital—The collective people and their knowledge, skills, creativity of an organization. The Human Capital create the Intellectual Assets and convert them to products or services and ultimately to revenue and profits.

Implied License—A License under IP that the courts will imply when there is no express (written) License and fairness (equity) suggests that a License should be implied. For example, if a company sells a Patented machine to a customer, there is an Implied License that the customer has under the company's Patents to use the machine for its intended purpose.

Infringement—The violation of an IP right.

Infringer—A violator of an IP right.

Integration Clause—The contract clause stating that "this is the entire agreement between the parties." Its use excludes parol (oral) or other extrinsic evidence to vary the terms of the contract.

Intellectual Assets—Codified, tangible, or physical descriptions of specific knowledge to which ownership rights can be asserted. Intellectual Assets are Intellectual Property that has not yet been protected.

Intellectual Capital—The collective Human Capital, Intellectual Assets, and Intellectual Property of an organization.

Intellectual Property—Utility patents, design patents, plant patents, copyrights, mask works, trademarks, and trade secret rights. Also called "IP."

Interference—An *inter partes* (between two or more parties) lawsuit conducted in the PTO to determine which of two or more Patent Applications (or one or more Patent Applications and an issued Patent) is entitled to a Patent on a single invention which is disclosed in all of the applications (and, where applicable, the Patent).

Invalid—Not valid. Usually used in reference to a Claim that, for reasons of Anticipation or Unobviousness, is not legally Valid. If a Claim is indeed Invalid it *cannot* be Infringed.

Inventive Step—The counterpart in many European, Asian, and other countries to Unobviousness. The meaning of Unobvious or Inventive Step varies from country to country.

IP—*See* Intellectual Property.

IP Bankruptcy Act—11 U.S.C. § 365(n).

Joint Ownership—Where two or more persons or companies each own an interest (called an *undivided interest*) in an IP right. The legal rights and obligations of a Joint Owner will vary, depending on the type of IP involved (Patent or Copyright) and the country. For example, a Joint Owner of a U.S. Patent may grant a non-exclusive license under the Patent for a Royalty and keep the Royalty for himself; in many other countries this is not the case.

Joint Venture—A broad term, used to cover a broad range of multi-party relationships. Often (but not always), each party owns 50% of a Joint Venture corporation.

JPO—Japanese Patent Office.

Know-How—Valuable unpatented proprietary information (e.g., an unpatented manufacturing process).

Know-How and Show-How—Know-How plus skills used in exploiting the Know-How.

Knowledge Management—The discipline of collecting, organizing, processing, and utilizing information, often using computer-based tools, to derive optimum value from the information for the information's owner.

Last Antecedent Doctrine—A doctrine of contract interpretation that a succeeding modifier of more than one noun applies only to the last noun, unless the context otherwise clearly indicates. For example, the Last Antecedent Doctrine will determine, in a License grant to "Licensee and Subsidiaries" and "successors and assigns," whether "successors and assigns" applies only to "Subsidiaries" or to "Licensee and Subsidiaries."

Letter of Intent—A document (often in letter form) stating (usually in outline form) the fundamental business and financial terms of a proposed contract, but not intended to be legally binding. Unless the Letter of Intent has language negating a binding contract, it might create a binding contract or at least questions about whether or not it is a binding contract (itself troublesome). *See* Heads of Agreement, Memorandum of Understanding, and Term Sheet.

License—A grant of permission to do that which, without the permission, would be a Tort. A right to use IP under defined conditions.

License Agreement—An agreement in which the owner of an IP right grants a License to another party.

Licensee—The grantee of a License.

Licensee Estoppel—A principle under which the Licensee is estopped (barred) to deny the validity of the rights licensed. Licensee Estoppel is negated as to Patent Licenses by *Lear v. Adkins*, 395 U.S. 653 (1969).

License Monitoring—A program for reviewing License Agreements and Licensee reports, and monitoring Licensee compliance with obligations, such as royalty reporting and payment and Patent Marking, under the License Agreements.

Licensor—The grantor of a License.

Literal Infringement—Patent Infringement (Direct Infringement) that occurs when the elements of an Accused Device or process correspond *100%* to the words or phrases of a Patent claim.

Maintenance—Periodic fees and other actions (e.g., proof of *working*) required to maintain protection of IP.

Marking—Placing a (1) Patent number(s), (2) Trademark notice (®), or (3) Copyright notice (©), as applicable, on a product or its packaging or label, to provide Constructive Notice that the product is respectively Patented, is designated by a registered Mark, or is Copyrighted, as applicable.

Marks—Trademarks, Service Marks, and the like.

Markman Determination—A proceeding before a judge, in a Patent Infringement jury trial, in which the judge interprets Claims of the Patent for later determinations of Patent Infringement of the Claims by a jury.

Means Plus Statement of Function Claim—Also "Means Plus Function" Claim. A Claim that includes the description of a Claim element by what it does (e.g., "means for fastening") rather than what it is (e.g., "a nut and bolt"). *See* 35 U.S.C. § 112 ¶6.

Memorandum of Understanding—A broad statement of the proposed terms of a contract, intended *not to be legally binding*. Used in international transactions. Unless the MOU has language negating a binding contract, it might create a binding contract or at least questions about whether or not it is a binding contract (itself troublesome). *See* MOU, Heads of Agreement, Letter of Intent, and Term Sheet.

Misuse—An equitable defense (unclean hands) to an infringement charge based on a violation of the letter or spirit of the anti-trust laws. Purging the wrongful act ends the defense prospectively.

Most Favored Licensee Clause—*See* Most Favored Nations Clause.

Most Favored Nations Clause (MFN Clause)—Sometimes called a Most Favored Licensee (MFL) clause. A clause granting a Licensee the right to have the same, more favorable terms (usually financial) as may be granted by the Licensor to subsequent Licensees.

MOU—Memorandum of Understanding.

Mutatis Mutandis—A Latin term used in contracts to designate a clause that is identical to a prior clause "with appropriate (obvious) changes."

Net Sales—Gross sales of (or revenue from) a Licensed product minus certain specified deductions. Used to determine a Royalty Base for computing a Royalty payment.

Non-Exclusive License—A personal, non-transferable right to practice an IP right.

Non-Obviousness—*See* Unobviousness.

Novelty—One of the statutory requirements for a Patent that the Claimed invention is new and was not previously invented by someone else. 35 U.S.C. § 101.

OEM—Original equipment manufacturer. A company (A) that manufactures a product for another company (B) to sell under B's Trademark.

Office Action—A formal letter from the Patent Office to an applicant Rejecting Claims of a Patent Application on formal or substantive grounds (e.g., "Claim 1 is unpatentable because . . .").

Omitted Elements Test—A Claim is Invalid if it omits an element that someone skilled in the art would understand to be essential to the invention as originally disclosed.

Option—A contractual right (usually for a specific time period) to acquire something (in the IP context, to acquire ownership of or a License to a Patent or other IP right) at a future date, upon exercise of the right by the Option holder. The Option grant, to be meaningful, should specify all of the terms of the Option to be exercised, including the period of the Option, the exercise price, and at least all other relevant business terms. Preferably, there should be a complete Option agreement specifying all terms of the Option grant; otherwise, there can be confusion about what are the terms of the Option.

Paid-up License—A vested License under which no further Royalty is payable.

Paris Convention—An international Patent treaty providing that a Patent Application filed in a member country on a given date (the "Filing Date") and then filed in other member countries within one year after the Filing Date, will be deemed in the other countries to have been filed on the Filing Date. Most industrial countries, including the U.S., are members.

Patent—An Exclusionary Right granted by a government, for a limited period of time, to an invention which meets the legal requirements of Statutory Subject Matter. Novelty, Utility, Unobviousness, and Enabling Disclosure. 35 U.S.C. §§ 101, 102 and 103. See Principle of Territoriality.

Patentable—Legally capable of being Patented. *See* Patent.

Patent Application—An application, filed with the Patent Office of a country, to obtain a Patent granted by that country. *See* Principle of Territoriality.

Patent Infringement Abatement Insurance—Insurance for specified Patents that, if the Patent is Infringed, will pay the legal fees and expenses of Patent infringement litigation. Typically, the insurance requires a prepaid premium and has a policy limit on fees and expenses paid. If the Patent owner is successful in the lawsuit, due to a settlement or victory, the Patent owner repays the insurance company the sum advanced plus a premium.

Patent Infringement—Infringement of a Patent by either (1) Direct Infringement, (2) Active Inducement, or (3) Contributory Infringement.

Patent Office—The government agency that examines and grants Patents. In the U.S. it is formally called the "Patent and Trademark Office" or "PTO."

Patent Prosecution—The interplay between an applicant for a Patent (or, more often, his or her Patent attorney) and the Patent Office, in which a Patent Application is alleged (by the Patent Office) to be improper or unpatentable for specified reasons and the responses.

PCT—Patent Cooperation Treaty. An international treaty facilitating the filing and prosecution of Patent Applications in various member countries (including the U.S. and most major industrial countries).

Permanent Injunction—A court order, entered in a trial on the merits, permanently barring a defendant in a lawsuit from doing an act, such as importing or distributing an Infringing product.

Pioneer License—A License with special terms offered to early Licensees.

Pioneer Patent—A Patent that represents a major technological advance is called a pioneer patent. When the Doctrine of Equivalents is applied to a claim of a Pioneer Patent, the Doctrine of Equivalents is interpreted broadly.

Plain Meaning Doctrine—Words in a Claim are, in the first instance, given their plain meaning.

Portfolio Analysis—The process of analyzing a Patent portfolio, to determine which Patents (or Patents and related technologies) are most likely to be valuable and therefore revenue-generating.

Portfolio Maintenance Analysis—The analysis of the Patents in a Patent portfolio and the Maintenance fees associated with each group of Patents (each U.S. Patent and its overseas counterparts), to determine which Patents, because of their limited value, ought to be discontinued by failure to pay Maintenance fees.

Portfolio Mining—The process of (1) Portfolio Analysis and then (2) developing and realizing revenue or other value from Patents in the portfolio or technologies represented by the Patents.

Portfolio Paring—Eliminating non-productive Patents in a portfolio by sale or by non-payment of Maintenance fees.

Portfolio Valuation by Sampling—A statistical technique for evaluating a Patent portfolio by sampling selected Patents in the portfolio, valuing those Patents, and extrapolating to determine the value of the entire portfolio.

Preamble Doctrine—A rule of Claim interpretation, under which, generally, the preamble portion of a Claim will not limit the scope of the Claim, but may shed light on the meaning of the Claim.

Preliminary Injunction—A court order, entered after an evidentiary hearing and before a complete trial on the merits, barring a defendant in a lawsuit from doing an act, such as importing or distributing an Infringing product, until the trial on the merits.

Presumption of Validity—The statutory presumption to which every issued U.S. Patent is entitled, that the Patent is Valid. 35 U.S.C. § 282.

Principle of Territoriality—The principle of international law that an IP right granted by a country (e.g., U.S.) is effective only within the territory of that country. For example, a U.S. Patent is effective only in the United States and its territories and possessions.

Prior Art—That body of prior Patents, Patent Applications, publications, and products which precede an invention or Patent Application and may be relied on to invalidate or limit a Claim.

Privilege—A legal right that protects certain communications (said to be privileged) from access to the adversary in a lawsuit. There are several types of Privilege, including attorney-client, priest-penitent, and physician-patient.

Provisional Patent Application (PPA)—An *informal* Patent disclosure (it may be no more than a detailed description of the invention) filed in the PTO, under 35 U.S.C. § 111(b), for a nominal fee. The PPA may be filed without a formal Patent claim, oath, or declaration, or any information or prior art disclosure. The PPA provides the means to establish an early effective filing date in a Patent Application and allows the term "Patent Pending" to be used. The PPA is preserved by the PTO for at least one year after it is filed. If, within that year, a Patent Application is filed, which refers to the PPA, the Patent Application will be entitled to the benefit of the earlier filing date of the PPA, *but only to the extent that the two applications disclose the same subject matter*. A PPA is a very useful way to preserve an inventor's rights for one year without the expense of filing a Patent Application. In any event, a formal Patent Application *must be filed* to obtain legal rights in an invention.

Reads On—A term used when each of the words of a Claim of a Patent finds complete (one-for-one) correspondence (1) with the description in a *single* piece of prior art (in which case the Claim Reads On the prior art and is therefore Anticipated and Invalid) or (2) in each of the elements of a product or process (in which case the Claim Reads On the product or process and is Infringed).

Reduction to Practice—Making a model or implementation of a patentable invention to demonstrate that it will work.

Regular and Established Royalty—An approach used in determining an appropriate Royalty, by determining regular and established Royalties (comparable Royalties) used in the industry (or closely related industries) for similar types of products, processes, and so on.

Rejection—A reason given by the PTO, in an Office Action, for refusing to allow the Claim of a pending Patent Application.

Return on Investment Analysis—An approach used in determining an appropriate Royalty, by assessing the amount the Patent or technology owner invested to develop the technology and the rate of return that the owner would expect to receive on its investment.

Repair v. Reconstruction Doctrine—A Patent Infringement doctrine that repair of a licensed, Patented article is permitted, but that reconstruction of the article is an Infringement of the Licensed Patent.

Reverse Doctrine of Equivalents—A rule of Claim interpretation under which, even if Literal Infringement otherwise *appears* to be present, there is *no Patent Infringement* because the Accused Device or process is *so changed* that it performs the function of the Claimed invention *in a substantially different way*.

Right of First Negotiation—The contractual right, granted by an owner of something (in the IP context, a Patent or other IP right) to negotiate exclusively with the grantee of the right for a specified period of time after the owner decides to sell that right. This is different from (and much less valuable than) a Right of First Refusal, because the grantee has no certainty other than a time advantage.

Right of First Refusal—The contractual right, granted by an owner of something (in the IP context, a Patent or other IP right) to present to the grantee any third party offer to sell the right that the owner is about to accept. This means that the owner must first get a complete offer to buy the right from a third party and, before selling to the third party, must offer to sell to the grantee on terms identical to the offer. This can have a chilling effect on the ability of the owner to get third party offers because the third party may be reluctant to spend the time and effort to decide whether to buy and then negotiate the deal and be preempted by the grantee. One way to make it more appealing to the third party is to offer a break-up fee to compensate the third party for its time and effort if the right is sold to the grantee.

Right of Publicity—An inherent right, recognized in many (but not all) states, of every person to control the commercial use of his or her identity. Protected by statutes in some states and by Common Law in others.

Royalty—A fee paid for use of Licensed IP, usually a specified sum or a percentage for each Licensed unit sold. *See* Royalty Rate. Some approaches used to determine (or aid in determining) Royalties are Discounted Cash Flow Analysis, Regular and Established Royalty, Return on Investment Analysis, and Twenty-Five Percent of Profits.

Royalty Base—The unit sales to which a percentage Royalty is applied (e.g., sales of widgets).

Royalty Rate—A percentage that is multiplied by a Royalty Base to determine a Royalty, or some other (e.g., fixed) rate.

Royalty Stacking—Multiple royalties payable to multiple Patent owners on a product which Infringes multiple Patents.

Royalty Withholding Tax—*See* Withholding Tax.

Secondary Considerations—A list of objective considerations which may be considered by the judge or jury (as applicable) to assist in the subjective determination of whether or not an invention is non-obvious, within the meaning of 35 U.S.C. § 103. The Secondary Considerations include commercial success, satisfaction of a long-felt need, and others. *See Graham v. John Deere Co.*, 383 U.S. 1 (1966).

Securitization—A form of lending in which an owner of Licensed IP grants a Security Interest in the IP to a lender in exchange for a loan which represents a portion of the projected value of License revenue from the IP.

Security Interest—A mortgage or lien on personal property (e.g., a Patent, Trademark, Copyright, or License Agreement) as security for an indebtedness or obligation of the owner of the property. Technically, mortgages apply to real estate and security interests apply to personal property.

Service Mark—A word or symbol that designates the source or origin of a service.

Set-off—The common law right of A to deduct sums of money that B owes to A from money that A owes to B.

Shop Right—A royalty-free, non-exclusive Patent License that courts will imply to exist, for the benefit of an inventor's employer, when an employee makes a patentable Invention using the employer's time, materials and/or equipment, and the employer does not own the patentable Invention (either under an appropriate contract or as a matter of law).

Shrink Wrap License—A non-exclusive software License which is not signed and is included in the software package.

Source Code—A computer program written in human-readable language.

Standards Licensing—A requirement of national or international standards committees (such as IEEE, ANSI, ITU, and so on) that the owner of an Essential Patent to the standard, which participated in the committee deliberations, grant Licenses under its Essential Patents to all companies on "reasonable terms and conditions, demonstrably free of discrimination."

Statutory Bar—Prior Art Invalidating a Claim under 35 U.S.C. § 102 and having an effective date more than one year prior to the filing date of a Patent Application.

Statutory Subject Matter—The categories of inventions that are patentable under 35 U.S.C. § 101, namely "process, machine, (article of) manufacture, or composition of matter, or any new and useful improvement thereof."

Structural Capital—The support or infrastructure of an organization which allows Intellectual Capital to be utilized productively. Structural Capital includes property, plant, and equipment.

Substantial Unlicensed Competition Clause—A clause in a License Agreement that provides for the deferral or forfeiture of royalties for so long as unlicensed competition continues unabated. This clause requires a definition of what is substantial (not always easy to do) and what are the conditions after which the royalty is deferred or forfeited, *for example*, notice of the competition, and an opportunity for the Licensor either to License or sue the unlicensed competitor.

Support—Answering questions and providing assistance about use of IP.

Term Sheet—A document setting forth the basic terms (usually primarily financial terms and fundamental definitions) of a proposed agreement. It is usually not intended to be legally binding. Unless the Term Sheet has language negating a binding contract, it might create a binding contract or at least questions about whether or not it is a binding contract (itself troublesome). *See* Heads of Agreement, Memorandum of Understanding, and Letter of Intent.

Tort—A civil wrong which *does not* arise from an express or implied *contract*. For example, Patent Infringement is a tort.

Territorial License—A License of IP that is restricted to a particular geographic area. For example, a License relating to a new pharmaceutical, as to which License A is restricted to North and South America, License B is restricted to Europe and Africa, and License C is restricted to Asia, Australia, and New Zealand. *See* Field of Use License. A License may be both a Field of Use License and a Territorial License.

Trade Secret—Any business information of value (technical, financial, marketing) that is treated as secret and is learned as a result of a protected relationship (employee, consultant, and so on).

Trademark—A word or symbol that designates the source or origin of a product.

TRO—Temporary restraining order. A court order for a brief time (e.g., 10 days) and without an evidentiary hearing, barring a defendant in a lawsuit from doing an act such as making, reproducing, importing, or distributing an Infringing product.

Twenty-Five Percent Rule—An approach used in determining an appropriate Royalty Rate, by estimating a Royalty Rate that would be twenty-five percent of the Licensee's profits for the Licensed Product.

Tying—Conditioning the purchase of one product or service on the purchase of another product or service.

Unbundling—Selling separately a product (often software) which is usually sold together with another product. For example, the Palm® operating system is usually Bundled with a Palm® PDA. However, it may be Unbundled and licensed to manufacturers of other PDAs, for use with their products.

Unlicensed Competition Clause—*See* Substantial Unlicensed Competition Clause.

Unobviousness—A statutory requirement of U.S. Patent law (35 U.S.C. § 103) that an Invention, to be patentable, must be unobvious to a person having ordinary skill in the art (technology) to which the Invention pertains. (Also called "Non-Obviousness.")

Unpatentable—Not meeting the statutory requirements for a Patent. (i.e., Novelty, Utility, Unobviousness, Enabling Disclosure, and Statutory Subject Matter) 35 U.S.C. §§ 101, 102 and 103. Not patentable.

Utility—One of the statutory requirements for a Patent, 35 U.S.C. § 101, that the Claimed Invention is useful.

Utility Patent—A Patent which protects a method or the functional (rather than aesthetic) aspects (what it is or what it does) of a product. *Compare with* Design Patent, which protects the aesthetic aspects.

Valid or Validity—Whether a Patent Claim meets the legal requirements of 35 U.S.C.A. §§ 101, 102, and 103 as to Statutory Subject Matter, Novelty, Utility, Non-obviousness, and Enabling Disclosure.

Willful Infringement—Patent Infringement which continues after actual or Constructive Notice of the Patent and without a legal opinion of non-infringement.

Withholding Tax—A tax imposed by some countries (e.g., Japan and Korea) on Royalties payable under a License Agreement. The tax statutes often require that the Royalty payer (Licensee) must withhold the tax and pay it to the taxing authority.

Working—A requirement of the Patent statutes of some countries (not the major industrial countries) that, if a Patented Invention is not commercially used (worked) in that country within a specified time period, the Patent owner must License the Patent in that country, on a Royalty-bearing basis, to any interested party or the Patent Rights may be lost.

Bibliography

Anson, Weston. "Valuing Intangible Assets." *Les Nouvelles* (June 1996): 45.

Arnold, White, & Durkee. "Patent Antitrust and Misuse Overview." Paper presented at LES Technology Transfer Seminar (March 1995).

Bramson, Robert S. "License Audits—Should Intellectual Property Licensors Conduct Audits of Their Licensee Records." *Licensing Law and Business Report* (March/April 1996): 13.

Bratic, V. Walt, Benoit, Bryan K., and Woods, James D. "Monte Carlo Analyses Aids Negotiations." *Les Nouvelles* (June 1998): 47.

Brealey, Richard A. *Principles of Corporate Finance*, 4th ed. (New York: McGraw-Hill Publishing Co., 1991).

Carney, Robert T. and McGavock, Daniel M. "Tax Strategies for Protecting Value of IP." *Les Nouvelles* (March 1997): 17.

Chant, Peter. "Lateral Licensing Offers Benefits." *Les Nouvelles* (June 1996): 89.

Clark, Kenneth A. and Sharron, Stephanie L. "State of the Art in Biotechnology Alliances." *Les Nouvelles* (June 1994): 100.

Davis, Albert S., Jr., ed., *Practical Patent Licensing*, vols. 1, 2, 3. New York: Practicing Law Institute.

Davis, William T. "Academic Interface with Industry." *Les Nouvelles* (March 1993).

Degnan, Stephen A. "Using Financial Models to Get Royalty Rates." *Les Nouvelles* (June 1998): 59.

Degnan, Stephen A. and Horton, Corwin. "A Survey of Licensed Royalties." *Les Nouvelles* (June 1997): 91.

Drinkwater, Don L. "Patent Audit Maximizes Return on IP." *Les Nouvelles* (March 1997): 1.

Erlich, Jacob N. "Ins, Outs of Transferring U.S. Technology." *Les Nouvelles* (June 1993): 79.

Fradkin, Henry E. "Launching a Licensing Program at Ford Motor." *Les Nouvelles* (September 1999): 129.

Franson, Paul. "The Market Research Shell Game." *Upside* (March 1997): 78.

Goldscheider, Robert and Finnegan, Marcus B. *Current Trends in Domestic & International Licensing* (New York, Practising Law Institute, 1980).

Grindley, Dr. June N., David, Chris, and Rule, Chris. "Making the Alliance a Success." *Les Nouvelles* (June 1998): 57.

Grindley, Peter C. and Teece, David J. "Managing Intellectual Capital: Licensing and Cross-Licensing in Semiconductors and Electronics." *California Management Review* (Winter 1997): 8.

Grose, Thomas K. "Brand New Goods." *Time* (November 1, 1999).

Hruby, F. Michael and Lutz, Mark. "Model Helps Set Value of Technology." *Les Nouvelles* (March 1997): 40.

Klein, Ira Paul. "Principal Tax Issues for Technology Transfer." Paper presented at LES Technology Transfer Seminar (March 1995).

Kline, David. "The New Gold Rush in Patents." *Upside* (May 1998): 58.

Lee, William Marshall. "Determining Reasonable Royalty." *Les Nouvelles* (September 1992): 124.

McGavock, Daniel M., Haas, David A., and Patin, Michael P. "Factors Affecting Royalty Rates." *Les Nouvelles* (June 1992): 107.

Mayers, Harry R., and Brunsvold, Brian G. *Drafting Patent License Agreements* (Washington, D.C.: Bureau of National Affairs, Inc., 1991).

Mignin, George D. "Processes and Principles for Technology Licensing." Paper presented at LES Technology Transfer Seminar (March 1995).

Monro, H. Alec B. "Disciplined Negotiation: Worldwide." *Les Nouvelles* (December 1997): 174.

Morrison, William F. *The Prenegotiation Planning Book* (Malabar, FL: Krieger Publishing Co., 1992).

Munson, Daniel C. "Figuring the Dollars in Negotiations." *Les Nouvelles* (June 1998): 88.

Murray, Charles K. "Guidelines for Marketing Technology." *Les Nouvelles* (June 1994): 82.

Neil, D. J. "Realistic Valuation of Your IP." *Les Nouvelles* (December 1997): 182.

Parr, Russell L. and Sullivan, Patrick H. *Technology Licensing: Corporate Strategies for Maximizing Value* (New York: John Wiley & Sons, Inc., 1996).

Prestia, Paul F. "Decision Tree: Good Tool For Analysis." *Les Nouvelles* (March 1994): 60.

Reilly, Robert F. and Schweihs, Robert P. "Trademark Valuation Methods." *Les Nouvelles* (June 1996): 52.

Reimers, Niels "Tiger by the Tail." *CHEMTECH* (August 1987).

Rivette, Kevin G. and Kline, David. "A Hidden Weapon for High-Tech Battles." *Upside* (January 2000): 165.

Smith, Gordon V. and Parr, Russell L. *Intellectual Property: Licensing and Joint Venture Profit Strategies* (New York: John Wiley & Sons, Inc., 1993).

Smith, Gordon V. and Parr, Russell L. *Valuation of Intellectual Property and Intangible Assets*, 2nd ed., (New York: John Wiley & Sons, Inc., 1994).

Sperber, Philip and Jarvis, Richard B. "Dealing With Licensing Infringers." *Les Nouvelles* (June 1990): 71.

Sullivan, Patrick H. and O'Shaughnessy, James P. "Valuing Knowledge Companies." *Les Nouvelles* (June 1999): 83.

Stewart, Thomas A. "Brainpower—How Intellectual Capital is Becoming America's Most Valuable Asset." *Fortune* (June 3, 1991): 44.

Stewart, Thomas A. "Your Company's Most Valuable Asset: Intellectual Capital." *Fortune* (October 3, 1994): 68.

Sullivan, Patrick H. "Royalty Rates Conform to 'Industry Norm.'" *Les Nouvelles* (September 1994): 140.

Szczepanski, Steven Z. *Licensing in Foreign and Domestic Operations* (New York: Clark Boardman Callaghan, 1991).

Thurow, Lester C., "Needed: A New System of Intellectual Property Rights." *Harvard Business Review* (September-October 1997): 95.

"US Department of Justice Antitrust Guidelines for the Licensing and Acquisition of Intellectual Property." Draft for Public Comment dated August 8, 1994.

White, Edward P. *Licensing—A Strategy for Profits* (Chapel Hill, NC: KEW Licensing Press, 1990).

Willis, John. "New Tax Rules Affect Licensing." *Les Nouvelles* (December 1992): 190.

Index